THE *7 DAYS* ART COLUMNS 1988-1990

PETER SCHJELDAHL

THE FIGURES

In memory of Seymour Peck

Cover photo by James Hamilton
Distributed by Small Press Distribution, Sun and Moon, Segue,
Inland Book Company, Bookslinger, and by Paul Green in the U. K.
The Figures, 5 Castle Hill, Great Barrington, Massachusetts 01230
This book was made possible, in part, by a grant from the National
Endowment for the Arts.
ISBN 0-935724-41-9

Table of Contents

PREFACE

My tenure as chief art critic of *7 Days*, from the Manhattan weekly's birth in March, 1988, to its sudden death in April, 1990, coincided with a period of growing muddle and malaise in New York, a sense of all-around entropy that I noted in my first column and that seems sadly confirmed by *7 Days'* demise (though the proximate cause of that event was the impatience of the magazine's billionaire owner). I enjoyed the job immensely. The experience of hitting the streets every week with my most immediately burning opinions and pleasures suited me fine, and any true New Yorker can tell you that dire omens are as often a goad as a deterrent to the spirit of enjoyment in our passionately perverse town.

At its best, weekly journalism seems to me a model of how to live in a city: with pried-open responsiveness to the fleeting moment (the moment, even, of overtaxed exhaustion). Column-writing, in particular, should amplify the non-stop, irascible, funny, serious talk that is the sweetest city music. "It was like every week you wrote a letter to your friends," artist Jane Kaplowitz has said to me. If it comes across that way, wonderful—keeping in mind that in a column the "friends" addressed are people you've never met or the unexpressed sides, hidden from you, of those you know. That's part of what distinguishes sitting down to write instead of reaching for the telephone.

The 76 columns, short reviews, and articles here (many of them abridged by me) are most of what I wrote for *7 Days*. I hope that this mass of journalism, conceived in the heat of many fleeting moments, adds up to a running chronicle of the art life of a specific period in New York. Whatever is good about it owes much to Stephen Greco, my editor on every piece, and to my wife Brooke Alderson, always my first and most generous reader.

June, 1990

HELLO

LIKE A PILOT TAKING AN AERIAL PHOTO prior to crash-landing, I'll use this, my first column, for a quick overview of terrain I'm about to be part of: the situation of art in New York, where almost everything appears to be going wrong and there are inklings of a new, probably glorious, era.

The incredible bull art market of the 1980s may or may not be softening—five months after the stock crash the evidence remains unclear—but the market is definitely glutted, with too much art chasing dollars that can't possibly be limitless. There are also way too many hungry artists for the available love and fame. Competition is getting hysterical.

The present avantgarde, the teeming horde of neo-this and neo-that, appears to have outrun its supply line of ideas. The late-1980s-model artwork—anything cool and strange, pretty and nasty, vaguely anti-commodity and very much for sale—may become the suddenest period-piece antique since psychedelic posters. Art has to be about something. Being about "being about" is an ulcer that has digested everything of New York's art body but the toenails.

Engaged critical impulses (apart from the numbskull establishment and the dithering media) have split among various coterie mentalities, forbidding anything bad to be said about anybody, and an academic leftism that is categorically negative. In either precinct, trying to tell the truth can get your head torn off.

What else?

The New York art world—really an archipelago of worlds, dozens of them—keeps bursting with wealth and energy, riding a phenomenal surge of public fascination and good will. New galleries (some of them moving from the more or less defunct Lower East Side scene) are stacked in high-rise Broadway buildings like planes over La Guardia on a foggy evening.

Saturdays in Soho look like Herald Square two shopping days before Christmas. Artists attain the tax bracket of doctors and lawyers. Museum attendance soars. Publications proliferate. Critics swarm. Collectors flash for society photographers the grin of the triumphant mountain climber (resting from the ordeal of writing checks). And yet there is this smell in the air: fear. New York, art capital of planet Earth, is slipping.

New York is losing marketing and institutional functions to Cologne, London, Milan, Tokyo, Los Angeles, Madrid, and other rising centers. (Stay tuned for Moscow and Prague.) Most gravely, New York is losing production. Aspiring artists can't afford to live here any more, of course, but ruinous rents only speed a decline of art culture that would be happening anyway.

There is no mystery about the root of this decline, which is national. The postimperial United States has trade deficits in spheres other than finance. The deficits include a hemorrhage of identity. The global triumphs of American popular culture, to take the biggest example, have effectively de-Americanized it. Andy Warhol is dead. The world has become hip to us. We're out of secrets.

American art now is roughly where European art was at the end of the 1920s: strip-minded of native intellectual and spiritual resources for coping with modernization and chaos. We are *exhausted*, folks. May we — unlike Europeans in the '30s, arrogant and suicidal — have the humility and sanity to admit as much.

Cars from Japan, paintings from Germany, ideas from France: the U. S. is still the world champion consumer, with an insatiable stomach. To reach that stomach, art must still pass through New York's big mouth. No multinational corporation lacks an office in New York. Contemporary art is now such a corporation.

So where is the glorious new era coming from? Everywhere. In New York, it will be — it is already — an era of decadence, which is often a good thing aesthetically. Everybody knows that. When things fall apart, you can see what they're made of. The poetic wafts from every gaping fissure. Sadness? Horror? Tragedy? Tones of the real to be grasped by sensibility and to be processed creatively in ways that suggest we do not regret having been born.

Why is visual art, more than any other creative medium, an apt context for reflections on such universal matters? Two reasons: 1) The dominant mode of all culture now is pictorial, and visual art (painting especially) is the queen of pictorial practices; and 2) Handmade visual art is the only major cultural practice unassimilable by mass media. It is simultaneously up to date and archaic, like the human soul whose vicissitudes it is peculiarly qualified to symbolize.

Now, go look at some art, and meet me back here next week.

GEORGE CONDO *Pace*

GEORGE CONDO, WHOSE FLAVORFUL SHOW at the Pace Gallery ends Saturday, is one of the new dumb painters, adherents of a fashion bidding to be a tradition. Thirty years old, he is the latest hope in the painterly romance that flared a decade ago with Julian Schnabel and Sandro Chia and has since made dozens of names in the U. S. and Europe. The romance is an infatuation with paint, distinct from any special use for it.

The new dumb painters of the 1980s are not necessarily unintelligent, but they are allergic to analysis. They bet that their own innocent pleasure in painting proves that painting (and they) will be immortal. Naively or defiantly, they plug into all the myths of genius —the painter as "radiant child," renegade, or gladiator —that theorists have pronounced dead, and now and then the result is electric. Buoyed by market demand, would their confidence survive a downturn? It's akin to wondering how tough heavyweight champ Mike Tyson will be when somebody finally hurts him.

The work of the new dumb painters refers compulsively to great dumb art of the past, time-traveling to such poignantly disreputable moments as the moribund post-war School of Paris (great talents like Miro and Masson burning out, minor ones like deStaël and Fautrier claiming succession) and the stillborn op-art vogue of the '60s. At the extreme reached by Condo, it is a cargo cult, presenting mockups of Picassoid, mid-'40s painterly surrealism as if to conjure the return of the real thing.

The new dumb painting makes historical sense as an adjustment to the decline of American imperial culture. Condo, a sure-enough expatriate in Paris (the first of significance, among American painters, since Ellsworth Kelly 40 years ago), shows how to leave the sinking ship of New York style.

Condo's lifeboat is the linear mannerism, painterly cuisine, and sentimental primitivism that were the last hurrah of the School of Paris before, in the words of grumpy French theorist Serge Guilbaut, "New York stole the idea of modern art." (The idea was lying around loose, actually: finders keepers.) That long-despised aesthetic proves well rested and rambunctious in Condo's hands.

The aesthetic pertains to beaux arts genres — portrait, nude, still life, etc. —fed to the furnace of modernizing form, especially cubism's frankly artificial, constructed visual space. In its decadence, signaled by Picasso's terminal, self-imitating, dumb phase (mid-'40s onwards), one gets an elegance so second-nature that the fiercest attempts to uglify it, by Dubuffet or by Picasso himself, merely amplify the tastiness.

Condo gets right to the heart of that in such paintings as the clamorous *Edith Piaf* (doesn't look a thing like her), in which the raucous contours of a studio nude jostle those of bold floral and totemic shapes in a steamrollered space, with passages of clashy red, yellow, and lavender. Up close, the surface is a congested mess. However, from any distance, the cubistic dynamics sing and dance.

Condo commands a brushstroke —with "touch" and "wrist"— that simultaneously delivers color and texture, describes form, and makes space and scale. Such stroking (de Kooning's forte) has had few notable recruits since Pollock revolutionized picture-making by drowning the local mark in the overall field. It didn't occur to anyone until the new dumb painters simply to rewind art history to the part where brushstroke is boss.

Condo's Gorkyesque *Expanding Color Painting* parades a lexicon of strokes, from loaded and languorous to thin and zippy. The picture's organic, sexualized shapes writhe and snarl smartly, while meaning nothing. They are heartless and brain dead, but if you like painting you get entranced by them. That's the point: to show that painting has a primordial vitality as unkillable as cockroaches.

If I have one major misgiving about Condo, it is that he may be having more fun with his paintings than I am. That's the standard new-dumb-painter way of failing: a precious self-indulgence that hogs the pleasures of art, then waits to be congratulated for being so pleased. This casts the viewer in the role of a doting fan and is likely to cause resentment.

April 13, 1988

"DUTCH AND FLEMISH PAINTINGS FROM THE HERMITAGE"
Metropolitan Museum of Art

Dutch and flemish paintings from the hermitage" is distracting and dissatisfying in the way of all masterpiece samplers. It is piety on parade. It is a lineup of prime suspects. It's cocktail party appetizers: some of this, some of that, you're welcome, go home. It is all but overwhelmed by curatorial packaging (decorator-color walls, sleeping pill labels, murmuring Acousti-guides) and diplomatic narcissism (smarmy glasnostalgia). It will be mobbed with people who never look at the works by the same artists, mostly as good or better, in the Met's permanent galleries.

None of this poses a problem for the old-master maven. He or she knows that the proper visit to such shows is a guerrilla operation that skirts many targets to take others by surprise. He or she knows, in crowded rooms, what elbows are for.

Rembrandt's *The Sacrifice of Isaac* is relatively unappealing, a melodramatic stunt with a gruesomely age-deadened paint skin, but it is a Rembrandt oddity, the sort of baroque machine he rarely went in for, so infernally clever as to be a lesson in greatness. Even doing something uncongenial, this Dutchman found ways to keep himself interested.

The picture is a narrative puzzle whose key is a knife in mid-air. At first it appears that an angel stops Abraham from stabbing Isaac by grabbing his back-stretched arm; the knife drops toward Isaac's body. Look again. The knife is round-pointed, not a stabber but a slicer, and Abraham shoves Isaac's head back to expose his throat (also probably to spare himself the sight of his son's features). He was about to cut the throat, and his arm is behind him because the angel, a mild girl who grasps it lightly, has yanked it back.

She is supernaturally strong. The shocked look the patriarch gives her from his very old face expresses something he has never felt before: physically weak, overpowered. The knife doesn't drop. Flung loose as his arm was retracted, it zooms out of the picture toward us. Duck!

Flora, a picture of Rembrandt's wife, Saskia, as the goddess of spring, is the best painting in the show, if not the universe. When bought by Catherine the Great in the 18th century, it was called

13

Portrait of a Lady Dressed as a Shepherdess. Later it showed up on Hermitage inventories as *The Young Jewess.* I think these are Freudian-slip titles, betraying different times' notions of sexy. It's a sexy image, all right, but with a meaning that feudal Russians were bound to miss: the bourgeois, domestic, married love that was one of 17th-century Holland's quiet revolutions.

Rembrandt has *dressed* this wife, this Saskia, in ravishing pale green and gold satin, silks, and brocade, and has made her a bonnet of spring flowers. He shows how beautiful every stitch and petal is. Meanwhile, he shows *her:* a plain, round-faced, 22-year-old Saskia, oblivious to the finery and distracted, maybe a little bored, as she watches something. What is she watching? Her gaze is directed out to mid-body level. She is watching the hands that hold a palette and brush. She watches what her husband is doing. They are alone in the studio (the background foliage is perfunctory, a backdrop), the young wife and the uxorious husband. She probably thinks he is the best painter in the world. He is. He takes joy in his power to envelop her young body in such beauty, and such symbols of fruitfulness, while seeing just her. Just Saskia.

JONATHAN BOROFSKY *Paula Cooper*

JONATHAN BOROFSKY'S SHOW AT PAULA COOPER, his first in New York since his retrospective at the Whitney Museum in 1985, may look like a capitulation by this progenitor of neo-expressionism to neo-geo fashion: hard-edged acrylic paintings of the flags of 51 nations surround a more recognizably Borofskian, huge blue fiberglass male statue with an exposed, audibly beating, flashing-red-light heart. The show isn't really a departure for him, but it also isn't Borofsky at his best. That makes two reasons to recall the kind and quality of artist we are dealing with.

A ringmaster of many mediums and, literally, a dreamer (who hatches most of his ideas during REM time), Borofsky hit the stagnant art scene of the mid-1970s like a blast of crazy, fresh air. With welcome-to-the-inside-of-my-head words and images drawn directly on walls and ceilings, he was at once shamanistic and goofy, somewhere between Joseph Beuys and the Little Rascals. He was grandiose and sincere, an apocalyptic poet who was also a convincingly nice, albeit an obsessive-compulsive, young guy.

Most of all — and this made his appearance timely — Borofsky was the avatar of all the weird kids in all the art schools in the world. Every class has one: the solipsistic genius who has been immersed in art since childhood and makes everybody else, professors included, feel dull and plodding by comparison. Such kids excite high hopes and generally go nowhere, because they never grasp that even artists, to succeed, must have some functional inkling of other people's existence.

But the 1970s was the Decade of the Art School, which institutionalized the formerly bohemian avantgarde. Conceptualism, the chief style, was institution-intensive, pitted against commercial culture. Borofsky's arrival was part of an invasion of the commercial gallery world by this art school ambience, so congenial to his weird-kid proclivities. In the course of it, Borofsky's ingenuousness set a tone for the hot figurative painting that presently erupted.

Borofsky has been big in Europe, where institutionalism remains the social-democratic rule for art. The peak of his career may have been the famous "Zeitgeist" exhibition of 1982, when he painted one of his trademark "running men" on the Berlin Wall. It looked perfect as an assertion, in that ghastly place, of the scared, irrepressible,

15

freedom-craving soul.

Then came his much-traveled retrospective, with its theme of protest of the U.S.-Soviet arms race —symbolized by, among other things, a Ping-Pong table, on which viewers were invited to play. Like most early-to-midcareer retrospectives, this one had dire effects on the artist's standing: by making him seem a known, summed-up quantity, it thrust him into the blind spot of an art culture with eyes only for the unassimilated. Changing fashion, bored with shaggy expressiveness, thrust him deeper.

The cool look of Borofsky's new show may signal an effort to adjust, but at root it's as sweet-souled as ever. It says, in effect, "My heart is open to the whole world." The bright, pristine flag paintings that represent the world are pretty, but oddly dead. They are like some middle term between "reality" and "art" that Jasper Johns sagely eliminated in his American-flag masterpieces of the 1950s.

The subject of world-consciousness is on time for this era of inflamed nationalism. We flat out do not know enough about people out there. It's interesting and humbling to find oneself, as I did, unable to identify most of the flags, the sight of which may rouse in the citizens of their countries exalted and potentially lethal emotions. And Borofsky's sentiment of personal sensitivity to the various world is impeccable. But the sentiment is inadequate to the subject, and the art isn't complex enough to compensate.

A sort of unreconstructed, make-love-not-war flower child at heart, Borofsky has always pushed naive political messages; but usually these have been neither here nor there in determining the impact of his work. The operative thing has been phantasmagorical, vulnerable, liberated subjectivity, amusing and heartening in a Whitmanesque or Chaplinesque kind of way. The new work doesn't share such feelings but only tells us about them. It is unengaging.

I suspect that Borofsky is going to be all right. He has one of the great spirits in contemporary culture, and he is on schedule for the crisis that visits most artists who, while young, have given their all and met with phenomenal success. Such artists often undergo dry, difficult years of struggling to find a new or renewed reason for working —in the face of an art culture they have taught, only too well, to expect a lot from them. Borofsky may need to reconstitute, on some unexpected plane (maybe in his sleep), his magnificent weirdness.

April 27, 1988

HANS HAACKE *John Weber*

Hans haacke is an installational showman, investigative reporter, circuit preacher, and doyen of agitprop within the politics-shy institutions of Western art. He is fearless, persistent, and skillful. He is also tendentious, prosaic, and coy.

For 18 years, Haacke has been rattling people with documentary works that blend art politics and politics proper. He had a well-remembered *succès de scandale* in 1971, when an elegantly deadpan project, detailing the slum real-estate holdings of some wealthy New Yorkers, was censored by the Guggenheim Museum. Never mind that Haacke used public-record material and pronounced no judgments. It gave the museum people a chill. The director of the Guggenheim, Thomas Messer, spoke of "an alien substance that had entered the art museum organism."

A sore spot of capitalism, which Haacke regularly pokes, is the way rich people indulge in art to feel better about themselves and, in the case of corporate sponsorship, to project a good-guy public image. His favored tactic is to link what such people are doing in art with something less pleasant that they are doing somewhere else. The results are often wonderfully informative, whatever their frailties as art.

A new piece called *The Saatchi Collection (Simulations)* links English advertising baron Charles Saatchi's promotion of "simulationist" neo-geo artists like Haim Steinbach (who presents shelves of intriguing commodities) and Peter Halley (bright, frigid abstract paintings) with work done by Saatchi affiliates for the South African government. Haacke festoons some "Steinbach" boxes and a "Halley" paint bucket with copies of nauseating anti-antiapartheid ads.

"Everything is connected to everything else," said Lenin. With cheekiness typical of the winning Saatchi advertising style, the line got quoted in an agency report. Haacke requotes it on an unflattering photo of Saatchi, hung above Steinbachian shelves that support, along with the aforementioned boxes and bucket, a Koonslike (but plastic) bust of Lenin. Below the shelf are mounted additional proofs of the South African connection.

Haacke shows impeccable journalistic instincts in going after Saatchi, paladin of today's multinational, management-intensive business and culture. Saatchi's collection is a lodestar of the art market

17

and of art criticism, and his agency is a global image machine of Disneyesque proportions. And neo-geo happens to be a faithful aesthetic mirror of the managerial-era capitalist spirit.

Aside from his muckraking coup in exposing Saatchi's indefensible South African involvement, Haacke's achievement in this work is doubtful. In particular, his heavy-handed parodies of neo-geo display poor understanding of that aesthetic of distilled material perfection. Haacke comes across as a square presuming to ridicule hipness.

Whatever its amorality, the best neo-geo is subtler and more potent than Haacke seems willing to admit. To call its pleasure fetishistic — the standard Marxist insult — changes nothing. The pleasure is real and its isolation in art, as witness the astonishing recent work of Ashley Bickerton, is a service to consciousness. To be immune to neo-geo's seductive tug is to have nothing useful to say about it.

How you feel about the main thrust of *The Saatchi Collection (Simulations)* will depend on how you feel about rich people in general, and the value of art patronage in particular. Is it okay to be rich? Is it a public boon to spend money on art no matter how the money was made? Does good work for culture excuse political badness?

"ALTERED STATES" *Kent Fine Art*

Altered states," a group show assembled by critic Rosetta Brooks, is only the latest incidence of a current fashion or syndrome that I think of as curatorial bondage-and-discipline. Like other such shows, this one forces miscellaneous artworks to illustrate a heady, none-too-comprehensible theme. Aesthetic edge and critical clarity take a terrific beating, under which they are presumed to whimper gratefully.

Though "Altered States" is typical of a genre, its mixing of generations and of big and little names (from Nauman, Artschwager, and Ruscha to Stezaker, Jones, and Brazelton, with some Joseph Cornell boxes tossed in for "tradition") and its high-gloss production values (including a coordinated issue of *ZG* magazine with apocalyptic musings by, among others, J. G. Ballard and Paul Virilio) make it special. We won't get a better gauge, as this overwrought art season staggers toward summer, of what passes for avantgarde mentality in the era of safe sex and market jitters.

Curatorial bondage-and-discipline is a pathology born of the contemporary art glut. When there are masses of artists with claims to fame — the fame, in particular, of hipness, sensibility's hot spot — problems of sorting and certification grow immense. It's all too fast and furious for any institution to handle, giving rise to the phenomenon of the independent critic-curator wielding, in theory, lightning bolts of instant illumination. In practice, the bolts turn into whips and chains, and the only thing illuminated is the certifying mechanism itself.

The theme of "Altered States," as developed in the issue of *ZG*, is the old reliable one of futureshock brought on by technological change. With some smart, sane exceptions (Vito Acconci's essay on video art is a must-read), the overall tone is self-indulgently hysterical, getting off on grim kicks of deracination by microchip: "We feel so dislocated, so disconnected, so uncentered," Brooks writes, not sounding terribly unhappy about it — as if "we" (whoever that is) haven't been feeling that way more or less since the invention of the steam engine.

Techno-doominess is enjoyable, conducive to a cold, sex-in-the-brain excitement and the sort of science-fictional perversity with

19

which Ballard, for instance, can term AIDS "a designer desease" that is "a metaphor for all kinds of processes." (Don't bother telling him that's repulsive: he *knows* it's repulsive.) The trick is akin to banging yourself on the head in order to see stars.

Fortunately, then, here comes summer, which is the time to go fishing.

Fishing is great. The technology is rudimentary but absorbing. Fish are interesting and tasty. You get, pleasantly, a little sweaty and smelly. You sleep like a log at night and do not think about art all day.

May 11, 1988

ELIZABETH MURRAY *Whitney*

IF YOU HAVE EVER WANTED ANYTHING as much as Elizabeth Murray wants to paint, you have it by now. Sensuous, lyrical, and given to domestic affections, she convinces us that, as a painter of buoyant, semi-abstract images, she just wants to have fun — but also that having such fun, in times hostile to painting for painting's sake, is a deadly serious endeavor. Struggling with skewed and fractured formats to keep her medium fresh and surprising, she squeezes dollops of joy from masses of toil. She is like someone who, wanting to dance, must build a city from scratch so that a nightclub can open to oblige her. Murray's strange combination of willpower and hedonism packs a punch in this brilliant installation (the last) of her much-traveled retrospective. The Whitney has added some huge brand-new work, more eccentric than ever, which hints that Murray's best may be yet to come. As always, however, the payoff of her art is not in its strenuous forms but in its fundamentalist pleasures of pungent color and, most of all, ravishing paint surfaces. Stand close when you look at the paintings. The sensation is like a full-body massage from a beautiful Swede who is on the verge of forgetting his or her professional detachment.

FORREST BESS *Hirschl & Adler Modern*

FORREST BESS, THE TEXAS PAINTER and crank's crank who died in 1977 at the age of 66, is often termed visionary, the kindest word we can think of for someone who "sees things." It is one of those euphemisms that deflect potential threats to our equanimity (such as creepy old Forrest Bess) by putting nice labels on them. It gums up thinking about what makes an artist like Bess interesting.

Bess's paintings make him interesting. I had forgotten how good they are, and when I got around to seeing his retrospective of 60-some pictures, it was startling. They are tiny, clunky things for the most part, but as dense as uranium. The harder you look at them, the more they stare you down.

The little paintings are imaginary landscapes, geometric abstractions, patterns, diagrams, and combinations thereof, painted thick, fast, and flat, mostly in pure colors, with palette-knife buttering and slathering, stippling and scoring. Blocky objects framed with strips of weathered wood, they feel packed with meaning — *Here Is a Sign* is the helpful title of one, in which yellow arrows spiral to gridlock inside a bulbous black form on a blue ground — while signifying next to nothing except, perhaps, painting itself.

Bess's work — like that of the great modern fundamentalists of the medium, from Malevich to Ryman — can make me feel that I've never before quite realized what a painting is.

What does it is the matter-of-factness of the knife- and brushwork. It reminds me of Malevich, whose surfaces often display a similarly blunt, whistle-while-you-work detachment, brusquely handing over ("Here is a sign!") an image you can't even begin to understand. It is painting stripped bare. You don't know what to do with it, but you're grateful.

Bess painted at night from dream drawings he made in the morning. In between, he worked as a bait fisherman around Bay City, Texas, on the steaming Gulf Coast. No wild child, he had studied architecture, religion, and psychology, with emphasis on sexological, mythological, and scientific esoterica. He corresponded with C. G. Jung and was an early devotee of L. Ron. Hubbard.

Bess had plenty on the ball in career terms, cultivating historian Meyer Shapiro, who gave him critical support, and Betty Parsons, whose gallery he joined in 1948. Myth and primitivism were artistic fashions in the '40s, of course. Bess's work then was right in step with some of the abstract expressionists, whom he despised (he accused Clyfford Still of plagiarizing him). He might easily have won fame as a sophisticated, lovable eccentric on the order of Joseph Cornell, except for one little thing:

Bess had these shy-making ideas about sex. He reckoned that a true hermaphrodite, balancing male and female orgasms, could, well, live forever. To prove it he underwent a number of operations that I'd rather not think about. Other writers, referring delicately to Bess's subsequent "disappointments," seem to find the subject similarly distracting.

It won't get you anywhere with the paintings, in any case. That an oval with a cross on it means "life (dilated urethra)" (a chart by Bess in the show's catalog says so) is a mental datum that just sort of sits there. Oddly, the sheer extremity and hermeticism of Bess's mania may have protected the integrity of his art, its usual concentration on "how" rather than "what" or "why."

The few exceptions include thematic pieces like *Untitled ("The Bomb")*, which freezes the mushroom cloud into a clublike black mass, and a gorgeous 1946 picture, *Dedication to van Gogh,* which suspends a solid blue sun over a field of orange and green zigzags. Van Gogh and — Forrest Bess? In instructive ways, yes and no.

I think Bess accurately recognized in van Gogh another painter who worked up "visionary" intensity with practical calculations of color and facture. (Pictorial organization, not "self-expression," is the Dutchman's cynosure.) Of course, Bess was walled up in his sense of specialness, where only his dreams seemed real. Van Gogh the man was wide open to nature and humanity, giving van Gogh the painter resources for a major art. That's the saintliness of van Gogh: in no matter how much pain, he never presumed to place himself above the world.

Yet on the single point of his radically direct approach to the act of painting, Bess bears comparison to van Gogh. When he put pigment to canvas — if only then — he was sane, strong, and whole.

"VISIONS/REVISIONS" *Marlborough*

THE CATALOGUE OF "VISIONS/REVISIONS" is like nothing so much as the last chapter of a typical textbook on modern art, the "recent trends" one that unwittingly reassures anxious undergraduates that, though they might not yet know what is going on in the world, their supposed educators sure as hell don't either.

Sam Hunter's dominant tone in his text is benignly befuddled "art appreciation" with a light dusting of buzzwords ("post-modern" being, as usual, to hard thought what the dishwashing machine is to after-dinner chores, getting the job done noisily and out of sight). Textbook-like arbitrariness is compounded, in this case, by a tacit demand to shoehorn as much of the Marlborough stable as possible in among the more or less illustrious invitees.

Still, the show is worth pondering as an instructive approximation of how contemporary art may look with the parallax of, say, Des Moines: a panorama of strange stuff flattened by the earnestly fair-minded mediation of cultural agents and agencies. It's art minus generative idea and passion, everything about art except why somebody would want to make it.

Dropping out of the show's dream of peaceful artistic coexistence like a rock from a cloud, Neil Jenney's *Venus From North America* (a slice of glittering, stylized wilderness centering on a dead tree) reminds me what a tonically obdurate presence this painter has been in art of the past two decades.

As advertised by Hunter, Jenney's *Venus* is sure-enough "allegorical" —a sort of autopsy of the body of wild nature in the era of ecological doom (something like that)—but its overriding value is as an assertion of individual, absolutely exclusive imagination. That's the significance, I believe, of the huge black frames Jenney crafts for his pictures: fortresses for his vision against everything that might horn in on it.

Jenney's obstreperous frames are a pretty good symbol of the beleaguerment of the individual artist in these curatorial-intensive times, when art is being loved not wisely—that is, discriminately, with a willingness to entertain and test its particular claims on us— but way too well. Literally at the edge between art and the world, and between one art work and another, our current reality is truly felt.

It is a fault line, ominously grinding.

GORDON MATTA-CLARK. *Brooklyn Museum.*

GORDON MATTA-CLARK, LAST OF THE UTOPIANS, died of cancer in 1978 at the age of 35, five years after Robert Smithson, the next to last, was killed in a plane crash at the same age. The mid-'70s made a wipe of the anarchic and messianic avant-gardism that had taken hold in American art at the end of the '60s. It would have ended even if Smithson and Matta-Clark had lived; their deaths just added an air of practically metaphysical disaster, as if the gods were angry.

Still, I was moved and stimulated beyond what I had expected when seeing Matta-Clark's retrospective. I felt the ache of an utter exuberance cut short, with so much left undone.

And I felt an inkling that much might be done even now — or especially now, in our money-sickened art culture — with hints from Matta-Clark and his "wonderful, socially redeeming harebrained schemes," in the words of Robert Pincus-Witten's catalog introduction.

I knew Matta-Clark in the frontier-era Soho of the very early '70s, when he was the most energetic of many "informalists" — guerilla auxiliaries of minimalism and conceptualism — who whipped up short-lived installations of urban detritus in alternative spaces also used for dance performances, poetry readings, and parties. Political rage was high and rents were low, making antibourgeois values both irresistible and affordable.

It wasn't all that much fun for someone given to critical thinking about art, or about anything. Though brainy in a flashes-of-genius kind of way, the mindset was hippie-ishly anti-rational — not that ratiocination was even possible given the prevalence of the substances with which we were disqualifying ourselves for Supreme Court judgeships.

Matta-Clark was one of the twin sons of Roberto Matta, the Chilean surrealist, womanizer, and, not to put too fine a point on it, jerk. (The twin committed suicide in 1976.) Bohemian-born and -bred in New York, Matta-Clark led a semicommunal life centered on nonstop cooking. (He was co-founder of the restaurant Food.) I regret having thrown away, as disgusting, my copy of his famous 1969 Christmas card: a photo of a Christmas tree, fried in grease.

Much of Matta-Clark's work, as documented by him in the bland photos-and-text format of the day, is of the you-had-to-be-there variety: obscure messes of one kind or another. Where he got onto something was in his cutting up of buildings.

Doyen of a group of architecture-trained radicals called Anarchitecture, Matta-Clark went in for acts of literal deconstruction that combined poetic inspiration and daredevil physicality. (His choirboy face topped a Superman body; and his lust for danger made dying in bed the least probable of ends for him.) Sometimes illegally, he took chain saws to abandoned structures, with results shocking, dizzying, and delicate.

Matta-Clark's most telling work, and one of the indelible images of our time, is his 1974 *Splitting*: the clean bisecting of a condemned two-story house in Englewood, N. J. He subsequently cut out the house's top corners, which are on display in Brooklyn along with other engrossing architectural fragments that look mightily prophetic of recent trends in sculpture that exploit materials with a history of social use.

That the Englewood house was a graceless and forlorn old clapboard thing only amplifies its "houseness" as nothing more or less than somewhere people live. Matta-Clark's elegant violence to this most basic human symbol makes for a drastic elegy, mingling sorrow and anger.

Anyone happily lacking personal feelings of dislocation and of some variant of "homelessness" might gaze on the photos and relics of *Splitting* with equanimity. I can't.

None of Matta-Clark's filleted buildings exist any longer, but his virtuosic photo collages of their interiors — in his later work, baroque shapes cut through floors and walls, communicating vertiginously from sky to basement and from backyard to front yard — readily convey a perceptual experience keyed to wherever, very carefully watching one's step, one would happen to be in them.

Matta-Clark's chain-sawed environments make meaning by intensifying physical self-consciousness to ecstatic or terrifying effect. They are symbols of a life in art conducted outside the upholstered prisons of commerce and institutions, an uncontained existence requiring moment-to-moment location checks: Where am I? Furthermore: What am I, and what am I doing?

I'm not eager for a return to the obligatory anarchy of the early '70s, when people were horrible to each other out of sheer distraction. But everybody knows that the present, market-tyrannized situation of art is intolerable. There has simply got to be another way.

WHAT DO THEY BUY WHEN THEY BUY ART? "They" meaning the
very rich individuals —not institutions, long since left in the runaway market's dust —who are paying these incredible prices at sales
where, for the fullest effect, the auctioneer ought to appear in cap-
and-bells and bidders' chairs should have whoopee cushions.

Or put it this way: are they —European business barons, American
financiers, Japanese I-don't-yet-know-what —buying anything at
all? Aren't they, rather, simply changing their wealth from one form
to another in public, where the transmogrification is a spectacle of
crazy alchemy?

A commodity's commodity, art in the marketplace behaves so
much like money itself that the differences —and don't worry, there
are differences —can get elusive. Like money a thing of no inherent
value, artwork has value assigned to it at the moment of exchange:
"This multicolored piece of cloth signed 'Jasper Johns' equals *x* million
of those green pieces of paper signed 'James A. Baker III.'"

Think of it next time you see a gallery price list. What you're looking
at is the going exchange rate for currency minted in this or that studio.

It's obscenely magical, the moment of exchange, and explains the
sick laughter that fills auction rooms when yet another painting is
knocked down for a sum —more than $40 million in 1987 for a decayed
van Gogh, nearly $5 million last month for an indifferent Pollock —
that might have cornered the world market in paintings not long ago.
It's a moment of indecent exposure of the arbitrariness, the sheer
pin-the-tail-on-the-donkey whimsicality, of assigned values.

The horror is not that art is overvalued but that, deep down, money
is worthless.

That's the best sense I can make of today's orgiastic art market:
a carnival in which the normally arrogant, intimidating dollar gets
"Kick Me" signs taped to its rear end. The sight brings raucous relief
—in an area safely cordoned off from other markets, where money's
authority is not to be questioned —from the intolerable suspicion
that money is our culture's only measure of value.

I'm not talking about speculative collecting, an epiphenomenon of
greed that is to the serious (or seriously insane) art market what
Chicago stock-futures trading is to the New York Stock Exchange.

I'm talking about buying behavior whose fervor suggests religious conviction. I'm talking about the kind of collector that any of us, if we love art, might become in a minute given unlimited pelf.

This market may have a sometimes blinding weakness for names, but they are good, interesting names, symbolic of values that are anything but frivolous.

Look at the artists today's collector has made auction superstars: van Gogh, Pollock, Johns—far cries from the genteel standards, mainly Impressionist, that used to set the pace. Beauty, tastefulness, skill, and other traditional values have been displaced as criteria of desirability. The big bucks now go for art with psychological and aesthetic edginess, brooding or ecstatic irritability, intransigent self-possession. The big bucks want *resistance*.

Whether they know it or not, many wielders of big bucks seem haunted by uneasiness about wealth's human consequences. They are going for tokens of the very values, like individuality and spirituality, that business and finance grind underfoot all day. To pay a ridiculous price for the token suggests a rite of purification: metaphysical money-laundering.

The Japanese corporation that plunked for van Gogh's *Sunflowers* keeps it in an office building open to a public probably meant to feel that in the poor, discolored, ardent, and irrationally expensive thing, they are viewing the *heart* of the company.

We may be witnessing, in the market, a sublimated, cosmopolitan equivalent of the world's current religious frenzies. If caught up in it, we become Shiites of sophistication, reacting in our own way against the values-shattering modernization that produces our wealth. Plowing wealth into an American-flag painting in New York and burning an American flag in Teheran may be alternate ways to soothe battered souls.

To confirm it, note how the edgy tastes of current big-time collecting mimic the edgy styles of current big-time art. The common feature of successful contemporary work is either a bitter pessimism about effects of modernity, as in Kiefer and Fischl, or, amounting to the same thing, a hyperintensified mockery of modernity, as in neo-geo. The spiritual compact between such art and the money that buys it is dark, neurotic—and sacramental.

June 8, 1988

ILYA KABAKOV *Ronald Feldman*

W<small>E ARE TEMPTED BY GLASNOSTALGIA</small> — morbid hyper-responsiveness to Gorbachev's open-window policy — to go gaga for all new things Soviet. Apropos of Ilya Kabakov, whose multimedia walk-in Russian novel packs the spacious Feldman Gallery, let's succumb! Kabakov is a great artist. He is a harbinger of phoenixlike glories in liberated Russian culture. If you miss this show, you'll feel obliged in the future to lie and say you saw it. John Russell wrote in *The New York Times* that Kabakov's theatrical warren — a dimly lit "communal apartment" containing relics and written accounts of fabulously obsessive-compulsive imaginary characters — is "closer to Chekhov than to Gogol or Dostoevsky." Wrong. Kabakov is in solid with all three, knitting their various fascinations together with the dream logic of souls unhinged by beleaguering social orders.

Be warned: the cabin-feverish *horror vacuii* of the work, initially elating, will get you down. When the characters' madnesses start feeling quite sensible, under the circumstances, you will know it is time to flee. But Kabokov's teeming weirdness seems the totally authentic note of Russian creativity so long muffled it's bound to jabber at first.

28

"CONTEMPORARY SCULPTURE" *Marian Goodman*

CHARLES BAUDELAIRE SAID OVER A CENTURY AGO that sculpture is boring. He was always right. Ad Reinhardt some decades ago said sculpture is what you bump into when you back up to look at a painting. He was always mean. What is it about sculpture that irritates us so?

I think it is a harsh demand we unconsciously make on anything that inhabits our own physical space: What is that? What's it good for? Why doesn't it go away? This is a modern phenomenon. Architecture and decoration once provided sculpture with cozy nooks and proud pedestals. Trapped out in the open, the medium has since had too much explaining to do.

The best modern sculpture always expresses some sort of existential gawkiness, capitalizing on the same intimacy of shared space that makes most sculpture irritating. It can have the spooky and lovable effect of reminding us of what, in grueling modern times, it is like to be a person — or just to try to be a person, in an inevitably losing battle that some of us fight with more honor and aplomb than others.

Bad sculpture may be correspondingly repulsive, beyond bad work in other mediums, because it reminds us of people whose idea of life tactics is to bully and whine (as opposed to blundering and whimpering — which had better be okay or else nobody makes the cut).

"MODERN TREASURES FROM THE NATIONAL
GALLERY IN PRAGUE" *Guggenheim*

BUT FOR ONE PAINTING, THIS SHOW is coals-to-Newcastle for
modern-art-flush Manhattan. That painting is *Dance on the Shore*
by Edvard Munch. Few Americans know that Munch (he of ubiquitous
Scream prints) was a great painter, because just a single work in this
hemisphere (*The Voice*, in Boston) confirms it. Ninety percent of his
paintings are stuck in Norway, constituting the one readily defensible
reason I can think of for visiting that nice, dull social democracy (my
ancestral homeland).

Sensual and lonesome, *Dance on the Shore* shows women at an
undulant seashore on or about Midsummer Eve, when the sun skims
the Scandinavian horizon around midnight and the locals get variously
frantic. It's the Munchian time of the year, when the secrets of all
hearts leap to the eye, ready or not.

Painted circa 1900, *Dance on the Shore* belongs to the declining
period of Munch's self-abandonment to themes of love and anxiety
that peaked in his 1894 *Madonna*, a lover's-eye view of a woman in
orgasm. Having exposed convulsive truths of sexual adoration, hatred,
and dread, Munch was retreating with shattered nerves. Thus the
lonesomeness, the elegiac and exhausted air, of the view of women on
a remote pink beach from a dark green foreground that heaves up
like a containing wall.

In Munch's symbolic lexicon, the blond woman and the redhead
dancing together would represent innocence and sexual appetite,
respectively; and the two women in black set apart from them would
be age and death. But the artist is no longer so interested in lexicons.
Leaking out of the symbolic patterns, his passion bubbles in every
detail of the scene, becoming general as it fades.

It's a gorgeous work, full of slow-motion-whiplash strokes and
colors as delicate as those inside an elbow, that gets wilder and wilder
as you look. It becomes less something you see than something that is
happening to you.

The picture is loaded with phallic, vaginal, ovarian, and spermoid
motifs so understated that you may dismiss them individually, until
the sheer number of them gangs up on you. Also hard to credit at first,
then unmistakable, are the "faces": at least three lurking, two-eyes-

and-a-mouth configurations that return your gaze with disembodied demonism.

Nothing in the depicted scene stands still. A high wind whips the dancers' hair and tosses the leaves that frame a blood-and-apricot-colored sun whose phallic reflection is chopped up by blue waves.

It is not a formally resolved composition. Its style vacillates between coarse and exquisite, bespeaking a rage for emotional truth contemptuous of aesthetic unity. What surely started out to be a fifth woman ends up as a sinuous red blob, and an eerie whitish form at the lower left is completely unreadable. It could be picnic litter or a corpse.

Your eye will return repeatedly to the center of the picture and an odd heraldic shape framed by the dancers' arms and skirts, a patch of blue water containing a reddish rock-eye-ovary. The shape seems to detach and press forward. You may feel that it is the painting's, or the painter's, heart, about to drop into your hand.

Swarming with comfortless life, *Dance on the Shore* is about being so alive you could die of it.

DAVID HOCKNEY *Metropolitan Museum of Art*

Sɪɴᴄᴇ ᴀʀʀɪᴠɪɴɢ ꜰʀᴏᴍ ᴇɴɢʟᴀɴᴅ ᴀᴛ ᴀɢᴇ 26 in 1963, David Hockney has had some lovely effects on American culture. He is a great, redemptive popularizer of the vaguely disreputable who has given tonic upbeats to things a lot of people didn't think they could or were supposed to like — from decorative painting and academic drawing to homosexuality, Los Angeles, and opera.

We're a little bit more civilized than we might be, on account of Hockney. He has done it all with elfin insouciance, a fierce work ethic, and a canny feel for the requirements of propriety. Though he has a mildly naughty streak, Hockney seems constitutionally incapable of offending. In his work as in his persona, he is this era's world champion houseguest, flattering his hosts with vicarious wit and tact equal to the challenges of modern art, naked boys, *Tristan und Isolde*, and other potential underminers of aplomb.

The unavoidable word to spring the transition I will now make is "alas." Alas, Hockney is his own worst (and probably only) enemy, driven by an overweening need to regret, somehow, the very nimbleness and finesse from which his blessings flow. With the rankling yen for Respect that sometimes afflicts innately lovable people, he has increasingly insisted on trying to impress with talents strictly suited to please.

The second half of Hockney's retrospective is leaden with strenuous and pointlessly tricky stuff — pastiches of neo- and pseudo-cubism, mainly — seemingly calculated to suggest an aesthetic deep thinker advancing art's frontiers. It's dismaying to sense Hockney so undervaluing a native flair that anybody else, deep thinkers included, would give a lot for.

Hockney's best work still is the cornucopia of interiors, swimming pools, still lifes, and portraits he painted, drew, and printed in Los Angeles and in London from about 1964-72. It is "realist" work, essentially, for all its extremes of stylization. It is about the joy of thoughtless absorption in gazing at pleasant, perhaps slightly strange people, places, and things.

Hockney's halcyon showers and pools let us know how wonderful it is to have bodies that can get wet. His fond and quizzical pictures of Henry Geldzahler and other friends call for a term akin to but milder than "love poems": "like poems," maybe. Throughout, delight in beauty and in having skills to render it make for a contented and seemly, sociable eroticism —a visceral niceness, if that's conceivable.

In 1973 Hockney moved to Paris for a couple of years and suddenly went arty, and it's been touch and go, in terms of his work's satisfaction quotient, ever since. He took it into his head that Western pictorial conventions needed revamping (after a century of modernist tinkering, a doubtful proposition) and that he was the one to do it (with his temperament, a colossal mistake). With plodding literal-mindedness, he proceeded to render subjects in reverse perspective, from multiple viewpoints, and so on along well-worn modernist paths: reinventing wheels, answering questions nobody had asked, and generally chewing more than he bit off.

At best, as in some of his photo-collages, the results are fun to puzzle out. At worst, in mural-sized treks through houses and landscapes, they are amazingly ugly. The one genre that rarely fails Hockney is drawn or painted portraiture. The presence of a congenial face seems to distract him from baleful urges to overturn conventions of representation. (A wit like Hockney *needs* conventions in the way outlaws, as opposed to revolutionaries, need laws.) Hockney's 1979 portrait of the late Divine is a knockout not on account of its borrowings from Matisse, but for how Divine's imperiousness holds all merely aesthetic appeals at bay.

FIREWORKS

IT IS THE FOURTH OF JULY WEEKEND as I write, art is elsewhere, and what I really love now is to set off fireworks. I'm talking backyard pyrotechnics with the traditional, bottom-of-the-line ordnance — cheap little gunpowder devices that blow up, zoom skyward, and/or emit colored fire — that is an everlasting miracle of human invention.

Thank you, ancient China, for the firecracker, upon which no improvements are anticipated or desired. Thank you especially for what we call in our vernacular the "bottle rocket," maybe the world's single most satisfactory manufactured object.

A contemporary bottle rocket ("Air Travel" brand, made in Kwangtung) is a 2-inch-long cylinder of paper-wrapped propellant and explosive attached to a splinter-thin, nearly foot-long, red-dyed stick. Stand it upright, ideally in a beer bottle, and ignite. Fsss. Swish, trailing sparks and smoke. A hundred or so feet up, a flash followed by a crisp bang. Then, if it's daylight (who can wait for sunset?), you see the bare red stick drifting down.

I know fireworks can hurt people, but so can a lot of other benignly intended things in an accident-prone world. I know they are illegal in New York State, but I assume law enforcers must be embarrassed to deny us simple, time-honored pleasures. Out of respect for the enforcers' feelings, I ignore this law.

Acquiring firecrackers may be dicey, entailing a Third-World-ish sojourn. It has led me at length, two years in a row, to smiling Chinese women in doorways — smiling, perhaps, because I am no kind of haggler. Even at sucker rates, however, bottle rockets should come to little above a nickel a pop.

You can get more potent items, too, and I do: rockets that scream, rockets that make semiprofessional-type fire flowers in the air, all manner of blazing gizmos that jump and spin, fireball-spitting (thup, thup, thup) Roman candles. The trouble with the more rare and expensive things is that you get too precious about expending them, making sure everyone is looking and so on. The optimum spirit of banging away is lost.

I leave out entirely the giant firecrackers like M-80s ("silver tubes" when I was a kid and their waterproof fuses made for low-effort, high-yield fishing in the town creek), whose specifications approach the military's. Fireworks should be dangerous enough only to encourage alertness.

Light a firecracker and, quick, toss it. Bang. A feathery burst of shredded paper. Repeat until sated. You will like to explode a few whole packs. Bbbbangbbang, bang. But that's too profligate —unless you could go all the way with it as they do on Bayard Street in Chinatown at the Chinese New Year, dozens or hundreds of people throwing masses of red crackers as fast as they can light them to produce a continuous roar.

After a day like that, it looks as if a red snowstorm has passed. In this city, Bayard Street filled with drifts of fluffy red paper is an annual sight as beautiful as Christmas lights on Park Avenue. It is a lovely, evanescent monument to hands-on, communal enjoyment, guaranteeing good luck.

Some will say that I would feel different if I had to live on Bayard Street. Some will be right. I do my exploding at an isolated rural place upstate in cahoots with my daughter and nephew. (To avoid feeling like an idiot, by the way, it is important to pretend that your fireworks are for the entertainment of children; if you lack kids, borrow one.) To the citybound who suffer the seasonal din, I can only extend a sympathy that they may well find unallaying.

Some, who are never wrong, will say further that my joy in fireworks is regressive. You bet it is —and none too soon after long months of approximating grown-upness. With fireworks, I discover old, inchoate excitements probably pertaining to a boy's dim anticipations of sex —an idea supported by Alfred Hitchcock, eternal sniggering little boy, when he mocked the coupling of Cary Grant and Grace Kelly in *To Catch a Thief* with cutaways to airbursts over Monte Carlo.

Do-it-yourself fireworks satisfy a limited appetite for the pyromaniacal. (Once a year is plenty for it.) The appetite is merely exacerbated, I find, by the remote, academic splendors of professional fireworks displays, which deliver the vicarious arousal and intrinsic bleakness of watching somebody else's fun. Watching professional displays, I know there are people out there having major kicks shooting the stuff off. I want to be one of them.

The alienating beauty of the professional spectacle impresses without moving. It can make you feel dead inside. Emotion is added, in dollops of gloppy sentimentality, by references to the ceremonial occasion. One may sometimes fall for this, as when, a few years ago, a centennial celebration of the Brooklyn Bridge was capped by having that totally adorable structure spew fire into the East River night. It's a matter of what symbols your heart will buy into.

No such thematic necessity burdens Fourth of July bottle-rocketing, which is bang-for-bang's-sake. Patriotism? Well, sure. It's a likable country that maintains such a tradition, when you come to think of it — but you're not obliged to. The point is not to congratulate America but to just go ahead and be an American in the classic mold: free, somewhat obnoxious, and up for a good time.

"ACT UP AT WHITE COLUMNS" *White Columns*

AIDS IS AN ANVIL upon which our culture is being battered into new shapes. They are shapes of fear and anguish, for the most part: grimaces expressing helplessness even to contemplate, let alone to ameliorate, the disaster. But there are emerging profiles of clarity and purpose, too.

A contentious but invaluable current special issue of *October* magazine argues persuasively that this climate is defined by more than physical illness. AIDS is functioning socially as a stigmatizing metaphor for the offenses of being homosexual or, increasingly, black or Hispanic and a drug user. The symbolism explains stony governmental neglect, institutional inertia, and general-public callousness —indelible blots on our era.

Art-world response so far has consisted mainly of fund-raising sales and auctions that have been very successful in today's lush market. Meanwhile AIDS has appeared as a theme in numerous works of art, such as the elegiac paintings of Ross Bleckner. By preserving and extending our capacity to feel, threatened as we are with numbness by the unrelenting plague, such art performs no small service.

What else, beyond money and emotional ministration, can be expected of the art world? A scruffy, intensely lively show of agitational and educational material produced by ACT UP (AIDS Coalition to Unleash Power), at the alternative space White Columns, suggests that one answer is an opening of institutions to AIDS activism, a lowering of art-world drawbridges for people who are doing something about the crisis.

ACT UP is a radically democratic, free-for-all organization in which "affinity groups" form spontaneously to develop actions. Dedicated to exposing entrenched prejudice, ignorance, and apathy (against lazy public assumptions that officialdom is somehow seeing to the problem), ACT UP is a model activist movement in ways visually palpable at White Columns.

The middle of the gallery is filled with huge black parade banners bearing motifs that include the now familiar ACT UP logo of a pink triangle (Nazi concentration-camp insignia for gays) and the words "Silence = Death"—a formula implying that life equals noise, which the surrounding show delivers in the form of hand-lettered signs, posters, fliers, videos, and other vernacular agitprop.

This tableau of call-and-response is the very image of how activism works.

But is it art? The question is pointless. Debates, always remarkably sterile, about whether "political art," when conducted in an emergency, can be "real art" are as sensible as fretting about the paint job on a lifeboat when your ship is sinking.

Political art is art purposefully shorn of concerns with beauty, complexity, individuality, and the other values most prized in the art of our culture. For this reason, political art should not be expected from most of the people we call artists, whose bone-deep allegiance to such values overqualifies them for the job.

Again, ACT UP shows a sure grasp of art's proper place in an activist movement: decidedly subsidiary and preferably anonymous, created by affinity groups that include art directors and other design professionals on the one hand and by inspired, street-politicking amateurs on the other.

Much of the material is angry. A favorite tactic is to damn political figures by the simple act of quoting their insensitive or downright vile words. (May William F. Buckley's clanking proposal to tattoo people who have AIDS be securely tied to his tail forever.) Other material is positive, promoting group morale and hammering away at educational messages.

The show is a kind of three-dimensional snapshot of growing efforts to light a collective fire under society's sluggish conscience. It gives rise to the thought that the AIDS emergency is an opportunity for society — for everyone — to change for the better. People don't like to change. I suppose most of us have hunkered down internally against the horror. At what point does the shame of passivity become more painful than the misery of consciousness?

August 10, 1988

ROBERT MAPPLETHORPE *Whitney*

IT'S TIME TO SAY THAT ROBERT MAPPLETHORPE is the greatest pure
studio photographer of our time and one of the most important
photographers of all time. He has altered the common meanings of
his medium. He has given definitive expression to historic changes in
the culture. He has created work of indelible truth and extraordinary
beauty. These are things great artists do.

Actually, it is none too soon to be remarking on Mapplethorpe's
greatness, as is plain to see in his Whitney retrospective of nearly 100
pictures produced since 1971. But allowance must be made for the
slow adjustment of even sophisticated eyes to the dazzling light and
no less dazzling darkness of Mapplethorpe's vision.

Allowance must be made, too, for the distractions of the legend
of Mapplethorpe as a punk dandy, *poète maudit* of the New York
demimonde, soul mate of Patti Smith, and so on. Anyone might have
suspected that the inevitable fading of early-'80s fashions in romantic
decadence, which boosted his work to heights of chic, would dim
Mapplethorpe's luster. As it turns out, with neo-expressionism,
neo-classicism, and the other period styles in eclipse, Mapplethorpe's
art is more radiant than ever, proving that he is onto something timeless even when immersed in the moment.

Mapplethorpe has been onto certain verities of photography,
certain metaphors: light/flesh, picture/body, studio/soul. Guided
by the demon of a cold erotic proclivity — a "feeling in my stomach"
he relates to his youthful experience of pornography stores on Times
Square — he has worked in a minimalist spirit to isolate and purify
those metaphors, with images that cut like knives.

Note, in the photographs of Robert Mapplethorpe, how light
molds naked flesh (even the flesh of flowers, the sexual organs of the
botanical kingdom) like a sculpting hand. Note how bodies, even
when clothed, dominate the non-space of studio-backdrop compositions. And note how the studio — invisible, assumed — comes to
seem a sacramental zone for the revelation of secrets.

Though large, the Whitney show feels more like a sampler than
an exhaustive survey, giving succinct glimpses of Mapplethorpe's
preoccupations: punkish little paintings and Polaroids of the early
'70s, minimal-conceptual constructions (direct forerunners of today's

39

neo-geo), his breakthrough theatricalizations of sadomasochistic rites in the late '70s, iconizations of black models, brooding portraits, his voyage of discovery on the body of muscle woman Lisa Lyon, and the most beautiful floral still lifes ever taken, with numerous surprising tours de force along the way. The one overall note is audacity.

Such audacity is rare, though the lust it serves, for Mapplethorpe the lust to know the secret and the forbidden, is purely human. The drive is especially powerful in recent American culture, which has associated privacy with constriction and loneliness. Mapplethorpe is a poet laureate of our violent wishes *to know*.

You don't have to feel any identity with the sometimes bizarre or disquieting secrets—the sexualizing of race, for instance—that Mapplethorpe chooses to explore. You get to be worried or upset. (I can now bear to look at his sadomasochistic tableaux, but only just.) But you will make a fool of yourself trying to deny the truthfulness of his art.

Radically amoral, in a way not so much art-for-art's-sake as *everything*-for-art's-sake, Mapplethorpe's work is ruled by the eye's appetite for perfect images of desire and fascination. As suggested by Ingrid Sischy, former editor of *Artforum*, in the show's catalogue, appetite has two components: "hunger" and "taste." Hunger craves union; taste demands distance. Mapplethorpe pushes these opposed terms to excruciating extremes, creating a magnetic field. His work is not about gratification, either sexual or aesthetic. Elegance spoils it as pornography, and avidity wrecks it as fashion. It is about a strenuously maintained state of *wanting*. The effect is a Keatsian, bittersweet, personal ache, given social bite by its kinship to the overstimulated demand that is the flywheel of today's consumerist, narcissistic culture.

Having already outlasted the downtown club world that gave birth to Mapplethorpe's career, his work seems a cinch to survive even this broader cultural era, in whose fleeting susceptibilities and frenzies he has found and caught, in photography's undying amber, the fossil of transcendence.

"DECONSTRUCTIVIST ARCHITECTURE"
Museum of Modern Art

Deconstructivist architecture" is a sly and brilliant attempt by Philip Johnson, modern architecture's eternal doyen, to expedite yet one more stylistic revolution in the international look of buildings. Aided by an eager assistant and propagandist, Mark Wigley, Johnson swoops down on some of the more far-out tendencies in postmodern design and hoists them skyward in his elegant talons.

Never mind that in the catalog of this jamboree of fractured, thrusting, jigsawed forms, Johnson denies attempting any such thing: "Deconstructivist architecture is not a new style," he writes. And never mind that his embrace of the work of Frank Gehry, Peter Eisenman, Bernard Tschumi, Daniel Libeskind, Coop Himmelblau, Rem Koolhaas, and Zaha M. Hadid is belated and superficial, coming well into the maturity of most of them.

Do mind the look and feel, the distinctive aesthetic wavelength, of the show. With sights plainly fixed on the corporate and institutional moneybags who are the people who matter most in world architecture — and whose tastes Johnson has been brokering for generations — the show says, in effect: "Get ready to love some crazy-looking buildings."

The chutzpah of this show is astonishing even for Johnson, last of a race of lyrically cynical, culture-mulching giants that included Henry Luce and Walt Disney. It follows his dominance of the whimsical, Robert Venturi-Michael Graves phase of "postmodernism" — that skittery term really meaningful only in the field of architecture, where it is defined precisely as a rejection of the International Style that Johnson (remember him?) helped establish with his epochal 1932 MoMA show, "Modern Architecture."

On this occasion, Johnson has picked spectacularly eccentric projects by architects of different national origins, with penchants ranging from cold structural analysis to crackbrained fantasy, and has repackaged them as a global smorgasbord of with-it sensibility. It's fun to imagine the poignant sensibilities of the architects thus dragooned, some ratio of "Oh, no, he's trampling on my ideas!" and "Oh, boy, here comes payday!"

The show is a textbook example of the ivory-towerish, decontextualizing, anti-ideological ideology that has always marked both Johnson and MoMA. In other words: modernism as usual, a continuing joke on the innocents who fancy that, in the real world, "postmodernism" can function as anything but another product label.

The curatorial coup of "Deconstructivist Architecture," lifting its subject from the mud of money and power where architecture happens up into a firmament of aesthetic moon-beams, is visual linkage of the featured architects with the 70-year-old traditions of Russian Suprematism and Constructivism (typically, with no distinction made between those mutually hostile tendencies of the revolutionary-era avant-garde). The show occupies three rooms: a stunning one of great work by Malevich, Tatlin, Rodchenko, Popova, Lissitzky, et al. and a bewildering two of drawings and models by the architects.

Johnson is quick to remark that the kinship of the so-called deconstructivists and the Russian avant-garde is pretty strictly formal, keyed to "the diagonal overlapping of rectangular or trapezoidal bars." Mark Wigley is less cautious, occultly suggesting that these contemporaries somehow do what those wonderful Russkies somehow meant to but somehow didn't.

If you try to think rationally about this forced historical conjunction, you are going to blow fuses throughout your cerebrum. I take this to be Johnson's plan, the better to reduce viewers to an addled state in which the mystical diagonals of Malevich and the jaunty ones of Gehry become congruent on a glamorous plane of sheer style.

Of course, the issues of architecture go beyond style for most of the architects here — including my favorite, Gehry, the rhapsodic rougher-up of sweetly human-scale spaces. (He's at the intimate end of a spectrum including cerebral Eiseman, technocratic Tschumi, epic Libeskind, and so on.) Johnson and Wigley observe the existence of the architects' differently serious intentions while pluralizing them into a sort of benign, blanketing fog.

Make no mistake. What's going on here is the soft sell of exciting new hemlines for skylines. Forget last year's demure cylinders and crenelations. The clock is ticking for buildings to go off like explosions in a shingle factory, never mind why.

August 31, 1988

BATTERY PARK CITY

Battery park city, the colossal landfill development on lower Manhattan's western flank, will make a great ruin someday. Parts of the complex still being built —"ruins in reverse," as Robert Smithson termed construction sites—preview the effect. But even the finished, Egyptoid towers of Merrill Lynch and American Express (designed by Cesar Pelli) feel already heavy with time, as if impatient to start crumbling picturesquely.

I used a humid Wednesday afternoon recently to check the current state of BPC's lavish public-art component: works in place by Ned Smyth, Mary Miss, and Richard Artschwager, with others in progress or still to come by Scott Burton, Siah Armajani, R. M. Fischer, and Jennifer Bartlett. I found that my thoughts about the art couldn't be contained by it but swelled toward the dizzying scale of BPC as a whole and what it means.

The meanings of BPC include manifest faith in the eternal robustness and imperial glory of the financial industry of New York—tones ringing hollow in this dawning day of the post-crash, post-Reagan, post-cocaine yuppie—and a touching belief in the magical power of something called "art" to react chemically with something called "the public"—a belief so incessantly disappointed that only somebody high on something can still entertain it.

On the plus side, at least BPC tells a story. Urban places should speak, and this one sure does—unlike such other contemporary Ozymandias-villes as the one upcoming in Times Square. That's the nice thing about early-'80s postmodern architecture, of which BPC is a suddenly dated, instant monument: it comes right out and tells you of the pride and mania of the corporate soul.

And you can't beat the view. I stood the other day on BPC's justly praised Esplanade, facing the Hudson. Sunlight was mother-of-pearl through mountainous clouds over Jersey, and the river was the dove gray of brushed aluminum. (At turn of tide, the glistering water was also charged with garbage.) I was nearly alone but for a day-care group of toddlers, whose glee among the terra-cotta pillars and arches of Ned Smyth's shrinelike sculptural environment made me reflect more kindly on that very self-consciously arty piece.

I saw lovers too, astroll and nuzzling. Even on a weekday afternoon,

43

the early-Sunday-morning enchantment of the place is guaranteed by a design that makes BPC a mammoth castle keep, moated by wide, roaring West Street and comfortably reachable only via two enclosed bridges that debouch in the intimidating gleam and click-clack of corporate lobbies.

Eventually a dense maze of high-hedged gardens complete with "guardhouse," the work of Bartlett in collaboration with architect Alexander Cooper and landscape architect Bruce Kelly, will secure BPC's southern salient near the scarily democratic old greensward of Battery Park. BPC will thus be assured of a network of public spaces roomy enough for the population of Vermont and usually empty enough for a visitor to hear the wind blow.

BASEBALL

IN THE VICINITY OF THIS LABOR DAY, at the annual nadir of the art world, with apologies and fair warning to the non-like-minded, I'm using this column as a paid vacation into my thing about baseball.

Actually, quite a few artists and intellectuals are hooked on baseball, probably because it is the least onerous of the major religions. Artists and intellectuals are compulsive skeptics, generally: what the majority believes, we won't. But like everybody else, we like a shared story of beginnings and ends and the meaning of it all. Thus baseball. Baseball explains everything except winter.

Initiation into the mystery of baseball is like initiation into the mystery of art, only backward: baseball looks like fun but is really serious, and art appears serious but is secretly joyous. The seriousness of baseball, like the joy of art, can't be taken for granted, let alone described with confidence. A lot of supposed insiders, in either field, never seem to get it at all.

In the news, as I write, the angst-ridden Yankees are in open mutiny against the man who pays them exorbitant salaries for the privilege of abusing them, George Steinbrenner. This era's living archetype of the Bad Boss, Steinbrenner does not understand that baseball is a ritual in which the spirit of observance is more crucial than the outcome of the games. If the spirit is proper, outcomes will be as good as they can be, given a team's talent.

The profligately talented Mets, meanwhile, have continued to display a strange malaise as they totter toward a division championship. Probably it's another case of pressure to win — coming not from above (Mets management seems exemplary on this score) but from all sides and from inside, blighting baseball's secret seriousness with the triviality of hyped expectations.

The seriousness of baseball (here it comes!) is about immersion in a compound time — immediate, seasonal, historical — that goes on and on, indifferent to hopes and fears and success or failure. You don't have to be an aficionado to grasp this. The snobbocracy of know-it-all fans is a cult, not a priesthood. Anyone who sighs contentedly at the sight of the great, green field is a congregant.

Like any religion or language, baseball is best learned by osmosis during childhood. My wife's mother took her to games of the then

New York Giants in the Polo Grounds. It was a lifetime gift. Our daughter, now 12, is entering what I think of as a baseball latency, as she emerges from the other kind. (Dwight Gooden is off her wall; River Phoenix is on.) But it will come back to her.

I wasn't much of a player as a kid, but I was into the game. I remember chasing a long fly ball at a school picnic in a Minnesota pasture. Other kids were shouting — with excitement, I thought. As the ball touched my glove, I rammed the barbed-wire fence they had been referring to. My torso, when they peeled off my shirt, resembled an organic pegboard. I sobbed because it hurt and because I had dropped the ball.

That's a sweet memory, of haplessness smiled upon by the gods of baseball. Normally a fool, I was for a moment a holy fool, St. Sebastian in the outfield. My friends laughed at me, but in an appreciative, wowed way. (There is a parallel to the self-immolating artistic genius.) I just still wish like hell I had caught that ball. It would have been nice to hang on to during my tetanus shot.

There are no barbed-wire fences in the majors, but there are other barriers, including built-in limits on human will, skill, and imagination. Fans live for instants when such limits are transcended either in lightning flashes of inspiration, when an ordinary player surprises everybody, including himself, or in the routine splendors of Ozzie Smith playing shortstop or Darryl Strawberry hitting very long home runs.

A certain kind of home run, taking off like a rocket and then drifting pensively in the upper air before descending far away, is commonly termed "monumental." It partakes of a timeless truth, like Euclidean geometry. Even opposing players watch it dreamily. It reminds them of something.

A fan cherishes that sort of payoff for hours and days and years of watching games. More than that, however, he or she remembers the self-suspension, the very forgetfulness, of those same hours and days and years. All the self you lose to baseball is collected in a safe place.

Art may be long and life short, but baseball is just there. A Steinbrenner or any other inappropriate intrusion can make you wish you'd never heard of the game, but only for a minute. All the idiocies heaped upon baseball, from artificial turf to Joe Garagiola, only prove its inviolability. Throw any kind of crap you want into the Mississippi; it will still float a raft past Memphis.

In 1992 baseball will become an Olympic-medal sport. Russians are playing it. This is confusing. It threatens intellectual fans' pet shticks, such as the one about the game as a working model of American democracy. But there will be no shtick shortage. A while ago, one enthusiast carried on at length in *The New Yorker* about the relation of baseball and Renaissance painting. The parallel even worked, sort of. They all do.

Intellectuals don't stop being intellectuals at the ballpark anymore than beer-soaked louts neglect to be beer-soaked louts. But a common grace tends to descend on most people along about the middle innings. It can look like boredom. It's really a merging into the wheels-within-wheels rhythms — quick and jittery, long and tranquil — of the game.

Nothing I've said here will surprise anyone who digs baseball, except maybe Russians. A mark of any true faith, as of post-structuralist art theory, is an allergy to the very idea of "originality." (For a celluloid catechism of baseball, by the way, see the miraculously correct movie *Bull Durham*.) It's a primitive thing: stories told around the same old tribal fires.

The following story concerns the essence of human endeavor.

Years ago my wife and I saw a minor-league game upstate (Class A, as in *Bull Durham*) in which a raw-boned Southern youth was pitching splendidly, with a big lead, until about the seventh inning. Suddenly he started walking men, then aiming pitches, then getting hit hard. His team's lead dwindled, and the manager assumed that unmistakable next-to-the-last-straw posture on the dugout steps.

Then, just as suddenly, the kid snapped out of it and mowed down the remaining batters with crisp, accurate pitches, securing a complete-game victory.

After the game, we had car trouble in the parking lot and were waiting for a repair truck when the players left the ballpark. A group of them moseyed over and asked if we needed help — nice young guys in their first summers far from home. I was saying no thanks when I spotted the pitcher.

"Wow," I said something like. "That was amazing! We thought you were totally out of gas. Then you reached back and really brought it."

The kid's wide-open face clouded with an unaccustomed effort of reflection. At last he hit on the answer and brightened. It was as clear as day to him.

"I had to," he said.

Next week I'll write about art because I have to.

JEAN-MICHEL BASQUIAT

"WHAT ELSE COULD HE HAVE DONE?" So said somebody in the art world to a friend of mine apropos the death on August 12, probably by heroin overdose (autopsy results have not yet been released), of 27-year-old artist Jean Michel Basquiat. My friend didn't tell me who said it. It doesn't matter. The repulsive suggestion that Basquiat died as some sort of career move belongs to the genre of cynical wisecracks passed around after any tragedy to reassure us that we're shockproof. In the words of John Donne, it is "A Valediction Forbidding Mourning" late-'80s style.

"What else could he have done?"

As well as being slimy in the way of such pleasantries, the remark is notably cruel as a parting shot at an artist often scorned, among the envious or otherwise meanspirited, as an upstart product of hype. According to this projection, Basquiat, who rocketed to fame in the neo-expressionist early '80s, had become a failure. He had worn out his vogue among the minions of fashion. His style was outdated. With the death of his mentor Andy Warhol, he lost social cachet. So presumably he needed to pull off something dramatic.

"What else could he have done?"

In point of fact, Basquiat could have done what he was already doing: making good paintings and selling them. Though not his best work, his most recent pictures have an undiminished, crackling edginess and authenticity. Across 9-foot-wide expanses of bare or colored ground, they deploy his familiar but always surprising stick figures, funny-savage mask faces, and block-lettered words. Their effect is kinesthetic, as engaging to our sense of bodily attitude and gesture as good dance.

Basquiat may be a martyr to nothing except the Russian roulette of a dope habit he vainly believed he could control without help. But there is no denying that his reputation, which will ultimately rest (rather securely, I think) on the quality and significance of his art, underwent weird inflations and deflations in the Byzantine art world of the '80s. It was a world that enabled his rise, that he helped to define, and that got bored with him.

I met Basquiat in March 1981 at the opening of a strenuously hip P. S. 1 show of scene-making artists and photographers called "New

York/New Wave." His work was the hit of the occasion. At that stage, it was still a fairly direct transfer onto portable surfaces of the frenetic and gnomic markings he had strewn downtown as leader of a two-man graffiti team named Samo, but the freshness of its spiky cartoons and stuttering nonsense writing was electric. At first glance, it seemed to clinch the breakthrough into art of demotic, up-from-the-streets energy that was a tenet of the then burgeoning (now defunct) Lower East Side scene (to which Basquiat never really belonged but which, like his contemporary Keith Haring, he supported in return for maximum exposure).

But the notion that this dreadlocked Haitian-American was an untutored wild child didn't square for me with the elegantly elliptical composition of his pictures—so unlike the formulaic centering and *horror vacuii* of work on canvas by the subway graffitists. His stuff looked awfully sophisticated to me. I mentioned Dubuffet to him.

"Who?" he said coolly. I got that we were not going to be friends.

Though a dropout and runaway, Basquiat was actually an upper-middle-class kid from Brooklyn who knew plenty about art from school study and from childhood museum going with his cultured mother. He was simply playing along with a mythologizing bent of the moment, when people were eager to see a whole truth in the half-truth of an innocent, hotly expressive, democratizing trend in culture. (Now it all seems like a very long time ago.)

There followed Basquiat's legendary months of working in the basement of the Annina Nosei Gallery; social shepherding and career guidance by Henry Geldzahler; entrance into a ravenous European market through Swiss dealer Bruno Bischofberger; erratic behavior that included a reported readiness, graying the hair of his dealers, to swap work from his studio for whatever cash or drugs he required on a given day; a tempestuous stint with the Mary Boone Gallery; and the improbable, temporarily sustaining father-son relationship with Warhol.

The eclipse of neo-expressionism by frigid, geometric modes around 1986 deprived Basquiat's warm, jazzy style of chic but scarcely invalidated it. He was a leader, not an epigone, of neo-expressionism, with an aesthetic sense rooted in New York big-painting tradition and with imagery drawn from heartfelt primitive and urban-pop veins. Nor was he a retailer of faddish angst. To the end, his graphic ferocity—typically with oil sticks rather than brushes, which he used mainly for erasure and filling in—had an unshadowed buoyancy.

He was a real artist, living to work instead of working to support a lifestyle.

The lifestyle was quite something, though. In 1985 I was asked to do an article on him by *Vogue* (which for some reason anticipated a hatchet job, as I learned when my piece was killed for being "too positive"), and I visited him in the converted carriage house he rented from Warhol on Great Jones Street. The dimly lighted place was a sort of busy womb, with a steady traffic of assistants and hangers-on, an attentive girlfriend, phones ringing incessantly, and a big table piled with Mediterranean delicacies and bottles of bordeaux.

Basquiat in the midst of it looked like a soft young African prince, imperious and wistful. "It was getting worse, but now it's getting better," he said of his work, in a tone of anxious self-assessment. He spoke nostalgically of his earliest days of making art in New York. He seemed to worry that what he called the "messy and earthy" feeling of those days was growing too far distant.

Basquiat was a young man plainly in for a tough time. He might well have come through it if he had kicked drugs, but it wasn't going to be easy. His artistic subject had been the passion of disaffected youth in a crazy metropolis. He was inevitably leaving that passion behind, even as its distillations were adorning the walls of rich, white, perhaps in every sense patronizing collectors from Dusseldorf to Tokyo. His later work displayed some resourceful use of African themes, to the possible end of developing a new identity as a black artist.

"What else could he have done?"

That's not the question now. The question, in these harsh and distracted times, is what Basquiat did do, which the art culture took up and then dropped so quickly and thoughtlessly.

THE NEW BUILDINGS

LET'S GET REAL ABOUT "ARCHITECTURE" in New York. The word is a euphemism for the peculiar activity that entails cranes and makes noise around here. Never mind our smattering of jewels, our Woolworth and Seagram and Guggenheim, our Grand Central and Central Park. Consider the average environment. This island is a river-to-river smorgasbord of sometimes charming, more often punishing mediocrities.

Big, though. And darn clever. The local substitute for architecture —artful alteration of the world of human use—is apt to be breakthrough engineering, as in the Brooklyn Bridge and the major skyscrapers. I have trouble thinking of skyscrapers as "architecture." Okay, Rockefeller Center is architecture. But Manhattan at best is a museum of technical whoop-de-do.

All this by way of prefacing my response to a coming crop of what promise to be mostly lousy buildings. These projects favor generically postmodern varieties of lousiness: square windows, formulaic setbacks, and melancholy arcades. But style doesn't matter. Spirit does. The spirit of building now is fanatically tame, obviously to dampen any possible excitement in a time when urban excitements invariably turn litigious. These are places designed by committees for committees.

Like most New Yorkers I'm a compulsive amateur building inspector. I've lived here 25 years. I am not an architecture critic, but you already know that because I'm not talking the stuffy, toneless talk of New York architecture critics—a civic-concern-speak with variants employed by everybody in the building racket, from developers' press agents to preservationists. I think this patois is a legacy of the Dutch and Anglo patricians who once ran the town. It says paternalistically to the masses who must struggle to survive here two things: 1) We have your best interests at heart, and 2) Fuck you.

Don't you love it when they carry on sensitively about the skyline, as if you ever see it? Like this, from flack for Solomon Equities' projected behemoth at 1585 Broadway: ". . . a prismatic crown at the top which will give the building a notable presence on the New York skyline." In other words, the criterion of Manhattan architecture is the view from Weehawken.

Your typical New York building—and the new ones will be radically typical—is defined by naked economic and legal calculation and cut-rate materials. Now and then some oddity of design gives the game away to an extent that's almost adorable. Take the 14-story public atrium awkwardly inserted in the side of a box called Tower 45. It emerged as a bargaining chip in a deal with said box's neighbor: an option to buy the 35-foot-wide strip of land the atrium will occupy in return for not blocking the neighbor's windows.

This is not a type of consideration that Brunelleschi had to deal with on a daily basis, but it's *echt* Manhattan. Love it or leave it. I don't know about you, but I personally plan to enjoy the dickens out of that atrium, secure that tears of gratitude will not be expected of me.

The number of proposed structures that sincerely contemplate civic benefits — notably the Harlem on the Hudson complex and Sam LeFrak's housing project for the Lower East Side — is so pathetically small that it only sharpens the pain of New York's catastrophic, never-to-be-met social needs. (Am I cynical? In Minneapolis, I'd be cynical. Here, I am not cynical.) One after another, the buildings are strictly about making money — and not even money for identifiable people (individualized greed often creates real architecture), but money for money.

This being the case, we might get better buildings by forgoing genteel pretenses and telling developers to just let 'er rip. The option is a real civic will to confront real problems. Meanwhile I like the colossal folly planned for Columbus Circle, though I preferred the even more colossal folly proposed earlier, and my heart fails to bleed for the we've-got-ours constituency that, while people are homeless and the public schools are in crisis, circulates petitions against *shadows*. Let's have world-famous monuments to New York's heartlessness, rather than all these banalities.

Even banal projects undeniably contribute, however, to the sheer velocity of change that is New York's cynosure. This is an unthinkable place to live — middle-class "livability" went out of the equation here a long time ago, if it ever pertained — unless both you and it are on the move.

One truly architectural phenomenon that makes New York a place of poetry is the demolition-construction site. Think about it. Your most powerful memories of your life here — love affairs, career events, nervous breakdowns — probably have in their backgrounds some partly finished structures whose progress was your soul's tempo. Do you suppose we could persuade some of these people, when their silly buildings are complete, to knock them down and start again?

PHILIP GUSTON *Museum of Modern Art*
NIGHT STUDIO: A MEMOIR OF PHILIP GUSTON
By Musa Meyer

PHILIP GUSTON'S LAST STYLE WAS BORN IN 1968 with cartoony images of Ku Klux Klansmen. Their raucous goofiness was very '60s, some-how, as if the artist were taking Bob Dylan to heart: "I was so much older then, I'm younger than that now." It scandalized most of the art world. Not only no kid, at 55 Guston owed his position of respect to a restrained and elegant, very grown-up abstract style undertaken in the early '50s. For many who cherished his hypersensitive abstrac-tions, including me, the new stuff was as welcome as a fart in a crowded theater.

The new stuff was anguished and a bit hysterical. Whose problem would that be? Would it be Guston's, marking one man's disintegra-tion? Or would it be the culture's, in the way that Cézanne's anxiety and Picasso's rage became psychic baggage for everybody incautious enough to love modern art? The issue see-sawed through the '70s as more and more young artists, but very few critics and collectors, found a hero in the later Guston. When he died in 1980, Guston had a cult following larger than many successful artists' mainstream audiences.

Eight years later, on the occasions of a show of his drawings at MoMA and of a biography by his daughter Musa Mayer, the verdict is in. The cult has dissolved into the mainstream like a dye, tincturing everything. Guston has won, meaning among other things that the base metal of his mania is transmuted into the gold of legend. "Guston-esque" now recommends itself, like "Kafkaesque," as a term in the lexicon of perversely poetic 20th-century feelings.

The Gustonesque is a mad love of Art rampaging like a bull in a china shop among the standard human emotions. You wouldn't like it in your father.

> One day, when I was very small, no more than three or four, my mother had made gingerbread cookie dough and rolled it out for my father to cut. Philip spent hours making a cookie for me, cutting up currants, marking the reins and halter of a beautiful Greek horse. It was put in to bake with all the other cookies. When I saw it, I cried, "Oooh, my cookie" and reached for it. "But you couldn't touch your horse cookie, that Philip had made for you," Becky

Phelps [a family friend] tells me now. "It was nailed on the wall, as a great sculpture."

As she tells it in her lively, honest, bittersweet book, Mayer never did get the cookie of her father's love. It wasn't for her. Nor was it for her mother, also named Musa, who emerges as an immensely poignant archetype of the Artist's Wife, endlessly deferring to her husband's obsession. Guston was vulnerable and generous, a pretty nice guy on the whole, and he did love both Musas, as the younger comes to recognize. But nothing was quite real to him, or available to anybody else, that couldn't end up on canvas.

Guston grew up in Los Angeles. When his father, a Russian immigrant junkman, hanged himself, Guston, ten years old, discovered the body. Jackson Pollock became his best friend and was expelled with him from high school for political radicalism. Embarking on an art career, Guston changed his name from Goldstein, for which he felt miserably guilty later in life. He came to New York in 1935 via an apprenticeship to the Mexican muralists and worked in various social-realist and symbolist styles that brought him national success into the late '40s, while alienating him from Pollock and other innovators of abstract expressionism.

Coming around to abstraction late in the game, he pulverized his conservative technique — a fruit of his eternally adolescent idolatry of Renaissance masters — into a delicate, trembling kind of not-quite-resolved picture. The aching tentativeness of his drawings circa 1952-65 can still take my breath away. I feel that it is about wanting something so impossibly good, a state of such grace and revelation, that achieving it would be a ticket straight to Heaven.

In retrospect, there may be something a little too high-toned to be true about Guston's abstraction. This was a man, as Mayer shows us, who was frantically self-absorbed, an alternately garrulous and self-isolating heavy drinker subject to wild mood swings. (The isolation was progressive, eventually confining him to the cinder-block studio of his home in Woodstock, N.Y.; he worked mainly at night with a turned-off telephone and was often unreachable even by soulmate friends who included novelist Philip Roth.) Lovely as it is, the abstract work is a mask.

So, too, perhaps, is Guston's post-1968 style, but this mask bleeds. When you attend the MoMA show, make yourself proceed slowly through the early stretches, the better to be set up for a visceral jolt when the facade of angelic aestheticism shatters and the demons

54

come out to play. Suddenly Guston's excruciating line finds, or stops fleeing, what it always yearned to confide: scenarios of childish terror shading into middle-aged abjection. The tone is one of vast relief and helpless joy: Guston finally working as and for himself, full-tilt.

Guston's bulbous Kluxers come by subterranean shortcut from political-protest art he made as a youth, only now they are figures not of indignation but of funny-horrible self-portraiture. They start out by whipping themselves and each other, then take spins around cities in bumptious cars, smoke cigars, do a lot of bang-bang-you're-dead finger-pointing, and paint replicas of themselves.

Gradually the slot-eyed, sutured hoods give way to lima-bean-shaped heads as heavy as cannonballs, with cyclopean eyes transfixed by paintings, books, and bottles or staring into comfortless space. Belligerent arms wield garbage-can lids, and several legs form grisly chorus lines on red and black killing grounds. Cigarette butts, old shoes, and studio detritus accumulate: junk for the junkman's son.

The feeling of the work is like the inchoate remorse, aimless anger, and impotent exaltation of solitary drinking, bursting into disciplined, improbable song.

Between heart attacks just before his death, Guston drew a gray boulder-head swatched with bandages and gazing dubiously up a slope, as if gauging the possibility of ascent or beholding something rolling its way. Like nearly all the late work, the picture is bold and vigorous, unquenchably alive. Guston had gotten the whole, sweet meat of his being exactly where he always wanted it — into the enchanted pictorial rectangle, where it could thumb its nose at the mere, perishing man wheezing at the easel.

The Gustonesque — a soul yanked inside out, guts on display, for art's sake — is now a permanent reference point for the spirit of our culture. Whether excited, repulsed, or indifferent, how you feel toward it is primary information about yourself. Having faithfully registered its human costs — what price glory? — Musa Mayer is entitled to a final word:

> Now that he is really gone, and not in hiding, pursuing his "sacred foolishness," now that it is no longer his hunger for painting that keeps me from him, but death itself, now that I can at last give up trying to get his attention, I find myself welcoming that passion at last, for what it has left of him for me, for the world.

MIKE KELLEY *Metro Pictures*

THE REPUTATION OF LOS ANGELES ARTIST MIKE KELLEY has been simmering in the downtown art world for years, and this could be the season when it boils over to a larger public. At 33, Kelley may be the most significant artist of his generation. You wouldn't call him "the best," because his performance-derived work shrugs off, when not insulting, conventional notions of "quality." That's part of his significance, and one of the things a lot of people will hate about him.

Attending Kelley's Metro Pictures show, some viewers may have a sincere inclination to flee the grotesque banners, assemblages, and paintings, with their themes of sticky sentimentality and bodily disgust. I can sympathize, because I gave Kelley's work a certain berth for a long time, vaguely hoping it would go away. But I've become convinced that he bears important news, at once socially dire and poetically fecund. He is an artist's artist for those artists — now in the making — who will matter to us in the '90s.

Kelley, a self-described "blue-collar anarchist," is from Detroit. He studied at the California Institute of the Arts, a major think tank of American art since the early '70s, and lives in Los Angeles. That's significant, too. There is a westward drift in art's concerns now, reflecting an ever more total identification of American culture with pop forms and mass media. In still-Europeanized old New York, the attitudes of our neo-geo and neo-conceptual artists toward masscult tend to be ironic and either romantic (it's exotic!) or paranoid (it's a plot!) — provincial, in other words.

In Southern California, wellhead of the commodity culture that is oozing around the globe, the facts of the matter are plain enough to be taken for granted. Kelley starts from a point well beyond fret or infatuation with the U. S. dream machine. In so doing, he awakens an old American myth of the candid and resourceful pariah: Huck Finn on the lam, rafting past golden arches.

Kelley's art is about how to be a person — and, taking ambition into account, how to "be somebody" — in a culture of manufactured fictions that numb our capacity to believe in anything. He makes do with whatever is left out of the fictions: shame, impotence, cruelty, hysteria, rage, failure, and all-around abjection. His work is funny, but with a sputtering kind of laughter that accompanies embarrassment and isn't far from a sob.

"PANTS SHITTER & PROUD" reads the lettering on one of 14 big felt banners loosely inspired by the work of Sister Mary Corita, the nun who in the '60s served a hapless movement to make Christianity groovy with modernistic, feel-good graphics. Each of Kelley's banners spells out a different malaise in the language of Sister Mary's idealistic kitsch. I liked a Matissean blue-and-white one in which a St. Francis figure ministering to animals stirs a thrill of revulsion when you notice the frog clinging to his foot, the dog humping his leg, and the snake about to bite him. In another, a sunny, UNICEF-type dove motif and the word "JOY" are reversed in clashing colors, like euphoria flipping over into anxiety attack.

Most of the work at Metro was shown recently in Chicago with a huge, controversial installation that incorporated portraits of Western thinkers who have spoken in apparent praise of criminality ("I want to sing murder, for I love murderers"—Jean Genet) and an amateurish clown painting made in prison by mass killer John Wayne Gacy. (Kelley wanted to include collection boxes for victims'-rights organizations, but all of the latter balked at the Gacy picture.) It sounds like a scrappy American version of the works in which Anselm Kiefer convenes German cultural heroes to confront the Holocaust.

A piece that does appear here, an assemblage of thrift-shop stuffed animals paired with a table bearing "novelty" candles, is tellingly described in the current *Artforum* by a Chicago critic named Laurie Palmer, in tones that speak to me of an emerging generational sensibility:

> The wall-hanging *More Love Hours Than Can Ever Be Repaid*, 1987, is made from handknitted, tatted, and crocheted effluvia (which resale shops have a constantly rotting supply of) in burnt oranges, limey yellows, and sour purples; it is accompanied by a pyramid of shaped and colored candles, melted into one obnoxious, perfumed mass. Redolent with the sickly-sweet sentiment of gifts that are less about giving than about incurring a bottomless debt in the receiver, the horror in these pieces comes in part from a recognition of the child's impossible position, forced to welcome even these treacly substitutes for love in exchange for a lifetime of feeling guilty.

Palmer's heartfelt sarcasm expresses a widespread and potentially dynamic pissed-offness with our culture of "treacly substitutes," though it doesn't convey the depth of Kelley's sorrow. You get that the degradation of religion, the awful glibness of cultural fathers, and the neuroses of popular handicraft are bleeding wounds for him. With obsessive fascination, he opens the wounds wider and wider, releasing a tremendous energy of unassuageable feeling. If you resist it, that's understandable, but if you try to argue with it you have dealt yourself a losing hand.

Kelley has jokingly termed his frieze of stuffed animals "my homage to Jackson Pollock." The joke seems to me at least half serious. Like Pollock and the other postwar abstract expressionists, Kelley struggles for self-hood as an artist in the teeth of frightening historical discontinuities. Forty years ago, the crisis was a disintegration of European tradition. Today it's the disintegration of practically everything, or so it can seem after an evening of television in which horrible facts mingle with idiotic "values" and you may catch yourself smiling at cute beer commercials tailored for children.

At the heart of Kelley's fiesta of morbidity and derision is an odd, sad tenderness, apparent in an assemblage that evokes the romantic life of a young girl: an "antiqued" pink chest of drawers standing on a mirror which reveals, in a net beneath the chest, copies of *Sex and Girls* and *How to Make Love to a Man* and a package of birth-control pills. Under the chest's glass top are photos of Kelley (a skinny, pleasantly homely guy) in "moody teenager" poses. It's easy to miss one tiny picture, from a performance piece, of the artist in drag.

Is a furtive girl in love with Mike Kelley? Or is she Mike Kelley in love with himself? Whom or what is anyone in love with, when anyone falls in love? This visual poem curls back on itself, becoming another link in a chain of meaning that Kelley is extending into a big, nearby, commonly shared darkness.

"IMPRESARIO: MALCOLM McLAREN AND
THE BRITISH NEW WAVE" *The New Museum*

I MISSED PUNK BECAUSE MY RECORD PLAYER WAS BROKEN, and because I was suddenly older. Back in the '60s the thought of not being up on a pop trend that big would have disgusted me, but by the middle '70s I could stand only so much distraction. I knew something was happening, as I looked out my Lower East Side window at the mohawks going by, and I tried to pay attention. But I didn't have anything to play the records on, and none of my friends cared much about new music.

Now here comes a show, documenting English entrepreneur Malcolm McLaren's machinations in pop culture, to drop broad hints that my mistake was not in missing punk music. Rather, I was naive in fancying that the music mattered a whole lot to a movement that was really a "swindle" insouciantly perpetrated by McLaren. Oh. Furthermore, that this grand scam, while being one small step for McLaren's enrichment, was somehow a giant leap for cultural revolution. Double oh. Not that I'm convinced, but braggadocio on such a scale commands a hearing.

The show's installation, by artists Judith Barry and Ken Saylor, is a mixed-media fun house retroactively promoting McLaren ventures, including his various clothes boutiques (most famously the 1974-77 store called Sex, with designer Vivienne Westwood) and rock groups (most notably the 1975-79 Sex Pistols). There are videos and mannequins and earphones and flashing texts in an architectural maze plastered with posters and luridly lighted —a deliberately tacky phantasmagoria attuned to the attention span of a hummingbird on amphetamine. It's all immediately engaging and instantly forgettable.

Far more fascinating is a distinctive verbal tone of the occasion, evident in celebratory catalog essays by art writer Paul Taylor (who organized the show), Jon Savage, and Dan Graham. The tone is one of preemptive self-slander, brazening words such as "swindle," "manipulation," "perversity," and "exploitation." Implicit is a sort of ethic for avant-garde capitalism: it's okay to cash in, as long as you do it as loathsomely as possible.

Actually, there may be a calmer way of assessing McLaren: as the doer of a dirty job that somebody would have to do — because something, of which punk was a focus, really did happen in the '70s. There was a new cynicism among the young, who drive the consumption of cultural goods like a flywheel, and marketing was bound to take note. That ex-art-student McLaren tapped in with hints from recent French philosophy and American art (an intellectual pedigree spelled out in the catalog) is incidental to the commercial equation.

McLaren's business acumen consisted in seeing unemployable, on-the-dole British youth as an underdeveloped market. His tactic was to flatter the bejabbers out of the kids with product lines that exaggerated what they were doing already. Were they into sex? He would provide gear from the darker closets of kink for them. Were they scruffy? He would sell them stuff to make them look like they lived in places where animals would die.

No big deal. Why is leisure-economy entrepreneurship as usual being covered on the art page? Partly because of the original art connection, which McLaren has maintained by beguiling art-worldlings with a heady sense of entree into the war room of mass culture. But this connection wouldn't be enough had he not committed one uncharacteristic blunder, which has immortalized him.

In 1975, McLaren hired a scummy-looking kid named John Lydon for the band of apparent no-talents, the Sex Pistols, that he had thrown together to promote his boutique. Purely by accident, Lydon, as Johnny Rotten, turned out to be a bright and driven, authentic rock poet and, of all things, a moralist.

Even I couldn't miss that. After walking out on the Pistols, Lydon gave an interview, which I read somewhere and took notes on, in which he spoke of waging "a losing battle permanently" against image-manipulators such as McLaren. "Image must be destroyed," he said, with a distillation of hopelessness and vehemence that is punk's lasting legacy, if anything is.

With enthusiastic support from the catalog essayists, McLaren has claimed to be a "producer-as-artist" and incidentally the true auteur of the Sex Pistols, whose profits he accordingly hogged for himself. When Lydon sued him, McLaren was deeply hurt. Lydon "didn't like his role, but that's what he was employed to be. That was his job," McLaren reasoned (quoted by Taylor), sounding like a rock 'n' roll George Steinbrenner. "Rotten has made the whole business of the Sex Pistols seedy and sleazy and turned the whole thing into an issue of money." Lydon won the suit. Yay.

The rest of McLaren's output is froufrou. Admittedly, some of it, mainly the original fashions and graphics he coaxed from Westwood and art director Jamie Reid, is once-in-a-lifetime froufrou. The nostalgia quotient of relics from McLaren's cottage-industry phase of obscene T-shirts and the like is high, but you wonder to whom the hard-sell display of them can possibly be addressed. The show is like a trade fair where trading has unaccountably been suspended.

I can believe that McLaren looks heroic, now and then, from the perspective of unhappy old England, where the rankling insults of class give drama to any kind of social mobility, be it only that of a brick through a window. And his own sense of injury is plainly not feigned. McLaren is a Jew who defiantly welcomes comparisons with Fagan, Dickens' corrupter of Christian boys. Where anti-Semitism ever flickers at the fringes of respectability, that's an appropriate provocation.

What we're left with is a stubborn cognitive dissonance between the U. S. and Britain as regards pop culture. Here, as Andy Warhol serenely understood, pop culture is more or less culture, period: the atmosphere we breathe, even if it gives us spiritual asthma. Over there, it keeps getting turned into some sort of alternative aristocracy, yet another charmed social status with a license to snub. That's what made the episode of British punk, with its swing-barreled rage against every pretense, so remarkable, though leave it to the likes of McLaren to make even punk pretentious.

DEGAS *Metropolitan Museum of Art*

AMONG MANY LITTLE-KNOWN AND SURPRISING THINGS in the Degas show, one thing shocks. It isn't art so much as evidence, the relic of an act of physical violence I can't believe I never knew about. Hold the art review until we get to the bottom of this. Why isn't the act in question a legend right up there with van Gogh's ear-ectomy, with which it shares the improper use of a razor?

I refer to a double portrait that Degas, then 34 or so, did of and for his friend Edouard Manet and Manet's wife, Suzanne, the former lounging and the latter playing a piano. More than a quarter of the painting, containing Suzanne's face, is missing, because Manet slashed it off. Degas got back what was left in the ensuing frostiness and later repaired the gap with blank canvas. He meant to repaint it but never did.

Now, exactly what the hell was that about? No one much knows, naturally. The bourgeois gentlemen of Impressionism were fanatically discreet, and all the giant Degas catalog's lowdown on private foibles of any sort wouldn't fill more than a column or two for a 19th-century Liz Smith. But I have a hunch about this thing.

Suzanne was older than Manet and perhaps a maternal figure for him, anyway a comfortable presence. She is nice, homely, and oddly blurry in his own pictures of her. I think outrage at the way Degas looked at her —no doubt coolly, as a matron of a certain class— made Manet grab the vandalizing razor. The younger artist's painting so violated Manet's feelings that he castrated it, incidentally injuring his own reverence for art.

Manet, the father of modern art, had a flash in which he saw his precocious colleague as a little monster. It was a flash of the future, because Degas was, and still is, the prime type of the great modern artist: obsessed, willful, and absorbed in style. Manet was all that himself, but not to the exclusion of common emotions. He was a mensch, you can tell —helpless to paint any subject with whom he lacked empathy and probably naive about people he liked. I bet his first reaction to Degas' Suzanne was fright.

Why isn't this little atrocity famous? That the painting has been in Japan since 1923 is no excuse. I think the reason is fear for cherished myths. The Impressionists are feel-good guarantors of modern culture, giving all of us our first intimations of aesthetic splendor and beaming comfort and joy into even the dullest hearts. Let *Post*-Impressionists like van Gogh, Gauguin, and Cézanne be flaky, but don't you tell us scary things about our daddies.

"Every 'original' genius has something a bit shady about him," Auden said, and I presume that most art lovers have had their epiphanies of realizing that Degas' ballet dancers are far from the spun sugar that middlebrow taste supposes. Rather, they are relentless looks at women torturing themselves to be relentlessly on display. Degas loves to watch them fight balky muscles and pitiless gravity, and he palpably doesn't give a damn about them otherwise.

I presume, too, that we've all heard Degas called a misogynist and an anti-Semite. The charges seem accurate, as far as they go, but they are beside the point of his art —which is where the true scariness comes in —and oversimple in judging him.

His mother died when he was 13, and he may have felt unconsciously that his puberty killed her. It would explain his eternal-bachelorish inhibitions with women, whom he pictured in the nude almost exclusively from behind. (You can practically hear him snapping at his models, "Don't look at me!") His vociferous siding with the army in the Dreyfus scandal may have reflected insecure pride in his aristocratic roots, through a half-Italian father he never rebelled against.

It makes sense to seek answers in Degas' childhood, because his "maturity" as an artist, seen in early works that are a revelation of the show, came so quickly. He didn't grow. He was born wearing a cravat. Degas is all there in a self-portrait at age 20, gazing sullenly from a head plainly programmed with every conceivably necessary aptitude. The student work he did in Rome is stunning. Want a John the Baptist? Bam. Next project. Right from the start, when you see the show, Degas is driving and you're just along for the ride.

His Salon-style history paintings are every bit as good in their way —meaning his way, nimble and icy —as his middle periods of realist portraiture, naturalist genre, and Impressionist dancers and racing scenes, and his last mode of virtual Expressionism with pastels. He was a medium-is-the-message stylist who had nothing to say except one thing, repeated with varying accents: behold perfection. If he roughed up the job in a hundred ways, mainly with weird compositions, it was only to make the final balance more impressive.

Through it all there is an awful coldness, which is nothing less than the thin, intoxicating air on the snowy peak of the capital A in Art. If you've ever breathed it, you'll do your share of gasping at the

Degas show, exalted by the finesse and incredible intelligence that mingle so strangely with the man's gross crotchets. He'll get to you, because it matters that much to him.

Degas had the same last phase that all the demonic male stylists do when they outlive their masks and their physical vigor. Like Ingres, Renoir, and Picasso, he went out in an explosion of female flesh, the core meltdown of what it had always been about for him: union with mother, sister, goddess, whore. This is Degas, so you get a voyeur's monument valley of turned butts, with breasts peeping out from under armpits, and it's mostly done not in fleshy oils but in dry pastels, colored dust.

But the colors go hot, hotter, hottest; and the models are killing themselves, holding those poses. He's an old man. How many more of these does he have in him? He's burning like a big meteorite trailing fire—and then winking out, gone. Nearly blind, he makes lovely little sculptures of dancers and horses from memory, touching them in his mind. Then that stops, too.

"It's amazing how indifferent you get in old age," he told a friend —a Jew he had shunned for years on account of Dreyfus—at an auction where one of his paintings went for a huge sum. His old American colleague Mary Cassatt soon described him as "a mere wreck." He lasted another four years. "I found him seated in an arm-chair, draped in a generous bathrobe, with that air of the dreamer we have always known," one of his last visitors wrote sentimentally. "Does he think of something?"

I doubt it. He would have been making something if he did. Art was dead in him, and there was never anything else about him worth mentioning. Even that could be dicey, as Manet had had occasion to sense. But Degas was as good as anyone gets at anything in the modern age, at a price reckoned on the standard rate of exchange: one soul in return for never being forgotten.

THE STARN TWINS *Stux*

THE STARN TWINS, 27-YEAR-OLD identical brothers from Boston who do poetical things to photography, have received what you could call a lot of press. A big spread on Doug and Mike in the *Times* magazine on Sunday the 5th somehow failed to rate the cover, which was given to some silly thing about nuclear peril, but you have to feel the setback is temporary. They are rock idols of art. I'm just waiting for the fanzine rumors. Like, you know, that Doug is really the smart one and Mike is really conceited, but Doug is too nice to say anything.

A naive tone seems appropriate for pegging the appeal of the Twins, whose transparent false-naiveté — a sort of wholeheartedly sincere insincerity — has refreshed an art world fatigued by the snarky braininess of neo-geo, neo-conceptualism, and other recent redolences of the art-school master's thesis. On sheer charm, the Twins have gotten away with murder in terms of overproducing for the market while retaining avant-garde cachet. Like beautiful children, they are indulged to a degree that probably isn't good for them.

Doug and Mike are given more credit for uniqueness than they merit, for one thing. As thoroughly collaborative art makers, they are only the latest of several prominent duos in contemporary art, including the veteran and still-champion tag team of the Brits, Gilbert & George.

You'd think people would note that the Starns follow Gilbert & George in assembling big photographic tableaux of treated fragments and in advancing grand romantic themes (the Twins brazen Christ crucified and the sea, among other love-and-death motifs) with a certain air of decadent exhaustion. But as far as I know I'm the first to mention it. That the Bostonians are messy and androgynous, rather than pristine and homoerotic like the Londoners, doesn't seem like a sufficiently categorical distinction.

I think the almost willful unthinkingness of the Starns' reception reflects a very American nostalgia for the recent past. It's a replay of the early '80s, a phenomenon along lines laid down by the sensational appearances of Clemente, Fischl, Kiefer, Longo, Salle, Schnabel, and Sherman — a generation that marked a truly new dispensation of art in the wider culture. That dispensation, accompanied by the fanfares of money and publicity, is entirely middle-of-the-road now. The Starns briefly make it feel young and innocent again.

Uncannily, the Starns seem influenced by every artist I just named, but the one most akin to their basic stance is undoubtedly Julian Schnabel. Like him, they are grandiloquent, sentimental, circusy, indiscriminate—and exciting. Their staggeringly prolific output displays a very high incidence of outright failure. But when one of their pieces comes off, the effect is exhilarating because it erupts in a context that is entirely theirs. You don't so much go to a Starn show as cross a frontier into Starn Country.

It is a country reminiscent of childhood. The device in their quilted photographic collages that everybody remembers is the "clumsy" use of Scotch tape, including the old, pre-transparent, yellowing kind. It evokes a kid trying to make something, oblivious in his or her rapture to the incidental cruddiness that is the first and maybe only thing an adult will see in the finished creation. The Starns are grown-up, elaborately art-schooled fellows who know exactly what they're doing, and to sense this, as we do, is to receive the primitive look of their process as a poetic aura, delicate with memory.

The Starns go in for what is known in the instant-antiques business as "distressing," using tricks to give an illusion of age. They get poignantly faded-looking images, to begin with, by projecting slides onto arranged pieces of photosensitive paper or transparent film. After developing, the pieces are variously toned, scored, and crumpled, then reassembled in funky frames, slathered onto boards, or push-pinned to the wall. The rough treatment nudges them, in a viewer's associations, from the class of new, studio-made things into that of old, found stuff.

As with their appearance of juvenility, the works don't aim to deceive with their pseudo-ancientness. Rather, the tone is a kind of joke we are let in on, permitted to have our cake of dreamy pathos and sophisticatedly to eat it, too. The Starns are wits, essentially, whose forte is keeping an audience off balance while slyly flattering its intelligence. The effect is quite civilized, for all the occasional spice of naughtiness (a tony erotic nude at Stux shows the Starns are loath to disappoint any taste) and intimations of moral grandeur.

The thing I like best about the Starns is the audacity with which they sometimes depart from their range of surefire, conventional genres. (Within said range are floral and architectural toss-offs that amount to the merest cash-and-carry accessories for chic decorating.) I have in mind an environmental piece that was shown at Castelli, incorporating small pictures of 49 historic victims and martyrs with a large one of Holocaust corpses. I can't say it "worked," exactly. With its joltingly understated title — *Lack of Compassion,* for heaven's sake — it mainly bemused. But the combination of convincingly earnest high-mindedness and damn-the-torpedoes gall seemed promising.

The Starns will ride the wave of their fame hard and well if they take it as an opportunity for risks rather than as a guaranteed trip to the shore of establishment approval. If worse comes to worst, and they are completely domesticated to the visual luxury trade, they'll have done something graceful. But they'll also have sharpened a growing sense of creative bankruptcy in mainstream art, which not long ago was abrasive and challenging.

ANSELM KIEFER *Museum of Modern Art*

FOR THE REST OF THIS YEAR, THE ANSELM KIEFER SHOW will be a city within the city of New York. It will attract artistic equivalents of tourists and pilgrims to its combination theme park and necropolis, its opera houses, temples, ancient libraries, and plazas where the living stroll with the dead. It is beautiful and clever, as a city should be. You will feel easy there, in good company, though your intelligence may sweat a bit from the credit being given it. Without the show's catalog as a map, you may get lost a lot, while always knowing you are in places poignantly familiar to somebody.

The city I'm describing is mental. Its landmarks are not visible things but tones, ways of thinking and feeling: some tender, some disquieting. (Any proper city has dangerous neighborhoods.) The images to be seen are largely rural or fanciful. Farmcountry landscapes and architectural ruins, crusted with paint, straw, and nameless crud, predominate.

There are watercolors of a frozen north and amazing, handmade books featuring dim photographs of peculiar stuff in a studio: a coffin-shaped bathtub, a toy tank. Many pictures bear written words that are like raveled ends of meaning. Tug on one hard enough (Mark Rosenthal's catalog essay shows how) and an avalanche of lore and association spills out.

This is the last stop for the Kiefer survey, which started in Chicago last winter and has toured to Philadelphia and Los Angeles. I've seen all four installations. (I've had a six-year minicareer of writing and lecturing about Kiefer since being excited by his work at a show in Germany.) This one is not as theatrically involving as the others, which tended to be cathedralesque and processional. It reflects an old MoMA preference for seeing artworks in contemplative stasis. Low ceilings in the museum's basement exhibition spaces have exiled the largest paintings to the third floor, further fragmenting a viewer's experience.

But MoMA's hanging, supervised by Kynaston McShine, is exceedingly elegant and more than okay, merely obliging viewers to provide their own rhythms to the unfolding of the show. That's citylike in itself. It's also civilized. This installation should scotch a misconception that Kiefer is some sort of brutal expressionist. It confirms that he is a discursive poet, ruminative scholar, and cottage-industrial craftsman. He is also, of course, a thematic daredevil who has jumped on subjects that some people, especially in his homeland, would rather not think about.

Kiefer, who is 43 years old and lives reclusively with his family in the Oden Forest south of Frankfurt, commenced in the early '70s to raid warehouses of German culture quarantined for its associations with the Third Reich. He embraced the associations, implicating the whole of the Germanic — 19th-century nationalism and Wagner, the Holocaust and Albert Speer, memories big and small — in a pageant of doom. Amid the ruins, he reared the fragile symbol of a palette, a self-portrait of the artist as a lone, truth-obsessed survivor determined to remember everything. The audacity of the gesture blinded many to its ironies and also to the preponderance of Kiefer's work that has little relation to World War II.

There is much irony, much panache, and some outright humor in Kiefer's art, but you wouldn't know it from public responses that yaw between weepy reverence and hysterical denunciation. The errors spring from gut reactions to his visual rhetoric, which is keyed to effects of unearthly light seeping through veils of darkness and clotted matter. People are either thrilled or threatened by a seeming invitation to abandon themselves to pathos, ignoring abundant evidence that Kiefer intends to cut obliterating passions down to the scale of individual understanding.

He pits pathos against pathos — fire against fire, which isn't to deny that his fire burns.

Several Germans over the years have tried to persuade me, in the bullying tones often adopted by that charming people to edify childish Americans, that Kiefer's work proves he is some kind of neo-Nazi. Germany has problems dealing with its past, and Anselm Kiefer isn't one of them. A pathological defensiveness is one of the problems. In relation to Kiefer, it takes the form of a reflex to kill the messenger of bad news. The bad news is that German souls were not wiped clean by a military surrender in 1945. The good news is that the bad news can be assimilated by a soul sufficiently sane and free.

Again, the astringent calm of MoMA's installation serves a wiser view. The show begins with a little watercolor from 1970 titled *Every Human Being Stands Beneath His Own Dome of Heaven*, which pictures a tiny figure giving the Nazi salute under a transparent dome on a vast, plowed field. I think this wry image asserts the artist's right to contemplate any idea at all in his own ambit — imagined universe, personal cranium — while granting others the same right. In everything that follows, we are addressed intimately and as equals by an incredibly engaging interlocutor.

The feeling, like the look, of all Kiefer's work is chiaroscuro: light and darkness, disembodied spirit and gross material. This polarity feeds his improbable fertility, popping out streams of inspirations like an intellectual Roman candle. The approach is playful even when the effect is devastating. The placement, in the painting *Shulamite*, of a menorah in a Nazi-war-hero monument is an act of wit that might make you cry, efficiently tapping depths of horror, rage, and sorrow untouchable by the concentration-camp photos that other artists have been exploitatively recycling lately.

It's only art. Remember that. I keep meeting people, slightly less exasperating to me than censorious Germans, who take vocal pride in remaining unmoved by Kiefer's work, as if this required heroic integrity. The fact is that communion with Kiefer comes only with patient concentration and a civilized willingness to be as respectful of his sincerity as he is of yours. Otherwise you're just a smug peruser of brown decor.

As for Kiefer's aesthetics — his omnivorous syntheses of Jackson Pollock, Joseph Beuys, conceptual and process art, photography, woodcut, collage and assemblage and montage, on and on — they call for no special analysis. You understand them intuitively when you grasp their purpose in communicating specific states of mind and heart. His technique is commonsensical, right to the point. The point may be erudite — Kiefer is bookish in every sense, to the verge of eccentricity — but, given a little background information, it is rarely obscure.

The drama of Kiefer's art is that of a mind struggling to know itself, to unpack its contents in objective form. The project has an old, Enlightenment cast, like the essays of Montaigne. It bespeaks a faith in humane intelligence that is exotic in these craven times, when few people dare to express anything without some communal permission. Kiefer can disturb, as when he confronts, in personas of Hitler or Nero, the megalomania lurking in every ambitious ego. But this is a guarantee of his honesty, which makes no exception of himself.

The putative "greatness" of Kiefer is an issue worried over by many, including myself in the past, that I am beginning to see as a distraction. His work may be best viewed as an antidote to delusions of grandeur, offering the modest virtues of a handmade, homemade world where the worst terrors and giddiest exaltations of life and time wait upon attention like a book on a bedside table. Kiefer's work is only art, but a crowded and eventful city of art affirming the capacity of a self-educating, independent mind to order, in some manner, practically everything.

His works are also lovely to look at, and they are getting lovelier. He seems bent on discovering just how virtuosic a painter he can be. I stress his art's ethical current only because it moves me so deeply, telling me that it is possible as well as necessary to be more true. Be a little brave, he seems to say. It may not make you happy or good, but you'll breathe free.

November 16, 1988

"DREAMINGS: THE ART OF ABORIGINAL AUSTRALIA"

Asia Society

A COUPLE OF YEARS AGO IN AUSTRALIA I visited Alice Springs, an unprepossessing burg at dead center in the vast, hot, hallucinatory bush. I remember aborigines. I remember how strange it was, shaking hands with an aborigine for the first time. His hand in mine was inert, like an object given by its owner on the understanding that he would get it back when I was through with it. I felt slighted for a moment, but he was perfectly benign. Hand shaking simply didn't mean much to him, evidently.

Another aborigine scared me by the way he stood inside a general store in the bush. Small and dusty, he had an unfocused gaze and a rangy posture bespeaking the immensity outdoors, as if the walls of the store did not exist for him. But for floorboards, he was in fact standing on the bush—and so was I, suddenly conscious of the store as something fragile and temporary in the bush's eternity. I felt a flare of hatred against him for his insulting attitude toward the reality of a building. Yet he was a mild man, only standing at his ease.

Between one thing and another, my equanimity was already in trouble by the morning, in an apartment on the edge of Alice Springs, when I was awakened by a terrific din. It seemed some aborigines disliked a policeman who lived next door. Stones flung by children were hitting the steel roofs and the steel stockadelike fence of the apartment complex. The kids didn't break anything and according to my host, who knew them well, probably weren't so much angry as gleeful, making percussive wakeup music with their stones. But it was a dreadful noise. What if the cop started shooting?

The ritual of the handshake, the substantiality of walls, the prudence not to arouse armed enemies—"universal" verities that I never leave home without were not being honored in the outback, and it toyed with my mind. I was shaken by the alienness of the place—and disgusted by what was familiar, by prosaic Alice Springs with its tacky shopping center, scorched golf course, and stockadelike fences. I became obsessed with the bottoms of fences, the straight lines where they jammed down into the reddish bush of otherworldly plants and lizards. The straight lines struck me as violent.

Literally, it seemed, *drifting* through Alice Springs, aborigines made the stolid, middle-class town, with its imported shade trees and World War I memorial, seem a temporary illusion, a heat mirage. I knew they were a decimated people, ravaged by alcohol and reduced to welfare dependency. But with the eternal bush at hand, their small, dusty, lithe demeanor had a power that made big, scrubbed, blundering whites seem flimsy. In the differences between "them" and "us," almost incredibly extreme within one species, I sensed the roots of racism in intimidation. I got a sickening hint of why white settlers had wanted to annihilate the aborigines: for their mocking grace.

Don't go looking for that power of strangeness at the Asia Society. It's not there, except faintly in a few old carvings and paintings on bark. Instead there is the violence of fences, unconsciously erected by people wanting only good things for aborigines. The show is an American boost for an Australian project to market symbols of the aboriginal religion, which has long been known by such pretty names: "songlines," "dreaming." The violence lurks in the straight lines of stretched canvases that aborigines are painting with acrylics, using motifs proper to the ephemeral sand- and body-painting employed in their rituals. Promoted internationally, the paintings are seen as a means to build independent wealth and self-esteem for a people gravely lacking both.

In problem-solving terms, the idea is impeccable. But the paintings are no good. They are turgid and nerveless, with their doggedly completed designs in plastic paint. They look like a type of abstraction briefly fashionable in the 1970s, when this project was born. Wall labels and a maudlin video, accompanying the show, assure us that the pictures are full of religious meaning, but what is religious meaning when divorced from religious practice and churned out in synthetic materials for export to nonbelievers? It is a symbol eclipsed by another symbol, to which it submits: here, the almighty white rectangle.

In its innocence, the Western mind fancies that the rectangle, divine form of the Parthenon, is purely neutral ground, rather than a template for mastering the world. Our way of looking at a rectangle is itself rectangular, congruent to it — such that the rectangle disappears. We see it not as a form but as a "universal" condition of form. Was there a true right angle anywhere on the Australian continent before the Europeans arrived? Those who innocently give an aborigine rectangles to decorate jam down fences they can't even see.

Aborigine painters don't know what to do with the edges and corners of rectangles, and why should they? Their bark paintings —

already suspect because the earliest surviving ones date from a century after the first whites —may be roughly rectangular, but in the roughness is the life: a slightly off angle carries throughout the composition as a compression or torque, making the picture squirm like an organic thing. On the crisp oblongs now in use, patterns burgeon absentmindedly to the edges and just stop there. The bush stops that way at the bottoms of Alice Springs' stockadelike fences —on the other side of which lawns and pavement happen to it.

White (and nonwhite) Americans should readily grasp a dilemma here. Our efforts to "help" American Indians, since genocide went out of style, have been similarly clumsy, to say the least. When we think of ameliorating ills, we seek progress and innovation, which are death to the absolute conservatism of tribal cultures. The helping hand brings only softer varieties of ruin. We ought to leave native peoples alone, but it would be too late for that even if, for once in a tradition of tampering older than the Acropolis, Western minds could tolerate such un-Western passivity.

One thing we have gotten good at, in our rectangular way, is preserving the legacy of what we haplessly destroy. I am thinking of a Plexiglas case at the Asia Society that contains a carved and painted wallaby, "attributed to George Ngallametta" (a delectably insane pedantry in context), that is the loveliest thing imaginable. The wallaby (a type of small kangaroo) stretches up and up in a series of vertical exaggerations that sing of horizontality: the creature is straining for a distant view across a vastness in which the Mojave Desert could nestle like a sandbox. It is also, perhaps, making itself visible to aboriginal hunters, who are elated by the sight.

Most of us imagine "primitive" people, though we no longer feel free to admit it, in terms of animals or children —for the excellent reason that only in sensations of our own animal selves and memories of our childhoods can we draw near to them. Their maturity and sophistication branch differently from ours and are inaccessible. In the wonderful carving of the wallaby, I understand the visceral insouciance of an animal and the childlike joy of a hunter. It is a tiny communion, like a flicker of light in darkness, but I want to remember it, in all its frailty, for the little seed of respect it nurtures. The carving was made for actual use in a ritual, which accounts for its dignity.

There is no such dignity in the aborigines' acrylics, whose pristine rectangles are semaphores of the rectanglar mind congratulating itself. It's excruciatingly sad. I was struck, in Australia, by the depth of guilty sensitivity felt by many whites toward the aborigines, in contrast to an old American callousness to the ongoing devastation of American Indians. It is an awful thing to confront crimes on which your culture is founded, and it is almost unbearable to think that you can make no amends to the victims without committing fresh offenses. As usual in our culture, which is not without resources, the answer is simply more and more consciousness, because only in the most painful knowledge does the idea of justice rise.

ED RUSCHA *Tony Shafrazi*

A FRIEND OF MINE RECENTLY CONGRATULATED Edward Ruscha on his current market success. Prices for his work have zoomed from nowhere in particular to something like $300,000 for early-1960s paintings like those (mostly borrowed and not for sale) now at Shafrazi. "That's me," Ruscha said, "the 25-year overnight sensation."

Ruscha gets to be sardonic about it. He is one of the major pop artists — maybe the most important after Andy Warhol, in the historical long view that is crystallizing now. Yet he has generally been regarded, if at all, as a marginal, special, "regional" talent: the best artist in Los Angeles, like the best French restaurant in Nebraska. Some people who have always known better, like epicures if there really were a three-star-worthy kitchen outside Omaha, have been content to keep Ruscha's brilliance to themselves. They will have mixed feelings about the present bandwagon.

A classic artist's artist, Ruscha has enjoyed the austere distinction of being appreciated most by those who understand at first hand the creative stakes in contemporary art. Now it is dawning on more-detached observers that many developments in the art of the last two decades make little sense without reference to his quiet influence. He is the primary anticipator, for one thing, of a wholesale convergence of popular imagery and conceptual, linguistic forms in art of the '80s. So penetrating has his influence been that the very eyes with which we now look at his work are, to some degree, Ruschavian.

If you had never heard of him, you would think the quarter-century-old pictures at Shafrazi were brand-new, the work of some semiotic-theory-intoxicated kid with a sensational knack for design. Most have splashy squarish formats and treat single, block-lettered words as images in colored fields. A ravishing one is *Annie* (1962), which imitates the title lettering of the *Little Orphan Annie* comic strip in black-bordered red on yellow, with a block of blue below. It's like the boiled-down essence — the erotic isotopy — of all the four-color newspaper graphics of all time.

Ruscha makes loaded words and phrases sit for their portraits as world leaders of the collective mind. He subjects them to sly poetic attacks in the form of puns, conjoined images, and material transubstantiations (drawings performed in such stuffs as gunpowder, blood, and spinach). A tiny 1961 oil, *Su*, reverses the initials of the United States to corral the French for "known," the name of a girl-next-door, and perhaps a hint of national litigiousness. The last half of *Damage* (1964) is on fire, bespeaking an epoch condemned to perdition.

Ruscha is 50, which seems impossible. As Jeffrey Deitch suggests in the Shafrazi catalog, he is a permanent avatar of the clear-eyed tyro — who once handed out business cards inscribed simply, "Ed Ruscha, Young Artist." He has that in common with Los Angeles, a place continuously verging on a future that never quite arrives. He is indeed a regional artist of Southern California, in the sense that Matisse was a regional artist of France. He concentrates and broadcasts strictly the aspect of his surrounding culture that is globally and charismatically modern. In the case of Los Angeles, that means the hyperspace of "communication" as industrial-strength seduction of planet Earth.

Ruscha went West from his native Oklahoma City in an old Ford in 1956, intending to be a commercial artist. (Symmetries with Warhol, who earlier headed East from Pittsburgh with the same ambition, abound.) He fell in with a generation of artists who would briefly put Los Angeles on the international map with feel-good variants of New York pop and minimalism, but right from the start there was something uniquely trenchant about his sensibility. His epiphanic decision to become a fine artist is one of the great legends, full of illuminating import for art to this day.

It happened in 1957, when Ruscha was transfixed by a magazine reproduction of a *Target* by Jasper Johns — a painting that itself was a sort of reproduction, a target-by-other-means. He dabbled a bit with an imitation of Johns's style — apparent at Shafrazi in an "abstract expressionist" rendering of his own name — but soon sensed the possibility of new form and content in the echo-chamber effect of reproductions of reproductions, the core of cultural experience in our age. So did Warhol, but with a New Yorkish, Europeanized allegiance to painting-as-icon (a point I owe to critic Christopher Knight). For Ruscha, the reproductive aesthetic is a common language, which he tosses around as insouciantly as a teenager talks slang.

Preserved until now in the amber of New York's blind spot, Ruscha's freshness won't last. I expect his art to grow old-fashioned in a jiffy, á la Dorian Gray, as the current pell-mell reevaluation of American art since the '50s proceeds. Market frenzies, notably for early Warhol, are symptomatic, though unreliable as to wisdom. (Seven figures for any of Andy's flailing near-misses, pre-Campbell's soup, is stupid, sez I.) The art history of the '60s is congealing into a new conventional version that will be unbudgeable for many years to come, and Ruscha will have his snug and prominent niche in it.

CARNEGIE INTERNATIONAL *Carnegie Museum of Art, Pittsburgh, Pa.*

I PROBABLY CAN'T PERSUADE YOU TO DROP EVERYTHING, including 300 or so bucks on transportation, and spend an afternoon in Pittsburgh, but just maybe I can make you feel bad about not doing so. Pittsburgh is home for the every-three-years Carnegie International, this continent's only rival to the big European contemporary-art roundups such as Documenta and the Venice Biennale. Any art critic who decides not to see it is declaring amateur status. I have now gone to the current Carnegie, and I'm glad. I'm also bemused and a bit dazed, which is the point of these things: by hitting you on the head, to change your thoughts.

I dislike institutional styles —high-minded, curatorial-intensive, public-sectored —of care and feeding for contemporary art. Let's get that straight at the outset of what will be, perforce, praise for an exhibition that makes the theatrical most of a growing feeling of crisis in Western culture. I much prefer the fecund hurly-burly of a teeming gallery scene — New York, in two words —for experiencing my contemporaries. But the latter has the drawback, at moments of complete bloody messiness like the present, of losing sight not only of the forest for the trees but of trees for twigs.

The show's soul is a room given to the two represented artists who are dead: Warhol and Beuys, ever more the twin deities of art now. Four versions of Warhol's 1986 self-portrait, with ghostly mien and wild wig, face a wonderful 1983-85 Beuys sprawl of 31 body-size basalt columns —soft-textured rocks with pluglike pieces removed and then, swathed in felt and sealed with clay, reinserted. The rocks are at once like corpses or mummies and like vessels preserving some vital fluid. The title of the Beuys is *The End of the 20th Century.* Yes!

Beuysian themes of death and sanctuary resonate throughout the Carnegie, which often feels like one great big mortuary of something or other. Direness comes down like a hammer in room after room. Three ravishingly ruined-looking huge new canvases by Kiefer, in materials brittle enough to make a conservator burst into tears, are almost upbeat in context. So, too, are three death-obsessed, likewise aircraft-carrier-scale paintings on weathered tarpaulin (one is about the late Jean-Michel Basquiat) by Schnabel, who shows signs of hitting a stride after all these years. For perfect effect, the sensuously elegiac Schnabels should be carried in a funeral procession behind a New Orleans jazz band.

The doominess of this Carnegie isn't entirely mysterious. What is being mourned, with honest clarity and in a big way, is the ideology implicit in the show's other name: "International." As at the finale of a Wagnerian opera, I am impressed but pleasantly detached, having no yen to be dissolved in any overaching collectivity of souls. How to breathe an individual breath in a civilization of corporate lumps and masses is the lesson, if any, that I seek in art. This show feels like the end of something whose survival never interested me much.

If the show contains one work that perfectly symbolizes both its sepulchral mood and my own disaffection, it's the masterpiece of the Swiss Barnums of inanimate circuses, Fischli and Weiss: *The Way Things Go*, a half-hour film of meta-Rube Goldbergian chain reactions in which exquisitely jury-rigged gismos of junk —powered by fire, water, pneumatics, corrosive chemicals, explosives, and gravity —sequentially self-destruct in endless, controlled catastrophe. The film thrilled ordinary museum goers when I saw it, while perhaps haunting more refined spirits with intimations of *Gotterdammerung*. It said to me that if everything insists on going to hell, you might as well dig the spectacle.

Speaking for art, the irrepressible Fischli and Weiss may also be saying something like this: "We don't know what art should do now. Meanwhile, we won't be gloomy. When we understand anything, you will be the first to know. Watch this space."

December 14, 1988

JEFF KOONS *Sonnabend*

JEFF KOONS MAKES ME SICK. He may be the definitive artist of this moment, and that makes me sickest. I'm interested in my response, which includes excitement and helpless pleasure along with alienation and disgust. As a professional critic, I'm thrilled. Koons' accurate blend of aesthetic perfect pitch and blazing sociological significance gives critical sensibility the equivalent of a new freeway system that will take you anywhere fast. But the critic in me must drive with irrational penchants — old ideals and new discontents — grabbing his arm and complaining in his ear.

As luck would have it, you don't need a whole-hearted guide to help you understand Koons' new work, which is as self-explanatory as a kick in the stomach: staggeringly vulgar statues of stuffed animals and smutty-joke tableaux in painted wood or glazed porcelain, and some grotesquely ornamented mirrors, all executed (largely by Italian and German craftsmen under the artist's direction) with staggeringly exquisite finesse.

The pieces faithfully reproduce the detail, while blowing up the size and infinitely amplifying the allure, of various grades of kitsch commonly found in living rooms with vinyl slipcovers, Toys R Us-stocked nurseries, and knotty-pine-paneled dens. They represent genres that educated folk tend to regard generically, with blanket disdain. But in Koons' hands, each tchotchke sings a specific, riveting, and excruciating aria.

To stroll into the Sonnabend Gallery today is to be gang-banged by a crew of inanimate demons. A simpering love-me bear sinks icy talons in the heart, and a nude grabbing her breasts in alarm at the surfacing of a snorkel in her bathtub stirs a brute laughter reflex that could drive you straight to a monastery. I defy anybody to shrug this stuff off. As a phenomenon, furthermore, it is somehow obviously a bell — or a carillon — tolling for thee, thee, and thee. Go look. Be your own critic.

When I first encountered a work by Koons in 1981 — two vacuum cleaners encased in spotless, fluorescent-lighted Plexiglas — I was amazed that someone had taken so much trouble to make a unique but, I thought, unnecessary pop-minimalist hybrid. Later I was only slightly more detained by his aquariumlike tanks in which basketballs disconcertingly floated underwater (something to do with liquid chemistry): vaguely nasty things with a metaphysical pizzazz that still seemed mainly eccentric.

I became a Koons konvert suddenly, in 1986, at a show of drinking paraphernalia cast in stainless steel and of liquor advertising posters reprinted in oil inks on linen. My physiological reaction to the kicked-up visual appeal was overwhelming: I wanted a drink! I got in a flash what Koons was after — what a lot of artists were then after, a con-crescence of the "commodity fetishism" concept much in the air — and that he had nailed it with his intoxicatingly beautiful works about intoxication (some of which, as sealed decanters, held actual booze). In a time given to heavy theorizing about "desire" (by critics seemingly immune to wanting so much as a chocolate chip cookie themselves), here was the living article: desire objectified, in objects wildly desirable.

This was, and is, the ticky-tum-tum part: the way Koons feeds off, and exacerbates, our culture's hysterical telescoping of all values into the seductiveness of things for sale, symptomized lately by a psychotic art market. Koons, 33, is a former Wall Street broker and an unabashed self-promoter who comes on with the sunny narcissism of a bubble-gum-rock star. He would like to be Michael Jackson, he has said, and he sort of is. He has the Gloved One's aura of naive decadence down cold, and he gives hints of similar don't-touch-me phobias about germs, dirt, and other sorts of imperfection, such as poverty and sex.

"The trick is to be outrageous but not offensive," Koons has said. For the record, I am offended by that sentiment, which reduces the artist, in my ideal a figure of freedom, to the slavishness of a court jester. It's a twerp's ethos, though I don't doubt that Koons is a one-in-a-million twerp.

The court is duly appreciative. Koons has positioned himself for wholesale production of multiples presold to today's insatiable col-lectors, who will crave one of each thing he issues. He is going to be rich beyond the dreams of contemporaries who, be they ever so glamorous, retain difficult, audience-limiting edges. You can love him or hate him. Either way, remember this: *it doesn't matter*. That's the awesomeness of Koons' success. He's like the greenhouse effect — toxic, unstoppable, and *here*. Get used to him.

The last time an artist had an analogous impact (though hedged by a more high-art quality), it was probably David Salle, seven or so years ago: imposing a paradigm on the art culture that seemed to preempt the most important new creative matters and manners. The paradigm of paradigms, in this connection, will always be Andy Warhol in 1962, ratifying Copernican shifts on all levels of art and society. Artists don't change the world. But any big historic development makes room for a creative personality who, understanding it sooner and better than others, will come to symbolize it. The appearance of such a personality is never guaranteed, and it always rightly feels auspicious, like it or not.

Koons symbolizes the apotheosis of corporate culture, the increasingly sacrosanct authority of money, the eroticizing of social status, and other emergent diseases not yet diagnosed. He does so with fierce poise and an irony so large that no single analysis can encompass it. In social terms, the loop of Koons' irony delivers, to an ever bolder upper-class hegemony, elixirs of repressed and debased content from working-class, petit-bourgeois, nouveau-riche, Disneylandish, Las Vegas-ite, and other compost-heap American sensibilities. With perfectly balanced condescension and celebration —a *noblesse oblige* so deft that none of his sources seems actually mocked —he concocts talismans of class-structural harmony that (lots of) money can buy.

So who is the joke on? Is Koons playing the fool for his audience or making fools of them? It's useless to ask, because his irony isn't a vector but a spiral, showing a special smirk to every available point of view. Only the incurably self-righteous, standing on quicksand and fancying that it is solid ground, will fail to see that Koons has their number, too. (Get set for some memorably shrill reviews from the likes of Hilton Kramer on the Stone-Age Right, from whoever will protest for the demoralized Left, and from various middlebrow ditherers.) I love it, and pardon me while I throw up. It's not that Koons promulgates any great truth. But he brackets a cultural ground zero whose very emptiness is faithful to current sensations of dizzying velocity in time, as day after day we encroach on unprecedented historical terrain.

Okay, how do I get all of this from the dumbest-looking sculpture you ever saw? I must assume that you have already toddled off to Sonnabend and dug the show, because there is no future in trying to reproduce Koons' diabolical magic in either photographs or words. The effect hits simultaneously above and below any reasonable expectation one brings to sculpture. The work's technical perfection and flat-out beauty are like divine redemptions of every luxury ever rejected by modern art in the name of authenticity. Meanwhile, the treacly subject matter, which would insult the intelligence of a relatively sophisticated 8-year-old, embraces emotions so hapless as to seem to obviate "art" altogether.

Between soaring ravishment and bottomless gross-out in the contemporary temple of the art gallery, you may feel possessed of a solve-it-yourself Delphic oracle on the present state and imminent fate of Western civilization. (I like a last-days-of-Versailles scenario, in which pseudo-shepherdesses traipse amid rococo bric-a-brac while an odd, troubling noise starts to filter in from distant streets; but that's just silly old offended me again.) What you won't feel is the pressure of an individual mind or the existence of any heart or soul at all. You will feel your own individuality being degraded and dismissed and your consciousness at once hypercharged and trivialized, like an interchangeable node of collective megabrain.

Koons' impersonality is stunning and refreshing. It is a slate wiped clean, a future that commences now. The future pertains to a new oligarchy which, after years of throwing money at art of all sorts, at last has in Koons a major artist specifically attuned to its finer feelings: lust for possessions and anxiety about the lower classes. This oligarchy has at least four more years to develop a really big-time style, the last I checked. It may well be a feast for the eyes, if you can stand the indigestion.

"COURBET RECONSIDERED" *Brooklyn Museum*

THE COURBET SHOW IS RIGHT ON TIME FOR US, but then, when wouldn't it be? We are always in the mood, whether we know it or not, for a brash, authentic arriver who is wild for our approval and, cheerfully absorbing all sorts of abuse, keeps on coming. Gustave Courbet was like that in mid-19th-century Paris—a swaggering fanatic importuning the public with paintings that Edgar Degas said made him feel he was being nuzzled by the wet nose of a calf—and Courbet is the same today in Brooklyn, which is a good place for him. He is to great art what a "dem"-and-"dose" accent is to American speech, and in Brooklyn, as in all else, he is off-center in a way that makes the center feel colorless and effete.

The show is a curatorial gem (by Sarah Faunce and Linda Nochlin), a neatly crafted container for Courbet's big, sloppy talent—necessarily minus the Musée d'Orsay's unbudgeable *A Burial at Ornans* and *The Painter's Studio*, his two stupefying masterpieces that, by failing to terminate art history, proved conclusively that no painting can do that. The show is also very racy, giving pride of place to Courbet's, shall we say, erotic or, well, pornographic—or, not to put too fine a point on it, *filthy*—pictures *The Origin of the World* and *The Sleepers*.

Seeing this show, I feel that I've finally met someone I had heard about for so long that I felt I knew him, but I didn't. Not that I really know him now, or ever will. Courbet was one of those blustering self-revealers who, maintaining a stubbornly childlike lack of self-consciousness, hide in plain sight. I think it's a shame that Courbet never met his exact contemporary Walt Whitman (they were born 11 days apart in 1819), who was like that, too, with an ego that embraced the world. The half-dozen most robust people of today, standing on each other's shoulders, wouldn't reach the kneecaps of those two.

Courbet billed himself a "Realist"—he promulgated the first, most naive, most often revived, and still most elusive of the "isms" that have jazzed and befuddled modern culture—and I went to the show with questions in my mind about what that meant and might still mean. I got that it was, and is, an artiartistic reflex, asserting—against art's constant tendency to grow precious and detached—the superior claims on us of actual, breathing life. I got this from the way Courbet's pictures are painted, which at best is thrilling and inculcates a restless disgust with the merely aesthetic. You want to run out and start a riot, milk a cow, have sex, eat an apple, die — do anything rather than stand around abrading your nerves with the angel-grit of "fine" art.

Technically and formally, Courbet pioneered nothing much in modern art except negatively, trashing conventional ideals of finish and finesse. Some of his pet stylistic tricks, such as making fast smudges with a palette knife to render highlights of "sea," "rock," and so on, predict nothing so much as the stuff of stores that advertise "1,001 Original Oil Paintings, Half-Price." To go for facts, in his way, is to seek effects that convince the imagination instantly, and when you see them operating before they grab you, the painting turns stone dead. Courbet's results are sometimes bizarre: you haven't the slightest idea what you're supposed to be experiencing even as the vastly self-confident effects swarm out at you.

Maybe largely because their colors have darkened with age, nearly all of Courbet's landscapes, which comprise about two-thirds of his total production but little of what we esteem about him now, have that sort of dumb, futile feeling for me. To succeed, his paintings have to be like sudden reminders of something you know already, such as what makes people interesting. Most of his portraits are fantastic, in exactly the way other people are when you're crazy about them. And his sexy stuff—the early, fully clothed *Young Ladies on the Banks of the Seine* somehow even more than the later, lascivious nudes—might just about make your knees buckle, remembering your desires.

Courbet made few drawings, going straight to work with paint. This was his sharpest break with drawing-based norms of painting that Ingres had taken as far as they could go. It wasn't a clean break. Nothing about Courbet was clean. (He wasn't the kind of man who takes a lot of baths, for instance.) As it was, he could fake up a very reasonable facsimile of traditional, figure-study modeling right off the palette, delivering figures with a panache that is like the word "Master" in blinking neon. But there's no delectation in it. He treated tradition like a powdered aristocrat on the day after a revolution, handing it a shovel and telling it to start digging.

Looking at the paintings, you can plainly see Courbet disdaining chances to realize art-for-art's-sake exquisitenesses — all tantalizingly within easy reach — on his way to colliding head-on with some messy truth. His intractable matter-of-factness excites me. We can use that now. We have a culture today suffocating under heaped technologies of fiction, and even to speak of truth is to arch most people's eyebrows. Courbet suggests that the trick to being true is no trick. Just do it. Julian Schnabel has that quality sometimes, though without much savor of a world anybody actually lives in.

Charles Baudelaire, who is my hero, evidently didn't like the portrait Courbet painted of him, and I think I see why. It's like a caricature of genius, in a way. The poet is perched uncomfortably on the edge of a seat, supporting himself with a clawlike hand as he reads a book with an intensity that could burn holes in it. I love the portrait, and I believe it. It doesn't even try to empathize with Baudelaire, whose loneliness must have throbbed painfully when he saw it. All it does is revel in this incredibly intelligent guy's eerie energy, as you would in a thunderstorm or a spectacular sunset.

Sex is the key to Courbet. Like Whitman, who celebrated what he called "adhesiveness" in all things, Courbet kept the business of life simple: possess everything that possesses you. When he painted *The Origin of the World*, a nude view for which the up-to-date term is the name of a clever animal that builds dams in country streams, he made an all-time philosophers' stone transmuting the lead of lust into the gold of awe —and vice versa, in a continual flicker. It is indefensible as art. Somebody should probably have punched Courbet in the jaw for it, as the only conceivably correct response of art criticism. It is a gesture of contempt for art. It is an idea indistinguishable from reality.

Courbet, whose public triumphs may have made him creatively lazy but didn't mellow him a bit, became an actual revolutionary in 1871, as arts commissioner of the Commune. He was associated with the famous toppling of the Napoleon column in the Place Vêndome, and the restored government, faced with the problem of how to punish a certified genius of France, sardonically opted to bill him for putting it back up: 323,091.68 francs. Taking refuge from the debt in Switzerland, he may have more or less drunk himself to death. It was a Falstaffian end-in-disgrace on a scale that befitted him.

Now he's in Brooklyn, inviting the public. He has a number of things there that he knows you are going to like.

AN AUCTION AT CHRISTIE'S

MAYBE BECAUSE IT WAS MY FIRST ART AUCTION, I was impressionable. I sensed historic wheels turning in the auditorium of Christie's on the night of November 9. The place was packed with citizens of the nation of money — Japanese and Europeans cheek-by-jowl with the local gentry, and I recognized several dealers and corporate consultants. I stood in a "press area" that did not communicate fawning solicitousness for the Fourth Estate: we were jammed sheeplike way off to the side in an alcove behind a velvet rope. All evening, I felt nearly nothing. It took me a couple of days to get mad.

The works of art — most notably, that evening, abstract expressionist and pop things from the estate of Burton and Emily Tremaine — appeared as if by cheap magic on a turntable next to the smoothie of an auctioneer and vanished upon the *thok* of his little hammer. As usual at auctions lately, previous record prices for most of the artists disintegrated in mid-bidding. Single works were bringing what would have been a good whole auction's take not long ago. A lovely but unastonishing painting from Jackson Pollock's hit-and-miss late phase, notable mainly for its rarity, topped out at $5.2 million (not counting the 10 percent buyer's premium), and an early, all-white painting of the American flag by Jasper Johns — a raw, strong work looking to me somehow besieged up there, and my heart went out to it ("This will be over soon, don't worry") — brought a money-is-no-object $6.4 million. I do not understand such sums, and when another Johns went for nearly triple that amount 24 hours later at Sotheby's the difference seemed trivial: three times a meaningless price equals a meaningless price.

Thok. A classic, absolutely ravishing Arshile Gorky in songful reds, yellows, and greens, attaining only a record-breaking high bid of $3.2 million, failed to better its confidential "reserve" and was withdrawn with almost palpable hurt feelings. Through it all, the vast audience (is that the word for them?) was hushed, tense, concentrated, repressed. Some of the bidding came from people at telephones, in touch with others elsewhere — bringing into the room a sense of the November night outdoors, as if the whole world were holding its breath from sale to sale. Closed-circuit monitors flashed close-ups of the works and the whirring, multicurrency tote board, and I briefly imagined the images appearing on television sets everywhere: New Delhi and Vladivostok tuning in to see how things were going. The Roy Lichtenstein comic-strip picture of a guy looking through a peephole and declaring, "I CAN SEE THE WHOLE ROOM! . . . AND THERE'S NOBODY IN IT!" fetched $1.9 million, $700,000 above the listed high estimate that would have seemed pure fantasy a year ago.

How could I have been an art critic in New York for 23 years and never attended an auction before? Easy. I was used to loving things that didn't belong to me and talking about them to people they didn't belong to, either. That the things might get shuffled around for money, somewhere out there, was a given, but the fact of their existence was all that really mattered. Nobody said that art was the common intellectual and spiritual property of humanity, because nobody had to. To have a smart and deep take on art —the drama of it and the fun — was once to be somebody in the art world, whether or not you had a dime. When I came to art, I wanted to become that kind of person, rich in that way. If I were starting out now, I don't think I would find the art world very promising.

Thok, went the perky hammer. A big picture by Franz Kline, a painter whose market appeal has been limited by his work's tendency to change color and fall apart, was knocked down for a merely staggering $2.1 million. *Thok*. A gorgeous, very small round painting of Marilyn on a gold ground by Andy Warhol brought $350,000, and I caught myself thinking, "Not enough!" Wait a minute. What did I care? *Thokketythok*. What the hell was this about?

It is about a spell of tyranny, I've decided. Tyrannies descend on culture every now and then, when particular social orders seize art as the symbol of their divine right. Royalty used to do it as a matter of course. Bureaucratic states have done it. Religions, too. Today it's money, whose glare is bleaching out the moon and stars of whatever other, financially irrelevant meanings art might show. The proof of it, for me, is that there I was finally standing —jostled, feet aching, dying for a cigarette — in Christie's velvet peanut gallery, hypnotized by the dazzling light of money.

I was there because the eating of art by the rich this year is a bigger story than anything that might conceivably be happening in studios, galleries, or museums. It is a big tail wagging a little dog. Paintings — pieces of cloth dirtied by self-appointed individuals acting on some strange, burning motive of pleasure, some inchoate inkling of glory

—are defenseless against annexation to the narcissism of money. I think that's what I felt when I saw Johns' *White Flag* on the block. It seemed so vulnerable, clinging to its dignity as a thing someone made for reasons it was trying hard to remember. It was like a blind-folded hostage surrounded by triumphant fanatics of an alien faith. I wanted to take it away. I wanted to hang it on an ordinary wall in an ordinary place, where it could recuperate.

Trying to grasp how this atrocious situation came about, I think back to the late 1970s, when the art market was flat — way, way down there on the plains from our present, Himalayan point of view — and art was transacted in stable institutional and professional worlds. Those worlds consolidated a cultural revolution of the '50s and early '60s, when art in the U. S. had stopped being a sissified European thing, patronized by bohemian heirs, and had been identified with the global apotheosis of American culture. The '70s were the era, in art, of the university syllabus and the government-grant application, furthering an all but official public good. It was a boring era, when "pluralism" reigned as a hopeless confusion of art values and democracy gladdening to functionaries. Recalling the '70s takes a bit of the sting out of the present for me, because that situation was pretty atrocious in its own way.

Most people's notions of the Golden Age evoke a remote past. Mine was a few years ago. I was happy in the early '80s, when an avid new art market — anticipating, topping, and ultimately outlasting the contemporaneous bulls of Wall Street — zoomed up out of no-where and changed everything. The new private money (small change by any present reckoning) agreed in essential ways with a wave of independent and brilliant new European and American artists. Money and artists agreed that art is about how we live, not ideally but really: enmeshed at once in the wider culture and in our own selves, subject to feelings of dislocation and hysteria, and driven by desire. Desire was the key. The definitive art work of the '80s was about wanting — and you wanted it, badly. In retrospect, my own most Zeitgeist-sensitive writing of the early '80s was that of checks for a couple of pictures I couldn't afford — a practice eliminated from my life when spending a few hundred dollars lost efficacy in terms of everything except groceries.

Meanwhile, the audience for art exploded, elating me as a journalist. Undismayed by '70s-type art people grumping about "hype and fashion" (pejoratives for genuine public ardor and an accurate cutting edge), artists and culture mavens of all sorts found each other and partied, and this elated me as a citizen of art's cosmopolitan metropolis. In the vivacious new art world, critics were cut out of the loop of decisive influence — okay with me, because I had no yen for power-brokering — and so were the art publications. They were too slow on the uptake — like museums and curators, who were also increasingly sidelined. Dealers were widely credited with the real clout, but that was a mirage. Collectors — and self-defrocked critics and curators rushing to advise them, and to some extent artists themselves, working the room like politicians — were making it happen. It was all very Byzantine and variously shady, but also passionate and entertaining, and the art was good. Then, gradually, the balance of the thing went haywire.

The '80s are a story of mutual addiction between art and money, starting in dalliance and proceeding to madness. The gray eminence of the decade has been Charles Saatchi, English co-head of the world's biggest advertising business (itself coming out of nowhere, avant-garde in the dark arts of public persuasion and corporate mergers) and co-pace-setter, with wife Doris, of the form and content of contemporary collecting. Early on, Saatchi bought out whole shows of the new art. His massive acquisitions, around 1980, of works by virtual unknowns named Anselm Kiefer and Julian Schnabel fired the starter's gun for an epoch. After him — in tribute to his prescience, for which he can hardly be blamed — have come ranked phalanxes of Midases and Midasettes flinging money at art with shovels.

Who are these people? Intriguingly, a very large number of them, like Saatchi, are media people, including the likes of publishing mogul S. I. Newhouse Jr. in New York and television producer Douglas Cramer in Los Angeles. (Hollywood is chockablock with paintings these days.) Have painting and sculpture become transcendent symbols for the era of what are laughingly called communications? Do these archaic mediums function the way gold in Fort Knox used to — backing with their glowing prestige the negotiable paper of flimsy, mood-diddling media?

As usual when a sociological trend inundates the culture, there are more than enough explanations: everything pushes synergistically in the same direction. Call it perestroikitis, the psychopathology of management-intensive, efficiency-obsessed competition that is eroticizing "creative" workaholism planet-wide. A new psycho-sociobabble, headlined "A Greed for Work" (a nice double entendre if you think of "art work"), was advanced by Laurence Shames in a recent *New York Times* business supplement. In this decade, Shames wrote, "the fashionable wealthy" have become "the slaving wealthy." "We put in 16-hour days, in part, because we don't want to share the work with others. We want the money, sure, but we also want the illusion of indispensability." As for recreation: "Spend enough money to establish where you stand, then jump back into the fray." By this measure, art collecting is the optimally time-efficient, glamorous-to-the-max way of keeping score among toiling oligarchs. So much tidier than the old, messy rounds of philanthropy.

Thok.

As the Age of Reagan segues into the Bush Episode, we are moving into uncharted historical territory for the relation of art and money, and for the values associated or confused with both. A central feature of the new terrain is an ever-more-exclusive concentration of cultural influence in wealthy hands. An art-world phenomenon of the '90s, already begun, is going to be a proliferation of private foundations and one-collector museums, as the amassings of art now filling warehouses are proudly displayed to a presumably grateful, admiring public. But I smell trouble. What we have here, symbolized by the art frenzy, is a proto-political situation in which Reaganomical plutocrats are 1) starting to feel secure and justified in their eminence, and 2) overplaying their hand.

I think our bouncing-baby aristocracy is going to run into all manner of grief. For one thing, no more than anything else in human history will the upward-spiraling art market rescind the laws of gravity. Like a pyramid scheme, this market will eventually stick a stratum of 16-hour-workers-come-lately with goods that may not decline in value — a nightmarish possibility everybody involved will heave and ho to forestall — but that will be effectively unsellable. New buyers won't materialize, and the existing players will tire of peddling to each other. This could take a while, what with the Japanese, but any other scenario overstrains the imagination.

Rich kids don't make art. That's another reason why the money-uber-alles art world, which legitimately arose because it reflected social reality better than '70s pluralism (which was based on perishing dreams of the '60s), is bound to become unreal in its turn and thus to crumble away. Look for a new, tattered avant-garde. Starving could be in again, both as subject matter and as modus operandi. The "slaving wealthy" may slave on. But slaving downward mobility, not to speak of leisured destitution, is a newer and larger actuality of economic life that will find expressions more compelling—and, at some point, more fashionable—than big money's story of with-it cultural munificence.

Finally, in more general political terms, American democracy is not going to stand for this shit. Few have noted that in the closing days of his hapless campaign, Michael Dukakis timidly ventured a little class-resentment stuff—and his polls jumped. Given an economic downturn to belie the trickle-down theory that has half-mesmerized the polity, there is going to be the darnedest populist rebellion in living memory. The rebellion will bubble up through the beleaguered middle class, brewing an art impossible to foresee but of an energy enjoyable to anticipate. It is a question not of if, but of when. And count on this: the longer the hegemony of the upscale, the more violent will be the inevitable return of the repressed.

All this has occurred to me in the aftermath of my genteel night at Christie's. In the corral with other out-of-the-loop critics, feature writers, and society journalists, I observed the finely tailored feeders at the art trough clutching their bidding paddles as sharp-eyed preppy attendants called the auctioneer's attention to the subtler bleats of want. Did I feel alienated? Let me put it this way: when I employ a rhetorical "we" in my art criticism, inviting empathy from readers, I don't fancy most of the folks who had the luxury of chairs that night, and they are the folks making all the difference in the world of what most concerns me. What's a middle-classnik art fan to do, then, short of identifying with the barbarian underclasses (not "we" material themselves) against the cultivated lords of, among other things, the art world? Nothing. Look for cues from the underclasses.

Meanwhile, follow the moving finger of money. To be an aesthete is always a bit schizophrenic. With exceptions like the Picasso *Motherhood* that recently shook loose about $25 million—a dog, if I ever saw one—I must admit that the artistic judgment of current big bucks is better than the average among, say, critics. (Like the prospect of being hanged, shelling out millions may concentrate the mind wonderfully.) Moreover, I foresee as a sure, short-term bet the rise of ambitious artists intimately attuned to the psychic wave-lengths of major money. Some of these artists, of whom Jeff Koons is a harbinger, will be very good, and I will like them—all the while dreaming of a great big set of scissors, in the hands of history, going *snip snip snip*, severing velvet ropes.

January 11, 1989

"VIEWPOINTS: POSTWAR PAINTING AND SCULPTURE" *Guggenheim*

GOING TO THE GUGGENHEIM IN THE SEASON of holiday vacations reminds me of being young and new to New York, to art, and to so many other things that life was more or less indistinguishable from a state of shock. Why especially the Guggenheim, of all possible mnemonic hot spots on this island? Because when you felt mainly awed and crazy, the Guggenheim really was crazy and awesome — and it still is, its ecstatic spiral the site of more than one kind of vertigo.

New Yorkers have strong feelings about the Guggenheim that pop up in conversation now and then but are generally taken for granted. Everybody should write them down. I'll go first, on the occasion of a show from the museum's collection of art since World War II that (eked out with loans) provides a fairly graceful gloss on the institution's often awkward history, as a bastion of transatlantic taste better at diplomatic ties and corporate tie-ins than at cogent and exciting views of contemporary art. But peace to all that. In the spirit of the season, and with deference to new director Thomas Krens, the museum's past foibles will rest as lightly on our minds as powdery snow.

Does the Guggenheim, as a building, memorialize Frank Lloyd Wright's disdain for painters and sculptures, tossing defenseless pictures and objects into a Cuisinart churning up puree of architecture? Does it fulfill that little whippersnapper's grudge against tall people with a balustrade that terrorizingly stops below the center of gravity of everybody except the Seven Dwarves? Yes. Yes. And it is eternally the most modern building — one hasn't the temerity to say *best* because the thing brooks no comparison — in New York and maybe the world, with a *newness* to outlast the ages. The building's indelible novelty may outlast even the building, a conservation and maintenance nightmare like many Wright structures. (Am I hallucinating, or has that old crack in the ground floor gaped perceptibly of late?)

Art lovers have tended to resent the place ever since it opened 29 years ago, but it does not lack pleasures. When he reviewed a show there in 1962, poet Frank O'Hara, greatest of American aesthetes, thought it might "be worthwhile, or at least different, to say something nice about the building itself," and he did: "It's wonderful looking from the outside, and when you enter the flat exhibition space on the ground floor the effect of the works near at hand, the ramps and over them glimpses of canvases and then the dome, is urbane and charming, like the home of a cultivated and mildly eccentric person. The elevator is a good idea too; I wonder if anyone has ever taken it down?"

I've taken the elevator down whenever a show was utterly uncongenial. My way of using the Guggenheim is to hike up the ramp, getting an overall sense of things, then to backtrack either briskly or lingeringly, as the art and my mood warrant—or, having had quite enough on my ascent, to punch the button for the cute little half-moon-shaped lift. (An obsessive people-watcher might ride the elevator all day for the kick of observing first-time Guggenheim visitors: they are nervous and excited, as if lining up for a roller coaster, and self-conscious, as if attending a social affair where something incomprehensible may be expected of them.) It just occurred to me that going up-ramp may be temperamental defiance on my part: behaving in the one way Wright permits that is not an option for a ball in a pinball machine.

One not-to-be-missed attraction of the current show is that it occupies the entire ramp, including the wide, giddy, dead-end segment above the elevator that is commonly closed off for storage or some other depressing purpose. Tucked right up under the great six-lobed skylight—whose 12 vertical divisions carry all the way down, forming the bays that mutate at each level like an organism of the primal sea trying to evolve into nuclear physicists—you know that Heaven must be like that: light-drenched, exalted, and embracingly secure (unless you're an acrophobe and make the horrible mistake of peering over the dinky balustrade at the *hardest*-looking marble floor in the world).

To concentrate on art up there is even less possible than it is elsewhere in the building, including the permanent-installation wings that feel vaguely like odd areas of department stores that house the lost-and-found and complaint counters. The Guggenheim has an effect even on great artworks that O'Hara noted in a Bonnard there, making them look "slightly washed-out" but, on the plus side, "what every sophisticated person let alone artist wants to look: a little 'down,' a little effortless and helpless." And that's the good stuff. Weak art there looks like a needy person even Mother Teresa would cross the street to avoid meeting.

Seeing a show in the Guggenheim is less like looking at art than like riffling through a coffee-table art book: a sequence of stimulating but shallow recognitions. This may be another reason I associate the place with youth: it's perfect for an art-drunk kid full of callow pride in his or her tyro knowledge of styles — pegging "a" Picasso, "a" Pollock, "a" this, "a" that. It takes heroically introverted work (Mark Rothko is the in-house champ) and a ferociously focused viewer to get it on together amid the distractions of wild walls, disembodying light, and the discombobulating message of gravity coming up through your shoes from the ramp's slope.

The current exhibition, a statement of the new Guggenheim regime's taste in its own holdings (and specific gift-hungers), merits a discussion longer and chewier than this column allows. Suffice it to say that the show starts, at the top, with Arshile Gorky and breaks off with Peter Halley. Some might term this a downhill spiral in spades, except for a strong foursome of big paintings by Anselm Kiefer, David Salle, Georg Baselitz, and Enzo Cucchi in what I think of as the museum's automobile-showroom, two-story alcove: a nicely calibrated parity (Cucchi at his best, almost, though not quite, holding his own with so-so Kiefer) making a provocative case about art of the '80s.

In between, there's plenty to enjoy and to wonder or snort at — unaccountable favorites like Jim Dine alternating with accountable ones, given the Guggenheim's traditional tilt toward cerebral abstraction, like Agnes Martin — and it's the holidays, so you'll see lots of dazed, vacationing students and people who have gotten out of their houses and offices in obedience to an annual urge to do something or other somehow special. It's a time machine, that place, if we let it be one: whirling us down into our memories and up into a lost Utopian future that Frank Lloyd Wright, who was there already, would have been the last to say we deserve.

ROBERT RYMAN *Dia Art Foundation*

ROBERT RYMAN—HE OF THE ALL-WHITE, ABSOLUTELY abstract paintings —is a pale presence who has haunted the biography of my art-love for over 20 years now, alternately moving and boring me half to tears. Like my conscience, Ryman's astringent art is congenial company when I'm feeling fine-tuned and calm, and a nuisance when I'm not. The first three months of his season-long show at the Dia Art Foundation's majestic digs in Chelsea have given me plenty of time to groom my ambivalence, and here in the art world's mid-winter doldrums —when the senses are sated, the mind circles, and the heart sinks —I am as ready as I will ever be to grapple with him.

It's a big show, of 33 mostly recent pieces in five wonderfully pro-portioned rooms designed by the artist on Dia's skylit top floor. A few earlier things, emphasizing the superficial variety and actual, monkish consistency of Ryman's gentle fanaticism, include two little canvases from 1958 and 1959, when he was 28 and already on track but still a decade away from being recognized as the painter most at home in the painting-allergic ambit of minimal art. Not for the first time, I can't decide if his single-mindedness, undeterred by inner promptings of expression and by outward imperatives of style, is mainly exemplary or mainly bizarre.

It makes for a very particular beauty, in any case, in the great, austere Dia space, whose soft gray cement floors and walls painted a warm white provide a melting atmosphere for the crisp edges and cool whites of the paintings. You don't so much enter as launch into that space, drifting in the wan effulgence of a New York winter after-noon amid works as plain and grave as protestant saints.

What you will be exploring is a long, slow course in the phenomeno-logical ABCs of painting. Like a mad grammarian compulsively parsing sentences, Ryman is transfixed by conventions that every-body else takes for granted: namely, the protocols of our culture that make it seem "natural," somehow, to affix one rectangular surface (usually canvas) to another (a wall) and to cover it with a third (a skin of paint). Ryman carefully maintains a mutual schizophrenia among these three planes of visual sensation, making each seem incessantly startled to find itself connected to the others.

To make the best use of the show's checklist, ignore Ryman's oddly vatic titles — *Messenger, Consort, Regis, Journal,* and so on — which betray the muffled beat of a romantic heart, and go straight to the list of mediums for each work. That's where Ryman's definitive poetry hangs out. For example: "Lascaux acrylic on gatorboard with steel," "oil on acrilivin with steel," "enamelac on fiberglass with aluminum." He is plainly the kind of man who blisses out in the aisles of hardware and art-supply stores. He seems never to have met a material he didn't like, and his evident care is to let each sing the song of its intrinsic visual qualities.

"With steel" and "with aluminum" in the lists refer us to the off-the-shelf devices — brackets, flanges, screws, and whatnot — with which Ryman ostentatiously attaches his painted surfaces to the wall: at corners or edges, on the back, or, sometimes, through holes drilled right in the middle. Never before in art has the charged juncture between architectural and pictorial space been so exposed, quizzed, and celebrated. Ryman's enchantment with the commonplace facts of "picture hanging" recalls the ecstasy of Moliere's gentleman at discovering that he has always spoken in prose.

Just as his methods of attachment energize the difference of wall and painting surface, so do Ryman's ways of deploying his invariably white pigments — with repertoires of stroking as formulaic as a game of solitaire — build tension between painting surface and paint medium. His fastidious distinctions between these two planes can be mentally exhilarating in a way that recalls the classic definition of intelligence as an ability to entertain contradictory ideas simultaneously. Each of Ryman's works is like an action shot of diverse matter obeying some sort of culture DNA to become the organism called "a painting."

Fairly often, Ryman's works go beyond being *about* painting to being lovely *as* painting. Take *Counsel,* a squarish "oil on linen with steel" 8 feet wide: with its cloud of furry strokes like a pillow slowly exploding in gray air, it is held out from the wall on flanges that seem to be saying, "For you! Here!" And spend a few minutes in the room occupied solely by *Resource,* a suspended, huge, slightly concave, smoothly painted sheet of material ("acrylic on fiberplate with steel and aluminum") whose hypersensitivity to the room's light and shadow may make you feel your eyesight improving by quantum leaps.

But Ryman's brand of pleasure is in every way wintry, a dried husk really gratifying only to the self-regard of the aesthetic mechanism in us, the click in consciousness when we see something part company with ordinary things to register as "art." It's a mostly negative pleasure —bracingly shorn of appeals to taste, style, and every other sweet tooth of our sensibilities—that preserves the rather overbearing, metallic flavor of minimal art in the '60s. A serenely unreconstructed '60s-type aesthetic radical, Ryman is so oblivious to every subsequent fashion that you may wonder either what world he has been living in or in what mazy paths you have gone astray.

I remember that about ten years ago, when painting was undergoing a brawny and sexy renaissance, I had an episode of feeling positively revolted by Ryman's art, as one might by bread and water upon receiving an invitation to lunch at Lutece. Now, after a decade of glutting overrichness in art, has the situation reversed? Does Ryman suddenly look wholesome and restorative? Not really. Painterly indigestion of the '80s demands its own designer antacids, not Grandpa Robert's trusty old Pepto-Bismol.

However, this Ryman show does give me a distinct feeling of being called to account, somehow, as if by some personal religious authority who knows my soul's waywardness and has reason to be concerned about me. He may be the last of the great modern artists who, believing that human endeavors partake of pure essences, once strove to put art on a philosophically equal footing with science. Certainly he's the only current painter who can turn my reminiscence of that perishing idealism into a specific ache rather than just a vague and global disillusionment. It's an effect of his radiant modesty, craftsmanly virtues, and incredible steadiness.

Ryman is painting's puritan—a whiplashing oxymoron, when you consider that painting as an art form is practically defined by sensuousness and fantasy. Painting is the last place to go looking for the sort of low-calorie, high-fiber aesthetic diet he offers, and I've always suspected people who praise him unreservedly of nursing a moralistic grudge against the lubricious joys of painting generally. But that's not Ryman's problem. He is an odd duck, but passionate in what he does. And what he does can exercise an amazing gravitational tug. It can take you clear out of yourself—whoever that is, dissolving in winter light in Chelsea amid the white paintings.

February 15, 1989

FREDERICK KIESLER *Whitney*

THE LAST TIME I SAW A BIG SHOW of work by mighty-mite Frederick
Kiesler—the very short (4-10), very self-confident Viennese-American
artist, architect, stage designer, and all-around visionary who died in
1965 after a long life of largely unfulfilled but irrepressibly grandiose
dreams—it was the late 1960s. Like a lot of other people, I had had
it with techno-artistic, save-the-world utopias keyed to far-out design.
Though always a sucker for the glamour of Kiesler's legendary interior
for Peggy Guggenheim's mid-1940s Art of This Century gallery, I
remember deciding that his labyrinthine *Endless House* and various
forced fusions of constructivism and surrealism were totally futile
and corny. Well. When I walked into the current Kiesler retrospective, which has been curated with great flair by the Whitney's Lisa
Phillips, I immediately wanted either to call up Kiesler's ghost and
apologize or find my own dyspeptic younger self and hit him. What
a great artist! Eccentric? Sure, but also poetic, searchingly intelligent,
and alert to possibilities that, today, feel as fresh as a daisy. A proto-
post-modernist seemingly from birth—*really* ahead of his time—
Kiesler maintained a silken, sexy irony toward modern styles even
as he played off nearly all of them in grand schemes now more than
ever full of surprising, funny, life-enhancing juices. Go see this show,
which is going to be big-time influential. In passing, note that the
pictures in a wonderful recreation of the Art of This Century gallery
—contrary to what one has read a dozen times—are *not* mounted
on baseball bats. We should do something, and soon, about the deplorable level of art historians' baseball literacy.

100

February 22, 1989

ANDY WARHOL *Museum of Modern Art*

THERE AREN'T ENOUGH FLOWER PAINTINGS.

How's that for hard-hitting criticism of the Andy Warhol retrospective? It will have to do. On an occasion so gaga it begs for curmudgeonly demurral, I'm afraid I'm just another happy face in the crowd. I love this show. I love Warhol, with a fan's love. It isn't so much a warm place in my heart, an organ not notably engaged by this artist, as it is a flat spot among the folds of my brain, from where said brain got run over in the '60s.

Warhol in the '60s had a steamrollering effect on the whole mental apparatus of Western cultural tradition. The weight that did the trick wasn't his, of course, but history's: newly gigantic American power, pride, affluence, idealism, social mobility, technology, mass entertainment — good stuff gone amok, lurching around and smashing things, running away with us. But nothing foreordained the appearance of an artist who would distill and clarify the melee, while it was happening, in icons of uncanny fidelity and total pleasure.

Warhol didn't change lives, but he gave sudden, lucid shocks of self-recognition to lives that were changing anyway. He thus imbued many of us with the stubborn, childish loyalty typical in the wake of conversion experiences, of which mine came in Paris in 1965. It was a show of the flowers.

Having bypassed New York from the Midwest, I was living out a year of unrequited romance with French culture. It was a gray day. I entered a gallery packed with those identical, flat images of pansies — big ones like billboards, little ones like ranked trivets — with their piercing synthetic colors never dreamed of in nature or in previous art. "Oops," I thought, "wrong city! Go home!"

So I did. I lived on Avenue B, took too many drugs, was miserable but too excited to notice, saw Warhol's films (saw *all* films, but Warhol's stand out as among the only slowed-way-down, contemplative moments of the decade), walked into galleries and was wowed, walked the streets and was wowed, gave or attended a thousand poetry readings, regularly felt on the verge of possessing important knowledge, didn't sleep a lot, confidently anticipated a revolution (didn't like the idea, but who was I to argue?), didn't argue, went with a flow that was like a whirlpool with riptides, and liked things.

Warhol had said that pop art was "about liking things." It was a sort of Eastern spiritual discipline keyed to dime stores, supermarket ads, and movie magazines, a way of levitating both to escape and enjoy the social earthquakes below. (It had very little to do with camp, incidentally, contrary to a standard intellectual line.) My temperamental compulsion to be analytical was a nuisance, so I took more drugs and entertained occult theories, beating it down. This was a poor idea that seemed commonsensical at the time.

Aesthetic emotion inhered in every particle of a world like an explosion, everything flying and tumbling. I had a couple of conversations with Warhol, who was so omnipresent you thought there must be a dozen of him. I talked in rushes and jumbles. He replied, as near as I can recall, "oh," all patience and never arrogant. He was nice. Not many were. Under the reign of peace-and-love, most people were basically abominable to each other.

Warhol got shot in 1968. Everybody seemed to be getting shot then, or hit on the head by policemen or shattered by the drugs. People fled each other and crashed. It was over. Exactly what was "it"? I forgot.

At MoMA now, I remember. I had expected the show to be beautiful and fun, which it is, and perhaps nostalgic, which it isn't really. The 300 or so objects, the vast majority of them from the early and middle '60s, are far too powerful for nostalgia, which is a feeling of being in control of memory. Their hieratic beauty, now as then, is like a light-house seen at night from a sinking ship. They awaken serious memories of a time absolutely not in control — bashed around by impersonal forces, staggering for balance, at best trying to make a dance of the stagger.

There aren't enough flowers. Only two big but rather drab ones, not counting a suite of prints in the members' dining room. The reason may be lingering sensitivity about one of MoMA's old pieties — the sacrosanctness of modernist abstraction — which Warhol's flowers sweetly wrecked. It seems plain in retrospect that, more even than the subversive strategies of minimalism, the cold aesthetic perfection of Warhol's flowers pulled the plug back then on would-be "mainstream," Clement-Greenbergian, color-field abstracton, long touted at MoMA. Is that still a sore spot on 53rd Street?

Never mind. The show is wonderful, and full of surprises. I didn't know that in his miracle year of 1962 Warhol did a painting of Natalie Wood: several dozen repetitions of her preternaturally pretty face in black and white with that fast and sloppy, there's-no-such-thing-as-an-accident silk-screening that abrades the senses like a fine erotic grit. He also made one I hadn't known about of Roger Maris hitting a home run: that big, grunting swing over and over in row upon row of mighty whacks you can almost hear. Each painting feels definitive of something or other, an all-time freezing of a fleeting euphoria.

I didn't know how great were the Marilyns, Elvises, Lizzes, Marlons, Jackies, electric chairs, car crashes, and "wanted" posters — and the flowers, where are the flowers? — which is odd because I thought they were all about as great as anything gets. So they are greater than I thought — not that thinking has much to do with a sensation of, mainly, rapture. Rapture is a feeling that engages the top, bottom, and all sides of yourself and homogenizes those dimensions, such that you don't know where the inside of yourself leaves off and the outside begins. It's like D. H. Lawrence's speculation about the sensory awareness of fish in water: "one touch."

Warhol's is a cold rapture, as if like a fish one took on the temperature of the surrounding element: in the paintings circa 1962-65, a chilled contemplation of molten desire and abysmal horror. The element is oneness with a generalized consciousness — yourself dissolving like Alka-Seltzer, with thought-bubbles, into a purely collective medium of "what everybody knows." Going and then *gone* like a home run, and the crowd on its feet is a single cheering organism.

The '60s were about erasing boundaries. Warhol did it best because the boundaries — between high and low, art and commerce, etc. — scarcely existed for him in the first place. Look at every other artist then, especially every other pop artist, and you see somebody clinging to some categorical distinction, some tradition, some irony. Warhol wasn't ironic. He was neither cynical nor naive. He was innocent and greedy. The ironic, cynical, naive middle-classniks of his audience tied themselves in knots trying to fathom the complexities of a mind whose secret was simplicity, as efficient a life-form as a shark, a cat, or an honest businessman (which he was). He gave himself with no strings attached, except for the price tag.

Warhol had a barbarian's unblinking detachment: a lower-class son of Czechoslovak immigrants and (it turns out, which almost no one knew) a lifelong devout Catholic. He became the artist laureate of capitalism, the system in which everything bears a price tag, because he regarded it matter-of-factly, as the natural order. Having grown up on the system's underside, with no middle-class sense of privilege and consequently no middle-class guilt, he didn't fret about its morality, though he was moral within it. He had the steady radiance of an undivided soul, so rare in this country as to seem otherworldly.

He ran into creative trouble in the '70s, it's true. MoMA's representation (decisively connoisseured by Kynaston McShine) of the mostly very weak later paintings is mercifully perfunctory. (I do like the society portraits, however—a peculiar genre that no one has properly characterized yet, though many of us have tried.) I think American culture simply became so permeated with Warhol's own influence that his responses to it picked up something akin to audio feedback, with deleterious effects. He did best with death (skulls), totalitarian and shamanistic sublimities (Mao and Joseph Beuys), and himself (the never-fail self-portraits).

Warhol had announced that the show I saw in Paris in 1965 was his last one of painting, and in a way that matters he was right. His next important outing, at Castelli in 1966, was a walk-in image of what he and the careening decade had come to: drifting silvery-plastic pillows that mirrored our blown minds, and cow wallpaper that showed us our faces, which were placid, stupid, and adorable. He then intended to abandon the art world for Hollywood and beyond. That eventually he had to come limping back to it is a bit depressing, still.

But far be it from a fan to emphasize a downbeat note here. Leave that to the curmudgeons, who are even now lining up for their swats at Warhol's maddeningly serene countenance. What they will miss, as usual, is that Warhol remains way ahead of them, as contemporary civilization's comprehensive visionary. He delivered the glamor-industrial goods with full cognizance of the "bads" inseparable from them, the petrification of life played by rules of economic transaction. (He thought it was a fair bargain for himself, but he wasn't pushing it.) Rapture and alienation aren't even two sides of a coin in his work; they are the same side, a ravishing surface with nothing—a black-hole-in-space, infinite nothing—behind it. Like clean glass, his art superimposes our reflections on the darkness of our vertiginous want.

THE MADRID ART FAIR

I HAD LOTS OF COMPANIONS LAST WEEK in Spain, whence I was
transported by the Spanish government with other foreign art folk
to swell the ranks of culturati at ARCO, the annual Madrid art fair:
nearly 200 chiefly European and American galleries peddling selected
wares under the eyes of tens of thousands — *masses,* mostly youngish
— of paying attendees. Given this publication's admirable policy
of Manhattan-intensiveness — it's what *I* look for in a weekly — do
I have a New York-ish justification for taking my column so far afield?
I do.

Supported by Spain's nominally socialist government hand in
glove with corporations and foundations, up-and-coming ARCO
(not yet on a par with the commercial frenzies of the Basel and Chicago
fairs but getting there) reflects a European trend in public-private
conglomeration of cultural activity that is steadily sapping New York's
art-world centrality. And it displays feverish new protocols, exploita-
tions, and meanings of the art game that make the New York scene
seem sedate by comparison. You have to see to believe, in Europe,
how the little engine of visual expression is being designated to pull
mighty boxcars of economic, diplomatic, and social freight.

Under the lovely stained-glass dome of the jaw-slackeningly *luxe*
Palace Hotel, by the Prado, I sipped *agua mineral* and viewed the
parading new international elite of dealers, collectors, curators, consultants, public-payroll culturecrats, indeterminate hustlers, and the
occasional working critic — a furtive and somewhat abashed creature,
this last, trying not to be either too grateful or too cynical in face of
the largesse that has put his fanny on one of the Palace's velvet sofas.
It had come about with the silken mannerliness at which the Spanish,
in my experience of hosting countries, are tops: a ticket in the mail,
a room waiting, invitations to receptions slipped under the door, and
no unsought contact with anyone official. Still, the sense of being
cast as a presumed spear carrier in a power-and-money opera is nerve-
racking.

I can't decide whether to be awed most by the size or by the nakedness of the production. No one I talked to could recall a precedent
for one wrinkle of ARCO: the expense-paid importation à la Las
Vegas of high-rolling collectors, compensating for the still malnour-

ished state of Spain's native market. Some of the collectors and the likewise subsidized corporate consultants, though a jolly bunch of party animals on the whole, were startled to discover in the fair's press packet a complete list of their names, addresses, and often unlisted home phone numbers. At least from an Iberian perspective, the art-commerce casino has rendered old gentilities of the trade obsolete.

March 8, 1989

"REFIGURED PAINTING: THE GERMAN IMAGE 1960-88"
Guggenheim

THIS SHOW HAS ALREADY BEEN CRITICALLY DEMOLISHED by Michael Brenson in the *Times,* but it is one of those occasions when you want to see the rubble jump. I can't remember a worse museum show. The honeymoon of Thomas Krens as new director of the Guggenheim is now strictly from memory lane. He is revealed as a curator with no taste of his own and no attentiveness to labors of discrimination already performed by others in the rich field of recent German painting. It's not just the badness but the *arrogant* badness of this show that will make it proverbial, a *Moose Murders* of the art world. Selections of Gerhard Richter, Sigmar Polke, and Jorg Immendorff at the top of the Guggenheim ramp and of Anselm Kiefer, Georg Baselitz, and A. R. Penck toward the bottom (the last two represented on a grotesque three-story kiosklike whatsit) are sloppy to the point of contempt. (Kiefer and Polke are great artists, and not all of Baselitz's later work is terrible, but you wouldn't guess it from what's shown here.) With the notable exception of Markus Lupertz, whose mandarin neo-modern-artiness looks better than it deserves to by contrast, almost everything in between is punishment for keeping your eyes open. One might want to protest on behalf of the gifted artist (Helmut Middendorf, say, or Rosemarie Troekel) in the mob of obscure names that can never be obscure enough, but it's hopeless. The good goes down with the bad and the ugly on this curatorial *Titanic,* which will make you forget why you ever liked painting at all. It's a disaster worthy of an "I Survived . . ." T-shirt and, as such, a must-see.

"FREDERIC REMINGTON: THE MASTERWORKS"
Metropolitan Museum of Art

WHERE DID I GET THE NOTION that Frederic Remington is some kind of cruelly underrated artist? The notion is buried by this show, which proves that Remington, turn-of-the-century maker of mythic images of the then recently housebroken Wild West, is rated just about right: terrific illustrator, erratic painter, lively but cornball sculptor — and beacon of macho-conservative, John Waynian nationalism. I have at least a column's worth of thoughts about him, but first I must sift through the wreckage of my overestimation to figure out how it happened.

It happened in a bar. The bar was — what else? — "Remington's," in basement rooms on Waverly Place now occupied by a bar called Nowhere. About 20 years ago Remington's was briefly the hangout of choice for younger, down-at-the-heels art people put off by the glitz, expense, and uptown tourists at Max's Kansas City. One spent beery evenings with negligently attired loft dwellers in an ambience of saloon browns, where the only reliable aesthetic objects were many reproductions of Remington paintings.

With a mind stimulated by conversation and standards made magnanimous by alcohol, I would look upon those images, my heart filling with a sense of something fine and lost. It was complicated nostalgia, probably drawing on my prairie upbringing — largely in Northfield, Minn., fabled site of Jesse James' unlucky last bank raid — and my old love of Western movies, a genre then mired in the exciting but terminal decadence of Sergio Leone and Sam Peckinpah. I think it was also a furtive yen for brushy narrative painting, which would resurge a decade later but was the ultimate taboo in serious art 20 years ago.

I have been relieved to confirm at the Met that the picture that most transfixed my tired and emotional regard at Remington's really is awfully good: *Fight for the Water Hole*, which still seems to me better than anything else by the artist except his one and only bullet-proof masterpiece, *The Scout: Friends or Enemies?* The latter is a moonlit snow scene in which your gaze, from behind, at an Indian scout is relayed into empty, blue-white depth, toward the tiny fires of a far-distant encampment.

An early work, done when Remington was only 29 or so, though already famous as a magazine illustrator, *The Scout* may be his only painting with a satisfying internal dynamic, neither ponderously arty like his later impressionistic pastiches nor, in the common way of his illustrational style, simply shoving something wild 'n' wooly in your face. Smoothly adapting a motif of European Romanticism — sort of Caspar-David-Friedrich-goes-to-Montana — it works on all levels. Even Remington's pedantic detailing of the Indian's costume and horse is poetic, for once, because the picture is about a desperate straining *to see.*

Fight for the Water Hole — five cowboys defending a nearly dried-up desert pool against circling Indians — is absorbing as a neither-fish-nor-fowl stalemate between painting and illustration. Its even tones of lavender-gray, butter yellow, and powder blue seduce the eye into a vast and indifferent landscape in which a deadly action is slowly unfolding. The illustration quality is given mainly by an implausible point of view, that of someone standing (suicidally, under the circumstances) outside the lip of the contested hole. In this regard, *Fight* relies on a literary rather than a painterly convention of narrative.

Actually, there's another word for that convention of a disembodied, omniscient narrative eye: cinematographic, the artistry of avidly obstrusive camera angles. Remington's bravura compositions are more than halfway from their sources in 19th-century painting to the movies of, say, John Ford. The distinctively angled cavalry column in *The Quest* could be a gussied-up still from *She Wore a Yellow Ribbon.* Considered as a cultural-industrial engineer — a technician of the higher cliche — Remington was major. As a painter, he was pretty hopeless. His stabs at Impressionism show the problem: formulaic figures dabbled with, rather than made of, feathery strokes.

As a man, Remington was a pig. And I don't mean just that he was carrying nearly 300 pounds on his 5-9 frame when he died after an appendix operation at the age of 48 in 1909. I mean this sort of thing, from a letter to a fellow oinker by the name of Poultney Bigelow: "I've got some Winchesters, and when the massacring begins which you speak of, I can get my share of 'em and what's more I will. Jews — injuns — Chinamen — Italians — Huns, the rubbish of the earth I hate." A New York native who did most of his work in New Rochelle, he lied about his practically non-existent exploits in the West, which he never visited for more than a month or two at a time. Teddy Roosevelt's reputation gains no luster from the fact that Remington was a pal of his.

(The above information, from a splendid catalog essay by David McCullough, does honor to a show that tempers its excessive claims for Remington with candid scholarship. In a related vein, an entertaining section of bronze sculptures cheerfully acknowledges that several "Remingtons" in the Met's collection for half a century have turned out to be unauthorized casts at best.)

Remington's career sheds historic light on the phenomenon, symbolized by Teddy R., of the U. S.'s turn to full-bore imperialism after the last recalcitrant Indians were crushed. As an artist-correspondent in Cuba in 1897, he was the supposed recipient of William Randolph Hearst's legendary cable: "Please remain. You furnish the pictures and I'll furnish the war." He did wonders himself for Hearst's jingoing with a sensationally successful propaganda sketch based on a false report about a lady stripsearched by Spanish soldiers. (It is one of his few images of women. "I don't understand them," he explained.)

Remington's thoroughly cinematic painting of the *Charge of the Rough Riders at San Juan Hill*—Teddy on a horse, the attentive leader of running and whooping men (one of them being inconvenienced by a Spanish bullet in the chest)—makes the affair "look more like a football game," as McCullough remarks, than like war, but there is a sickening truthfulness about it. Precisely that rah-rah spirit sent America galloping into this century with a whole new style of geopolitical mischief—from San Juan Hill to the Tet offensive. (Teddy, meet Ho Chi Minh.)

Still and all, it makes sense in the present twilight of American globalism (Teddy, meet Toyota) to look afresh at the culture of its dawn, in which Remington was a morning star. The re-examination ought to cure nostalgia while perhaps intensifying fascination — in the way of the startlingly good recent TV miniseries of Larry McMurtry's *Lonesome Dove*. Little else that might happen in the '90s would make me, for one, happier than a big revival of the western, a consummation made thinkable by the McMurtryesque principle of looking each messy fact of the epoch and its heritage in the eye. Dead as a motive force (knock on wood), the romance of the West seems newly retrievable as a metafact, smoky forge of American destinies.

REMOVAL OF THE TILTED ARC

THERE IS SOMETHING NEW THIS WEEK on the plaza of the Javits Federal Building: nothing. It's worth a visit. You may never in your life see anything more vividly *not there*—quintessence of *gone*, Absence City—than Richard Serra's *Tilted Arc* now that it has been lumbered off in pieces to a Brooklyn warehouse, leaving a 12-by-120-foot slice of sparkling vacancy. You may or may not feel, as I do, sweet relief, like that of a child when the school bully moves away.

On the bright, cool afternoon after the big removal, passersby gazed at the long slit in the plaza where the sculpture stood. They seemed amazed, as I was, that a thing so overpowering could have fit into such a narrow and shallow fissure. This being New York, a spontanous symposium was under way, with citizens person-on-the-street-interviewing each other. There was a mood of wonderment—not quite believing the witch was dead—and maybe the odd twinge of regret, such as the loss of an old enemy may entail.

A woman with frizzed hair and cowboy boots said, "I liked walking by it. I liked the graffiti on it. I liked everything about it." A group of (probably) young lawyers listened. One demurred quietly, "Richard Serra didn't want you to *like* it." An old guy, courtroom-gofer type, seemed moved by an automatic grievance against anything done by the government. "I didn't like it for years," he said to no one in particular. "Then I got used to it. It just turned into another thing." But he was smiling.

I never stopped hating the arrogance of *Tilted Arc's* installation. That it was a good sculpture in Serra's brooding and obstreperous manner just made it all the worse for an already oppressive environment. I said as much in an article when it went up in 1981, with the result that I got screamed at at dinner parties by people who deemed it treason to impugn the carte blanche of an artist by implying that the public should have a say in public art. Did *Tilted Arc* make office workers feel every kind of pushed around? Some art mandarins thought that was swell. "It'll do them good," a famous artist said to me of 1,300 petitioning workers. "They'll quit and get new jobs. It will change their lives."

With characteristic finesse, Serra told an interviewer at the time that my opposition smacked "of fascism. . . . When people say they want *Tilted Arc* removed, I can smell the books burning." But it was never an issue of his free expression. It was a matter of the government providing an amenity for its employees that turned out to be a disaster. Parallels with Salman Rushdie do not apply, unless you imagine a federally mandated recitation of *The Satanic Verses* over loudspeakers in a public place 24 hours a day forever. Which sounds kind of neat, actually, but anything is apt to until you have to live with it.

No longer Berlinized, Federal Plaza now looks its banal and naked self, badly wanting the benches and greenery that you'd think someone back then might have seen as preferable to Serra's steel cancellation mark. The festering split in our society down the middle of the phrase *public art* — a wound that *Tilted Arc* rubbed salt in but hardly inflicted —won't be fixed so easily. Think about it while having lunch from a bag there, as I did the other day. That plaza has become one of the great philosophical sites, its voluptuous void a monument to the cultural *tsuris* of democracy.

CINDY SHERMAN *Metro Pictures*

Art NEVER SEEMS TO MAKE ME PEACEFUL OR PURE," Willem de
Kooning once lamented. "I always seem to be wrapped in the melodrama of vulgarity." The remark is subtle, because no artist in our
culture is more "pure"—purely an artist, investing his whole existence
in art—than de Kooning. In effect, he warns us not to envy him,
cautions against the dilettantish superstition that art is somehow
about "the finer things," and implies that he feels worse about it than
anybody.

De Kooning could have been speaking of, and for, Cindy Sherman,
who after a decade of consistently astonishing photographic art has
proved as pure—and as unpeaceful, "wrapped in the melodrama of
vulgarity"—an artist as we have today. I think she is heroic. I feel
no inclination to judge her work, preferring simply to learn from it.
Her problems are more interesting than other people's solutions. The
more eccentrically particular—bizarre, raw, dicey—her work has
become, the more exemplary it has seemed to me of the general condition of creativity now.

Sherman's new color photographs of toys and other cunningly
arranged and lighted studio props, including vomitous-looking substances, are sensationalistic beyond anything that can be savored
even as "bad taste." She has been upping the ante of grotesquery in
her art for several years, frankly defying her own reputation as an
enchanting woman-of-a-thousand-faces. After hundreds of pictures
that enlisted her extraordinary acting talents, she no longer appears
in her work, which was always about painful mysteries of identity
but often got regarded as seductive light entertainment. She's fixed
that. Her nine new works are ferociously weird, in-your-face tableaux.

In the two-panel largest picture, a face that originally belonged
to a Styrofoam jack-o'-lantern has glass eyes and a painted tongue
and is almost illegibly embedded in an oleaginous, gleaming mass of
melted candy. A geek mask in another big work is hauntingly personal-
ized with painted flesh tones, romantic wisps of blond hair, plastic
breasts, and an intruding human hand. Elsewhere, a small toy monster
seems to be dissolving in a greenish bath, and an eviscerated teddy
bear shows what (ghastly gunk) it is made of.

A series of three pictures using old-fashioned baby dolls seems intent on debunking the sweetness of early childhood. Slime-covered on wet fur, one doll may just have been born from something you would rather not think about. Viewed from the low angle of a doll-audience, a grinning performer-doll exudes sheer menace. Yet another doll, cute little destroyer of worlds, sprawls amid shattered electronic gear.

This brings us to a *really* disquieting new photograph. It shows a partially deflated, life-size plastic sex doll loosely held on a sort of rack with metal cables, suggesting bondage, amid piles of party favors. Her silly, cartoon face dangles upside-down, smudged with lipstick. A mirror doubles the scene, confirming what is at first hard to make out and then hard to believe: a clothed, living man is going down on her. (Another photo — an obstetrician's-eye-view of a pregnant nude assembled from doll legs and arms, a witch mask, and artificial breasts and belly, the latter sporting, in lieu of the navel, a pig's snout — had been planned for the show but was left out at the last minute.)

What is all this about? It is not about cinematic genres and fairy tales. Horror movies, *Blue Velvet*-type film noir, and tales of Grimm creatures may legitimately come to mind, but they are not of the essence. The essence is pictorial. Except in her earliest "film stills" — one-frame movies, starring herself — Sherman's work has always functioned, aesthetically, more in the here-and-now way of painting than in the there-and-then of photography.

At present, it is absolutely paintinglike: confronting the viewer with powerfully scaled and colored, totally considered compositions that symbolize consciousness. You don't so much look at as enter into and *live* them, as if they were your idea, for as long as you can bear.

To say that the works are meant to shock seems true but beside the point. Shock is their element, a territory they inhabit. As always with Sherman, they entail questions of identity — "Who am I?" "What am I?" — posed by images that are receptacles of emotional identification. Her current receptacles are broken and degraded, merging personality with insulted bodies, bodies with organic substances, substances with mineral and synthetic stuff, and everything with the yakking flux of bad dreams. And yet she does it all with virtuosic, transparent, festive artifice, letting us in on her harrowing explorations as a form of play.

Formally, Sherman's pictures are masterfully ordered and perfectly gorgeous. This is important. It points to the aesthetic seriousness —

a seriousness about play — with which she has laid hold, one after another, of our culture's most potent pictorial tropes, from the presumably high forms of art photography, baroque painting, and operatic theater to the presumably low of B-movies, fashion advertising, centerfold erotica, fiction illustration, and the party snapshot. No cynical appropriator or parodist, Sherman has surrendered to each mode in the apparent belief that, given a selflessly passionate spirit of participation, it can be made an oracle of emotional conviction. She is like a scientist mixing unstable chemicals in search of a life-saving medicine, undeterred by her experiments' tendency to explode.

Her laboratory explosions yield the grotesque, which is the inevitable aspect of anything human that is studied with sufficiently prolonged and fearless detachment. Try it with your own hand, say, asking yourself, "What *is* this?" and accepting no abstract thought in answer; you will scare yourself sick.

Using the full resources of our culture's pictorial lexicons in combination, now, with the prefab fantasies of gross-out paraphernalia and, always, her own polymorphous imagination, Sherman pushes her scrutiny of the uncanny to the psychological equivalent of higher mathematics. A state of shock, in the result, simply guarantees the honesty of the procedure, guarded against reductions to easy irony.

Frigidly hot, Sherman's work brings together in one expression the polar extremes of adventurous art in the past decade: the contemplation of collective images by media-oriented artists and the dramatizing of individual emotion by neo-expressionists. Both extremes are in art-world eclipse now, submerged by a wearily sophisticated muddle of hybrid means and uncertain ends aptly termed by critic Ronald Jones "hover art."

Sherman's intensity consequently feels acutely unfashionable — much as Willem de Kooning's has since about 1960, when he proved helpless to trim his creative sails to please changing sensibilities. But she may very well emerge in eventual retrospect as the single most important American artist of the '80s — even as, "wrapped in the melodrama of vulgarity," she bears constant witness to a blessing of genius that can be indistinguishable from a curse.

SIGMAR POLKE *Mary Boone*

I FEEL IN GOOD HANDS WITH SIGMAR POLKE, which is kind of peculiar because the man is a nut. Actually, there's no paradox here but instead a lurking truism: artistic genius tends to be a shifty, shady, half-crazy phenomenon in our civilization, where to keep your head while all about you are losing theirs is not to grasp what's going on. Reflect on this lesson while enjoying yourself at Polke's current show of 14 strange and beautiful two-sided paintings. The show is flat-out innovative and insouciantly masterful. It has made me high on hope for art.

Polke is 48. From East Germany, like so many of the best German artists, he sat down in Dusseldorf in 1963 with fellow painters Gerhard Richter and Konrad Fischer (who would become a major dealer) and concocted a seminal response to American pop art. They called it "Capitalist Realism." As hip to anticapitalist critiques by Walter Benjamin as to capitalist icons by Andy Warhol — and jet-fueled by trashy romances with science fiction, hallucinogens, and hippie mysticism — Polke commenced to play at painting rather like Jerry Lee Lewis plays the piano: none too exactly and incredibly well. Ever since, he has gotten torrents of exciting music from an instrument he often seems bent on smashing to bits.

I've met Polke once, at the opening of the West German pavilion, with his show of colossal mineral-flaked resin paintings, at the 1986 Venice Biennale. In a naked bid for public sensation, the opening was delayed until the last officially allowed moment. Masses of people, including swarms of paparazzi, attended. A chubby elf in a frantic Hawaiian shirt and green satin trousers, Polke bounced around, giggling, with a huge shoulder-mounted movie camera that he whirred at anyone trying to photograph him. (I've often thought that must have made a nifty film — if, in fact, the camera was loaded.) Perhaps miffed at such grandstanding, the Biennale prize committee split their "best artist" award between Polke, whose show was astronomically superior, and the dreary English painter Frank Auerbach.

I had just published an essay on Polke in which I wrote of "primordial fear" in the way his art seemed to flirt with psychic disintegration. Introduced to me amid the Venetian clamor, he thanked me warmly for my praise — then abruptly seemed exasperated with himself, perhaps for being so uxorious to a critic. "Are you really *frightened*?!" he cackled suddenly, making like a Three Stooges bug-eyed maniac. With that, he moved off, working his big camera.

Later that day I encountered Polke wandering like a dazed tourist, with a woman friend, in a narrow street. He looked deflated inside his preposterous duds, lost-little-boyish. He smiled weakly and nodded. I wanted badly to talk to him — I was full of curiosity and a sort of appalled admiration — but the best I could manage was to smile back encouragingly.

Polke's public performance reminded me that in Germany artists are often vested with a faintly magical, shamanistic prestige, as figures emanating some ratio of the prophet, the jester, and the sacred monster. Joseph Beuys was the champ at this, of course, but even before Beuys' death Polke was starting to run him a close second. (Anselm Kiefer, an artist avowedly influenced by both Beuys and Polke, is the flip side of the type, reclusively abjuring any public role whatsoever.) My glimpse of Polke's vulnerability brought the pathos of the high-stakes game home to me. All in all, I was confirmed in my belief that Germany enjoys an art culture singularly luckier, and way weirder, than the American.

Polke's new works will surely add to the influential coups by which he has energized painting with heterodox supports (every sort of noncanvas fabric), materials (witches'-brew chemicals in place of paint), technique (e.g., overlay drawing), and imagery (e.g., sleazy cartoon jokes). The most perversely irreverent painter since Francis Picabia, he seems fascinated by how painting's aesthetic unities gamely reassert themselves under no matter how much abuse. He keeps making things that are paintings by default — because you can't imagine what on earth else they might be — and the result is somehow a heroic affirmation of a medium whose demise as something central to our cultural experience always seems just around the corner.

The new paintings — on both sides of semi-transparent silk rectangles of medium size, clamped in stretchers that are temporarily enclosed by free-standing racks vaguely reminiscent of auction-house display easels — are metaphysical conundrums. All but one are initialed by Polke on both sides and thus have, in effect, two fronts and no back. Much but not all of the marking on one side will show through on the other, making each unit a sort of Siamese-twin set of symbiotic pictures that endlessly inform, subvert, and refresh each other. I can think of no true precedent for this device in the whole of art history.

As always, Polke works here in a disjunctive sequence of procedures that add up without really blending. You can see exactly how he slathered orangish artificial resin, doodled drawings in black marker (faces, expressionistic stick figures, a rococo entablature, a Dufyesque landscape, a Mayan idol, etc.), suspended pigment in wet resin (drying in lovely cloud-crystal patterns like *Scientific American* illustrations for an article on chaos), and painted mock-ups of the Ben-Day dot screens often featured in his earlier work. Viewed from either side, the accumulations of seemingly slapdash operations are arrested in states that almost always feel achingly perfect.

The effect of the drum-tight silk darkened and made more transparent by the resin, like greased paper, is no cinch to describe. In my notebook, I scribbled "tender glow — suavity — parchment — unhealthy skin — old bruises — dirty stained glass — hard candy — amber." It is intimately riveting, in any case: an erogenous membrane that nudges a viewer directly into reverie. Lest you forget the kind of guy you're dealing with, the occasional stupid joke jumps out and bites you. A turd-like shape turns out to represent Mount Rushmore, which Boone told me was Polke's idea of a greeting to America.

Seemingly an unusually resilient type of the carefully deranged '60s leftist — erecting barricades of and amid his own brain cells — Polke at times has seemed out to test the bourgeois stratagem that Herbert Marcuse termed "repressive tolerance." This is not to give him any points for ideological purity. He seems a cheerful enough compromiser, despite a legendary fecklessness about administrative and business matters.

Simply, Polke is a temperamental violator of any sort of purity. As a leading light, now, of Western art, he is like a parasitic growth that makes its afflicted host feel goofily good. Is it bourgeois of me to be so deeply reassured by Polke's continuing triumph? No doubt. (Painting is still *the* bourgeois medium in a lot of ways, which is why leftists since Benjamin have kept trying to blow it out of the water.) At any rate, the reassurance hardly seems sentimental — laced as it is with tones of decadence and, yes, *frigh-tening* hints of real disturbance. Polke's triumph remains radically provisional, as moment-to-moment as life feels today, like walking in a haunted house where the next step could drop you straight through the floor with a burst of mad laughter fading away.

1989 BIENNIAL EXHIBITION *Whitney Museum*

THE 1989 WHITNEY BIENNIAL CONFIRMS what many of us have suspected: at some point in the last couple of seasons while no one was watching, maybe late one night in summer, American art had a nervous breakdown. In the general impression it makes, the show is a trauma center—antiseptic, literally almost colorless, hushed, and twitchy. It isn't much fun, but it is unusually cogent, as Biennials go, and grimly informative.

In the words of the astonishingly candid catalog introduction by curators Richard Armstrong, Richard Marshall, and Lisa Phillips, the show displays "vulnerability, delicacy, and instability"—dire mental symptoms, right? The introduction is a cry from the heart of 1989 that's a keeper. Reread it in a few years to remember how things were in today's bad or—perish the thought—good old days. It expresses beleaguerment, alternately whimpering and snarling between obligatory, tellingly listless upbeats.

"Today's art world is troubled, yet resilient, something like the society it reflects," the curators begin gingerly. Then they go for it: "We have moved into a situation where wealth is the only agreed upon arbiter of taste ... a system adrift in mortgaged goods and obsessed with accumulation ... a public forum geared to journalistic hyperbole ... the greed and impotent theorizing that have choked so much contemporary art."

They're right, you know. The art world's ongoing glut of money and prestige is increasingly hollow at the core. It no longer has the backing of any ideas, any style, or any life-enhancing vulgarity, only nerveless momentum and a spooky conviction of invincibility. Creativity danced with wealth through much of the '80s, but the tempo has exhausted creativity. Wealth is on its own. The truest new art at the Whitney is shaky and frail. It has discovered the one sure way to discourage checkbook avant-gardism: be boring.

(Some people are bound to rejoice in this boredom as the end of '80s-type "hype and fashion." I think such people will like being dead.)

I refer to younger, emerging artists, properly the topical focus of Biennials. Several veterans in the show, such as Brice Marden and Joel Shapiro, are in great shape. Marden's webby linear abstractions—classics of American matter-of-fact lyricism—are my favorite things in sight. (They are slow and elusive at first, then steadily more powerful: give them time.) Shapiro's chunky bronze shapes on poles are prodigies of strength and wit.

Ross Bleckner's darkly perfumed nocturnal paintings and Sherrie Levine's inscrutably satiric plywood panels (which feature the timely image of *Krazy Kat*'s Mr. Austridge, an ostrich with his head in a bucket on wheels) show these two phenoms of the mid-'80s qualifying for the longer haul. Meanwhile, Ashley Bickerton probably and Jeff Koons indubitably ensure that the late-'80s paroxysm of art-as-commodity will leave lasting memorials. The only remaining question about Koons has been whether his insolent genius marks a new departure or a last hurrah for this epoch. The correct answer is: last hurrah (loud, though).

A few other artists merit consideration as sturdy contributors to what might be called the upper-middle range of American art. Among them: Martin Puryear, stylistically unfocused but estimable master of sculptural form; Donald Baechler, last of the neo-expressionist painters to receive, and to deserve, mainstream recognition; and Saint Clair Cemin, Brazil-born maker of art-nouveauish bronze furniture-sculpture with nastily sexy clay pots.

All such special cases aside, the message of this Biennial is one of distress, at best. About a third of the 42 artists (not counting 34 in the film and video section, which I haven't seen yet) evince present neo-conceptual and neo-minimalist trends that acutely register today's malaise — as does, in another way, a peculiar current flavor in painting: melancholic fantasy, from the lonesome-child daydreams of William Wegman to the soundless-because-no-one-is-there-to-hear landscapes of April Gornik. (Other painters in this seductive cul-de-sac are Mark Innerst, Joan Nelson, and Tom Wudl.)

Some of these artists are very good. Most aren't, because they're stunted by the terms of what they're up to: escaping the present for moments in the past, often the early '70s (if not the 19th century), that probably weren't so wonderful in the first place and will not be coming around again. At its deadliest, the impulse gives us Cindy Bernard (photos of the patterned insides of governmental and corporate "security envelopes"), Kate Ericson and Mel Ziegler (heady meditations on American institutions, involving broken windows and jars of paint with sand-blasted rubrics), and Hirsh Perlman (linguistic riffs on modern architecture, with photos and text). With its peremptory need for professional explaining, such work bodes only a return to art-schoolish casuistry, which may soothe museum curators but will suffocate pleasure.

Less programmatic graspings for straws of tradition are apparent in some ingenuously revived geometric abstraction, by Cary Smith and Andrew Spence, and other sorts of what I think of as "I-love-painting painting": generic romances with the old medium that derive their poignance from a sense of vagabondage in time. For instance, David Reed's deftly slathered arabesques on long panels suggest fragments of some lost baroque plenitude.

In contrast to these small gestures toward big pasts, two theatrical show-stoppers prove the ever-ready ability of American artists to redeem weakly obvious ideas of the present with sufficient bravura. Forget the tedious "commentary on the artwork as commodity" attributed in the catalog to Allan McCollum's *Individual Works* — 10,000 grenade-shaped plastic whatsits, no two identical, on a black velvet table — and dig its lake of a marvelous color that a friend of mine decided is "fortified aqua." Even better is Chris Burden's *All the Submarines of the United States of America*, 625 ceiling-hung, gold-painted cardboard subs composing a sinister and delirious psychedelia. Not to suspend judgment and simply to wallow in such spectacles would betray an ill-bred sensibility.

Also spectacular, in a mysterious way I can't make up my mind about, is the single piece by Charles Ray, an *echt*-Californian artist of mechanized Zen: a disk-shaped section of wall that looks motionless but is in fact revolving at a terrifying 3,500 rpm. It's a nifty stunt, at minimum.

Are there signs of hope for the future in the Biennial? No. This show is strictly from downside — as in the work of Christopher Wool, whose paintings using old-fashioned stenciled lettering are jejune replays of a device that sang with energy when Jasper Johns adopted it over three decades ago. One quite clever Wool picture, repeating the word "PLEASE" six times, could be the logo not only of this Biennial but of the whole Zeitgeist of insatiable need and desperate ingratiation it signals.

One of many things I like about Mike Kelley, probably the most important younger American artist after Koons, is that he takes the despair of the moment head-on, in a spirit of no-future fiesta. You won't get any hope from Kelley's radically pessimistic congeries of maudlin stuffed animals and images of excretion and death, but you may be reminded that creative fierceness and honesty are their own reward in the worst as in the best of times.

American art has gone passive-aggressive, the Whitney informs us. Low spirits are in. Professionalism is the most you can expect. The muses are staging a sit-down strike. A lot of people who have become convinced that they care passionately about new art are about to have serious doubts. The future, turning murky, may begin to rehearse one of its old, lately neglected tricks: taking us by surprise.

"GOYA AND THE SPIRIT OF ENLIGHTENMENT"
Metropolitan Museum of Art

Everybody I TALK TO IS DISAPPOINTED by the Goya show. It's a dull show, keyed to numbing amounts of information about politics in Spain during Goya's career. Goya's art is forced to illustrate this information, which one does not necessarily care about. Nor is any reason for caring proposed. The show was conceived on the Planet of the Scholars, where every question is considered except "So what?" There is the nice touch of a reading room halfway through. It should have oxygen tanks.

But part of the disappointment must be laid to Goya himself, a painter commonly overrated in this century. He is disappointing even in Madrid's Prado Museum, where his strongest paintings unbudgeably reside. He is one of the greatest graphic artists who ever lived (a distinction best savored in the intimacy of a book, not in endless ranks of little prints at a mobbed exhibition), and he is a heroic historic figure: appalled discoverer of the modern condition, the first old master who feels like one of us. But the sludge of a degraded baroque tradition weighed heavily on his painting, whose victories — despite an extraordinary use of color — are generally Pyrrhic.

Putting the best face on it, we might term Goya the artist *of* disappointment, the poet of smashed hopes. Some such thesis could have given point to the show at the Met, had not its co-directors in Boston and Madrid been allergic to anything resembling a critical idea in their eagerness to portray Goya, that dark angel, as a public-spirited social progressive, sort of an Iberian Henry Fonda.

I have no problem with the facts laid out in a half-dozen all but unreadable catalog essays: Goya (who was a nearly exact contemporary of Thomas Jefferson) belonged to a late 18th-century liberalization in Spain that, after many defeats, was effectively obliterated in 1814. But it's as an artist of defeats — not a watery liberal evincing "sympathy for the common man," as in the Met show's treacly version — that Goya looms over the past two centuries.

I can guess why an upbeat myth of the Enlightenment might be favored in Spain today, still only 14 years into that snake-bitten nation's post-Franco perestroika. However, everybody's got problems. The sinister social scene in the U. S. gives a Pollyannaish cast to old-fashioned liberal idealism. All of this is moot, in any case, because the show and its catalog disdain to touch ground with the here-and-now of anybody anywhere.

We are left to have what experience we can of Goya's art amid a didacticism that's as energetic about the many inferior works as about the few masterpieces present. (A tip: seek out the five Goyas in the Met's permanent collection, better than almost anything in the show—and also the superb 13 drawings and 10 prints in a lovely current Met mini-exhibition called *Spain*, a well-kept secret that, after elbowing through the main event, I shared with two other viewers.) This is one of those times when art-love is a guerrilla operation.

My favorite picture in sight is *Maja and Celestina on a Balcony* (1808-1812), featuring an ambiguously winsome young prostitute and an ambiguously gleeful old procuress. It is about seduction of men in the person of the (male) viewer—which describes a lot of old-master paintings, but this one is astounding. A good-news/bad-news proposition—symbolically, the girl and the crone read as two sides of one truth—it is a lure and a warning. The triumphant figures glimmer out of the black background full of an awful knowledge that dawns suddenly: the lure is already taken and the warning is too late. Having just looked, one is *had*.

The thought is as good as the deed. This is a very modern sort of idea—or exaltation, or sickness—which arrives full-blown in history with Goya (and William Blake). All the Met show's nattering about issues of liberalism is cold cant compared to the molten lava of traduced subjectivity that is Goya's message about "Enlightenment" individuality. Deaf for the last 36 years of his life, he *saw* the irrepressible beast beneath modernizing rationality. More than that, he detailed its ravages within his own soul.

The first thing many people note about *Maja and Celestina* is its prediction of Edouard Manet, who, as a painter, learned from and improved on Goya while, as a poet of successful modernism, domesticating Goya's beast. Manet's world is enfevered with sex, but people don't go around overtly brutalizing each other. What would we make of Goya if Manet had not picked up on him? We can't know, any more than we can really imagine Cézanne without the retroactive gloss of Picasso and Braque.

The single most definitively Goyaesque tone is, to put it directly, gross-out: hilarity plus shock, with an aftereffect of feeling pawed. Mocking the show's prissy wall labels, the *Disasters of War* are a delightful encyclopedia of homicide: garroting, hanging, stabbing, shooting, axing, spearing, stoning, starving, and poisoning, not to mention fun with corpses. And what of the print from *Caprichos* about pedophilia: a witch wielding a naked boy like a bellows, using his farts to swell a fire? One can only hoot or tremble, or both.

Goya inhabits the moral twilight of expressionistic satire: ambiguity of being "against" things whose pleasures you have profoundly imagined. He groans and cackles in the attic of modern culture. The Goya who will haunt us until the end of time is beyond politics, and even beyond art. He is one scary hombre.

DAN FLAVIN *Leo Castelli*

GUESTS TO A RECENT BIG PARTY at a collector's house uptown were momentarily blinded, at the top of the stairs leading to roast beef and asparagus, by a phalanx of white fluorescent tubes by Dan Flavin. This provocative placement irked many, which I assumed was part of the plan for a lively evening. An artist obliged by yanking Flavin's plug. This artist later allowed that he might have been partly motivated by an old pique at having had work in group shows more or less annihilated by the presence of Flavins, which tend to affect their ambiences like aesthetic machine guns.

Flavin's fluorescents have been logging kilowatt hours and group-show kills for 27 years, their configurations of factory-fresh components composing one of the really durable product lines in serious contemporary art. They are definitive works of minimalism, which is still the last — the terminal — great modern movement. Like Carl Andre and Donald Judd, Flavin, 56 years old, is a minimalist founding father stubbornly loyal to a principle of making the viewer's self-consciousness the bull's-eye for all (if any) meaning. Like minimalism generally, he has lately been nudging back into art-world prominence after an eclipse by picture-drunk styles of the '80s.

Flavin's show of prints, drawings, and project diagrams at Castelli's new Broadway annex is unelectrified and unelectrifying, but instructive. It follows the April installation, in Castelli's main digs on West Broadway, of *To the Citizens of the Republic of France on the 200th Anniversary of Their Revolution*, a huge, spankingly handsome, rather sentimental congeries of red, white, and blue tubes. Flavin — who once dedicated to his pet dog a big piece in green and blue, evoking a grassy hillside against a summer sky — has given ample evidence of being a cornball at heart. Somehow this ought to damage his standing as a minimalist paladin, but it doesn't. He's had an idea so good — his fluorescents — that not even he can fall out of it.

No amount of self-indulgence — including that of some hopelessly dopey sketches of sailboats (seemingly made in a wave-tossed dinghy) and a runaway penchant for maudlin dedications, both in the present show — can spoil the authority of Flavin's ideas about art and the world, so impersonal that the mere good or bad taste of the artist's could neither improve on nor ruin them. It has been enough, in the fundamentalist rigor of Flavin, Andre, and Judd, that the artist understand the ideas and make them aggressively manifest. All the rest may be eccentricity, like a scientific genius's absentminded hygiene.

Minimalism ratified a situation of art and culture that became the case in the 1960s and is pretty much still the case now: art as a phenomenon of "public" (in feeling, if not in fact) environments, something happening to people in real space and real time. Orthodox minimalism makes the raw reality palpable at gut level, never more so than in Flavin's creations of "not so much an art object as the phenomenon of the piece's existence in a particular location, at a particular moment in time," as critic Gregoire Muller once elegantly put it. The fluorescents are art only when installed and turned on; betweentimes, or when a rival artist freaks out, they are just hardware.

All of this is old news, perhaps, but it bears repetition at a time of looming confusion over art's role in the world —except as a new form of liquid asset, juggling numbers on balance sheets whenever it is moved from one bank vault to another. Not that minimalism is "pure." At the recent Chicago Art Fair, old Flavins were aglow seemingly all over the place, blushing courtesans of the mighty resale market. But the old minimalist insistence on art's necessary relation to somebody's specific experience, at a specific place and time, may provide at least a glimmer of philosophical sanity in the present money-sick madness.

I only wish that Flavin —and this goes, too, for Judd, who has lately been inflicting dumb furniture and architecture on us —were content to recognize and make a virtue of his limits. The silly sailboats and other wishfulnesses in his new show may symptomize the malaise of an artist oppressed by the strictness of his own best idea.

Attempting to extend his range, Flavin is like a bird fancying itself a virtuoso but naturally programmed with just the one song. That song is beautiful and strong, in Flavin's case, and he has managed against any reasonable expectation to freshen it repeatedly with coups of design and lovely effulgences of color. But you get that he resents its hold on him.

ARNULF RAINER *Guggenheim Museum*

TRUE TO ITS KARMA AS THE PRESIDENT GERALD FORD of New York art institutions, the Guggenheim gives us yet another show with "Kick Me" written all over it: an indiscriminate retrospective of the Austrian Arnulf Rainer, an artist I used to think was sort of interesting and may deem so again when the effect of this event wears off. The most intriguing aspect of the show is the list of sponsors — a mighty array of Austrian governmental and corporate bodies — for the promotion of a determinedly hysterical native son. Note that this aspect is just a little bit intriguing.

The exhibition is only mildly awful when compared with the Guggenheim's recent "Refigured Painting: The German Image 1960-88," a never-to-be-forgotten milestone of curatorial haplessness. But then, the museum had no hand in curating the Rainer show, a job done surprisingly badly by the usually adept European impresario Rudi Fuchs. Is there a miasmic vapor on 89th Street that addles even the best of minds?

The show's big fault is inflation. With 140 pictures — endlessly repetitive and often mediocre, though selected from an output of 36 years — it quickly exhausts attention. I was eventually reduced mainly to reading the wall labels, which reveal that about 100 of the works belong to the artist or to a gallery — marketable imports, in other words, being anointed with the cachet (which can't be worth a whole lot, surely) of having been shown in the Guggenheim.

It's too bad, because an exacting retrospective of Rainer — which you might want to curate in your head while viewing the present one, if you have the pep — would keenly dramatize the lot of a provincial but driven post-World War II European artist burdened with grandiose myths of capital-C Creativity while stuck with worn-out formal conventions. Rainer, who is 60, is essentially an abstract expressionist infused with the theatrically self-lacerating spirit that is a frequent feature of Viennese modernism from Egon Schiele to the present. His works are either dark flowers of anguish or garden-variety blooms of frustration, depending on your willingness to play along.

Rainer is often compared to his contemporary Yves Klein, star of the rather gimmicky European avant-garde of the late '50s and early '60s. But as a showman he is in no league with Klein, who used naked women as brushes to make electric-blue paintings. Rainer's signature device of that period was "overpainting," the monochrome obliteration of existing paintings by himself or someone else (Sam Francis was among the artists contributing works to be thus immolated). The results, as art, are lots of glumly color-fieldish abstractions, some handsome. As antiart, they are timid: lurkingly genteel, really, in the sacredness they assume for painting even as they make a big deal about violating it.

After a spell of what the catalog dryly terms "experiments" with hallucinogens, Rainer had an intermittently impressive run of pictures in the late '60s and early '70s that involve feverish finger painting and/or photographs of himself grimacing maniacally. These works can be genuinely eloquent about frustration: the artist seriously worked up about something and expressing his inability to express it. If only there weren't so many! The sense of a tantrum indulged for years gets old fast. You wonder that Rainer never developed a hobby, or something.

Do you buy Fuchs' assurance, in the catalog, that Rainer has often used red paint for his violent finger painting "in case the hand started bleeding"? (Dried blood isn't red.) Fuchs falls in with a romance of the wigged-out genius that Rainer's own writings in the catalog avidly advertise: "I began crawling from picture to picture, slapping and stroking paint on the surfaces. (Having become a 'painter animal' I would employ bear and fox paws or tiger claws to stamp the paint on.) . . . I was a catch-as-catch-can wrestler fighting adversaries en suite."

Yawn. It may be very pragmatic-American of me to say so, but how paint is delivered to a surface seems properly a professional matter of no special concern to us laypeople. Rainer gets a wonderfully snarly graphic look with some of his altered photos and an occasionally gorgeous stitchy-smeary texture with his finger painting. So the techniques served him well, as dripping served Jackson Pollock well. But Pollock always insisted that the picture was what mattered.

Rainer is no Pollock, as well as no Klein. He is even no Cy Twombly, an artist whose emotionally more subtle graphism Rainer's work often recalls. Nor is he the equal of the Germans Sigmar Polke and Gerhard Richter, whose slapdash painterliness transcends "expressive" bathos with bracingly matter-of-fact irony. Rainer is a minor artist whose apparent lionization in Vienna says nothing encouraging about Austria's art culture.

This brings us back to the Guggenheim, which as usual messes up its potentially invaluable role as a New York mediator of European art by flattering the vanity of its overseas sponsors rather than honoring the acumen of its local audience. Somebody should have told the Austrians and Fuchs that only a small, taut Rainer show could fly in this town. But what the nabobs of Europe don't know is plainly no skin off the nose of the Guggenheim, whose message to New York continues to be: drop dead.

June 21, 1989

"HELEN FRANKENTHALER: A PAINTINGS RETROSPECTIVE"

The Museum of Modern Art

THE DOYENNE OF "COLOR FIELD PAINTING" (an overblown, under-nourished styloid of the 1960s), Helen Frankenthaler has long been ascending to an eminence strangely reserved in this culture for older women artists of maximum pretension and minimum real vitality, such as Georgia O'Keeffe and Louise Nevelson. (This fate rarely threatens perennial live wires such as Louise Bourgeois or Nancy Spero.) Her 36-year retrospective of 40 big paintings at MoMA makes sense as part of her official elevation. As an art show, it's dull.

Frankenthaler gives attitude. She can say (in the MoMA catalog) of one of her paintings that it is "considered and formal, yet the spontaneity shines throughout." She can say, "My work is never playful" —a remark only too true, and a crack of doom for art that mimics the improvisatoriness of watercolors on a huge scale. What, if not playful, are expanses drenched in shades of mauve, pink, mint, tangerine, and the blue of mixed-berry-flavored popsicles? They are solemn teases, is what they are.

Color field painting was invented by Clement Greenberg in 1953 when he showed a stain painting by Frankenthaler —a delicate mess of a picture called *Mountains and Sea*, which kicks off the present exhibition—to Morris Louis and Kenneth Noland, a couple of striving provincials from Washington, D. C. They went and did likewise, and by the early '60s dozens of painters were doing likewise: staining miles of canvases that advertised Greenberg's cultish rhetoric of "flatness" and "opticality." It was a bizarre episode in the history of taste, inspiring Tom Wolfe's *The Painted Word* and memorably skewered by minimalist Robert Smithson as a mania of dried-up professors who long to press their faces into wet grass.

Never an orthodox Greenbergian, Frankenthaler can't be blamed for the derivative inanities of color field. But only an overconfidence buoyed by that orthodoxy explains her relentless inflation of little ideas to giant size. And her style of personal hauteur, hinting that her art may be entirely too good for the profane eyes of this world, owes a lot to the winning-through-intimidation critical routines of Greenberg. This is not to belittle the style, a big-town snobbism that makes

Frankenthaler a sacred-monstrous living treasure.

She was even a very good painter for a while — now and then in the late '50s, despite a pseudo-emotiveness in the fashion of "action painting," and solidly in the early '60s, when she combined the best of that declining period style (its make-it-up-as-you-go-along nerviness) with the best of the cool, heraldic period style that was replacing it. *Yellow Caterpillar*, 1961, and *Seascape With Dunes*, 1962, feature rhythmical lollops of intense color as fresh as cold water and hanging together with the vernacular rightness of great jazz.

Frankenthaler's painting then went limp at least partly because she switched from oil to acrylic paints, joining a rush of painters to the miracle plastics that made Greenbergian "flatness" a foreordained cinch and an instant cliche. Colors in oil are translucent and volatile, tough to handle in ways that gave Frankenthaler's fast-and-loose work with them a risky edge. Colors in acrylic just sort of lie there. It's funny, I remember how spankingly contemporary the matte opacity of acrylics looked in the '60s. Now that look is hopelessly dated.

From 1963 to the present you get a sense of an intimate talent (Frankenthaler's works on paper are often dandy) being forced to make "major" statements. Until the middle '70s, these tend to resemble overwrought preliminary sketches for banners or supergraphics. Since then, the style has been that of a nearly forgotten color-fieldish submovement, called "lyrical abstraction," that peaked in the early '70s. This kind of work exploits the fluid properties of acrylics, manipulated "wet-in-wet" to yield flashy atmospheric effects: instant cloudscape, fog bank, sunset, you name it.

Frankenthaler's readiness to take credit for the God-like association of these effects — asserting that one of her paintings "is resolved in the way nature is resolved" — goes over well in hauteur-admiring quarters like *The New York Times*. For a recent Sunday magazine profile, Deborah Solomon (while showing signs of indigestion) lapped up bowls of such talk from Frankenthaler; and John Russell has given the MoMA show one of those elegant reviews of his that seem murmured by a courtier on bended knee.

Her images "don't cloy," Russell's review ends truthfully enough. Frankenthaler's images can't cloy because she takes so few chances in the direction of delight. Her colors tend to be sourish, tipped toward the medicinal rather than the candied. This may qualify her as "serious" for some. But the upshot for pleasure-seeking eyes is that her paintings aren't only not beautiful, they aren't even pretty. This is an achievement of sorts, given Frankenthaler's lush palette, but I wouldn't call it a wonderful achievement.

Restraint is a buzzword in Frankenthaler criticism, but restraint in art, as in manners, is only as impressive as our sense of what — a temperamental wildness, perhaps — is being disciplined. There's no great trick in training a dead dog to play dead. But then, evidently somebody has to do it: providing passionless symbols of controlled passion for the comfort of polite society. It's interesting that this is a role set aside for women.

July 26, 1989

"LAFAYETTE, HERO OF TWO WORLDS: THE ART AND PAGEANTRY OF HIS FAREWELL TOUR OF AMERICA, 1824-1825" *The Queens Museum*

DID YOU KNOW THAT LAFAYETTE was 19 years old when commissioned as a major general in the Revolutionary War and turned 24 while setting up the endgame at Yorktown? I didn't know that, and I love it. At the Battle of Yorktown, remember, Cornwallis was bottled up by the French fleet for decanting by Gen. Washington. Can you even begin to imagine the music and magic, the poetry, of that phrase *the French fleet* to Colonial ears after five years of war? And the fleet was there largely due to this French *kid*.

If I seem kidlike myself here, chalk it up to hot weather and a patriotic nostalgia that comes back on me now and again. I suspected I'd thrill to the Lafayette show at the Queens Museum, and I do. The museum is a winningly strange little place, to begin with: a professional island in vast Flushing Meadow, ghostly site of the 1965 World's Fair. Summer is always a season when the present weakens and the past refluxes, and Flushing Meadow is a wide breach in the local time dike through which floods of old summers drench the heart.

Back to Lafayette, of whom the show provides over a hundred portraits in media ranging from painting on canvas to printing on the backs of ladies' gloves. You get that he was a star in the USA, whatever his ups and downs in French turbulences from 1782 until his death in 1834.

He first-drafted the Rights of Man, ordered the razing of the Bastille (sending Washington the prison's main key in care of Tom Paine), lost everything to the Terror, was jailed as a subversive for five years in Austria, survived persecution by Napoleon and the Restoration to broker another revolution in 1830—you get the idea: what a guy! In 1824-25, a planned four-month American visit became a 13-month, 24-state national love orgy, relics of which compose most of the show.

He was French, all right, with quick eyes in a big-nosed, sensual Gallic mug that got fleshier, rosier, and more adorable with age. In late pictures, he is the Platonic ideal of a favorite uncle, which is sort of what he was to the U. S. —virtual kid brother as well as intimate sidekick to Washington, whose patriarchal austerity he leavened with pure charm. It is nothing but wonderful to think of him arriving

133

in Philadelphia in 1777 as a teenager with ideas so perfect he would never have to change them and, which didn't hurt, a personal fortune big enough to buy himself into history.

What has this got to do with art? I don't care, if you want the truth. I will just contentedly endorse the Queens exhibition's thesis that Lafayette's tour was a benchmark in forming American high and popular arts, a moment of raised national consciousness when art, politics, and civic ritual meshed.

All our top portraitists then had a crack at Lafayette, and the show is a chance to register the relative quirks and merits of Samuel F. B. Morse, Raphael Peale, Thomas Sully, et al. Morse wins in a walk, for those keeping score, with a virtuosic full-length job of our hero in yellow trousers posed with busts of Washington and Ben Franklin against an orange sunset. Sully, as usual, overdoes the sugar, making even democracy's warrior seem a glamorous simp.

But the main creativity of the event was in the streets. Cities competed in pomp, meanwhile fretting about the proprieties of republican, egalitarian demeanor. (It was generally decided that some young men who unhitched the horses from Lafayette's carriage and pulled it themselves had gone too far.) The tour occasioned renovation of Independence Hall and spurred monument building everywhere.

What a pity to have missed the parade in Philadelphia, which wound through 13 temporary triumphal arches that made of the city an instant pseudo-Rome. Or not to have been in New York when Lafayette held daily receptions for anyone who dropped by to say hello, and entrepreneurs churned out souvenir tchotchkes à la Elvis. Everything was employed except photography, not quite yet invented. It's interesting how the absence of one mechanical gizmo makes the tour seem so much longer ago than it was.

The point is, for me, that I didn't know about most of this until I saw the Queens show and read its lushly informative catalog. One of the compensations of a crappy American education, I've decided, is the capacity later in life to experience manifold wonderments of basic knowledge that you were spared in grade school.

"Lafayette, we are here," said Gen. Pershing in 1917, at the grave in Paris where Lafayette is buried in American soil he brought back in a trunk for the purpose. (Sentimental morbidity was in then, as witness a circa-1828 crystal brooch displaying mingled hair of Lafayette and Washington.) It was a nice thought. Especially nice —an exalting upbeat for summer time-travel—is a sense of moral and political convictions so tough they can always tell you where you are, and why.

Today the idea of such conviction is travestied by people whose notion of revering democracy is an anti-flag-burning amendment. But it is also renewed by the drama in Tiananmen Square, where Lafayette, firebrand for democratic revolution anywhere (and fervently antislavery, by the way) would somehow have gotten in the thick of things. His answer to the more knotted human woes was always the same: *Liberty*. Just liberty. Never argue with a Founding Father.

August 2, 1989

A TREASON OF CLERKS

THE RECENT PUBLIC OUTCRIES AGAINST ARTWORKS by Robert Mapplethorpe and Andres Serrano, the ongoing flag furor (including outcries against an artwork by Dread Scott Tyler), and the distinct possibility of a nationwide wave of anti-cosmopolitan populism remind us that political controversy is like a speeding train. It has one aspect when passing by (vicariously stimulating on *Nightline*, say) and quite another when it is coming directly at you.

Long comfortably marginal to public debate, the sector of the art world reliant on government funding has had particular reason lately to feel tied to the tracks in front of a political runaway freight. But anyone living the American life of art is apt to glimpse in a general uglification of attitudes toward artistic license the mesmerizing glare of an approaching headlight.

We are in for something. What it will be and how bad it will be are shrouded, but we are in for something. And we —meaning those of us committed to art as not only a refined pleasure but also an oracle of worldly change, a redeemer of things debased, and a cosmopolitan communion —are going to make whatever badness there is worse, because we can't help it.

Two weeks ago the House of Representatives nibbled $45,000 from the National Endowment for the Arts' $171.4 million budget for next year, withholding only the pittance spent last year toward the offending shows of Mapplethorpe and Serrano. It was a chilling but elegantly understated threat, engineered by liberals to finesse conservatives who were out to gut the agency, that as much as said (or pleaded): "Do not come to our attention again." How do you think my kind of art person, who identifies with art's ambition to make a difference in the world, will receive that message?

My kind of art person will be happy that art has had such an impact. To come to people's attention is what all artists always try to do, and what almost no artist ever does on a substantial scale in this country. We have had nearly three decades now of a liberal dispensation that abides almost any expression so long as it stays within its proper little red-light district of the culture.

Those of us who have chafed at this, grumbling about "repressive tolerance," may soon have our chance to put up or shut up in the face

136

of conservative intolerance that rejects the notion of any sanctuary for sinners.

Nothing so terrible has happened yet. By themselves, the scandals of Serrano's urine-immersed crucifix in North Carolina and Tyler's flag-on-the-floor provocation in Chicago might be isolated rages of a sort that can happen in the U. S. when normally separate cultural spheres accidentally jostle. And Congress has signaled the preference of its majority for simply shoving the spheres back apart and stuffing insulation in the restored gap. In this context, the demagogueries of redneck-as-art-critic Dick ("morally reprehensible trash") Armey of Texas and art-critic-as-redneck Hilton (protector of children from homo-propaganda) Kramer of Connecticut might seem passing squalls. (If you missed Kramer's astonishing screed in the July 2 Sunday *Times*, track it down. It's a classic.)

The single event so far that makes a fading away of the stink improbable is the decision by the Corcoran Gallery of Art in Washington, D. C., on June 13, to cancel a Mapplethorpe show for fear of upsetting Congress on the verge of considering the NEA budget. On one level, this grotesque act succeeded mainly in letting blood into waters crowded with right-wing sharks, who seem to find artistic turpitude even more delightfully frenzying than the tasty but lean meat of flag desecration. But the Corcoran's display of weakness is ominous on another, subtler, and deadlier level: its save-the-NEA rationale.

Precisely that rationale has galvanized initial responses to the crisis by art institutions and even political activists. "Don't Take Away My NEA!" was a slogan emerging from a rally I attended at Artists Space on July 12. Thus is an issue of artistic freedom turned into one of a special interest group's claim on federal largesse.

The question of the NEA's fate (involving as it does the agency's mighty influence on state, local, and corporate funding policies) is serious for art people much as the possible closing of an auto plant is serious for auto workers, but it is beside the point of art's role and prerogative in American society. Just you watch. That point is going to split the art world between grant-protective Corcoranists — or more likely crypto-Corcoranists, who will mouth a liberal line while pursuing conservative agendas (never mounting a show that anyone could object to, for starters) — and my kind of art people, who will borrow trouble to pay dues as believers in actual liberty.

Though heretofore nameless, Corcoranism is not new. It is a tacit doctrine that preserving the means of cultural support justifies suppressing the ends of culture. Under Corcoranism, bureaucratic insularity and institutionalized self-censorship are good, and art's spontaneous fermentation of ideas and passions is bad. Corcoranism is a treason of the clerks. It is a formerly obscure treason whose exposure in the present emergency makes this an occasion not for defensiveness, in the cause of art, but for attack.

Let's keep a sharp eye on our institutions now. Do demand that they pledge anti-Corcoranist allegiance to artistic freedom, but don't heed what they say so much as look at what they do. In an era of conservative hostility, artists may be counted on to put new edges on their own disaffection. Keep tabs on the responsiveness of the institutions to those edges, as also to specifically controversial artists — Mapplethorpe, Serrano, Tyler, and the many more to come — whose cases can no longer be regarded as peripheral.

Things may get dramatic presently here in our cosmopolis. Forces of brain and brawn on the American right — the stuffy but powerfully aggrieved Kramers and the stupid but powerfully numerous Armeys — seem to be getting in rare sync, no doubt pooling enemies lists that toll for thee and me. So what? You don't abandon your principles just because some louts are in a mood to resent them. We aren't going anywhere. And a fight for the soul of American art culture may be just what is needed to clear a lot of lingering cobwebs, immediately including the uncertainty of who, in the culture's ranks, is or isn't artistic freedom's friend.

GALLERY-PHOBIA

LET'S TALK ABOUT HOW INTIMIDATED WE ARE by art galleries. Admit it, first of all. Especially when alone, you have a queasy, shriveling feeling in those pristine bivouacs for beautiful and intelligent objects. There, sensory overload vies with sensory deprivation — hot art thrust into architectural ice water, causing steam — and the ozone of the aesthetic burns the sinuses.

You feel gawkily self-conscious. You are convinced that the svelte young person behind the front desk does not like you. You do not for a moment imagine that this place is maintained for the likes of you.

Oh, but it is. I am here with good news, friends, which it took me a couple of decades to figure out for myself and which, taking advantage of summer's dearth of shows to review, I am going to share.

Gallery going is a definitive feature of present urban culture — what theatergoing used to be, perhaps, back when there was theater — as everybody knows including the many who never avail themselves of the experience because it makes them twitchy. Gallery going is poorly understood. (Art is poorly understood, but that's another matter.) The upshot is one of those universal miseries with which each individual feels uniquely afflicted.

The misery is basic to capitalist culture: a ragged fissure between Mammon and Eros, or money and meaning, that quite literally runs through the middle of commercial galleries and is not *your* problem (just everybody's reality). This gap defines the two physical zones of a gallery: the back room, seat of Mammon, and the front room, playground of Eros. Of course the two rooms function in sync, but in nothing like the simple bait-and-hook manner of the showroom and office of a normal shop.

You must understand the nature of a collector and the nature of an artist, between whom the dealer is middleperson. A collector, at least of the high-rolling type that dominates the art world now, is not lured by front rooms into back ones but proceeds on a beeline to the latter, where barbaric rites of flattery and abasement are practiced. Note that the Mary Boone Gallery — semiotically most informative as well as among the most successful of '80s art emporiums — maintains a locked "back door" on the street near its open front door.

(Boone's design is about stages of initiation, starting with the double-glass front doors that offer four theoretical possibilities of ingress: pull the right-hand door, pull the left-hand door, push the right-hand door, and push the left-hand door. The fourth and, for Americans, invariably last-attempted expedient achieves entrance. Observing the *nope-nope-nope- YES* dance of Boone goers is reliable Saturday-afternoon fun in Soho, varied by the immediate left-hand pushes that call attention to members of the cognoscenti.)

A gallery's artist, too, is admitted directly to the back room, there to have baroquely ambivalent feelings of which the most intense involve the front room's raison d'etre: The Show. Whatever murk of mind and spirit a career in art incurs, the Show reminds an artist of what the whole thing has seemed to be about from the beginning: get love, respect, or revenge via your talent, but get something emotional back from somebody. Make the world respond.

What entree is for the collector, The Show is for the artist: it's the dealer's bargaining chip. This is especially apparent now that so many exhibitions are sold out in advance, as is evident by the rosary chains of red dots on the legally mandated price lists (we adore those mightily demystifying lists, keeping in mind they may not be scrupulously candid). The Show is less about selling art than it is about propitiating the artist, serving the artist's dream of front-room consummation in return for desirable, back-room-fueling wares.

Much as television networks sell viewers to sponsors, therefore, galleries barter viewers to artists. You are nervous, comrade gallery goer, because you don't grasp that your presence is a perk in the contract between dealer and artist, a provision to earn the dealer's 50 percent commission on sales. If simply selling were a point, a dealer would need only a room somewhere with a telephone —and there exist many such "private" dealers, parasitic on the life of art. "Public" dealers support the life of art —hosting sure-enough culture in their front rooms —in order to command good artists.

Most dealers do not, as a matter of fact, like you very much. Most rather resent their services to the unwashed masses, because most at least half-believe one or more of the myths about belonging to an aristocracy that are catnip to their actual customers. The threatening hauteur of much gallery design is a passive-aggressive expression of this resentment. But hey, gallery-going pal, no sweat. It's part of the free spectacle.

I invite you to contemplate the majesty of the gallery phenomenon, which forces mutually repelling values of love and money into proximity—but not quite together, leaving a narrow, wild margin in which the craziness of our culture crackles. For an analogy, think of a nuclear reactor: a sealed core of primal energy, whose heat is drawn off indirectly to make electricity. Also by indirection, the erotic magma confined to a gallery's front room aids the generation of cash and prestige in the back.

Naturally this is discomfiting. Life is discomfiting. And culture under capitalism is a whoopie cushion, booby-trapped with unwelcome recognitions. But precisely this play of mixed emotions explains the dark glamor of visual art, a wavering institution about which the most idealistic and the most cynical statements will be both true and contradicted by their opposites. If you are nerve-racked in galleries, congratulations. You are onto some major truth about us. Just don't take it personally.

"THE DESIRE OF THE MUSEUM" *Whitney*

DON'T GO SEE "THE DESIRE OF THE MUSEUM," a high-concept group show assembled by a team of the Whitney's Helena Rubinstein curatorial interns who are students of theory-mongering critic Hal Foster. Read about it. Better yet, hear about it. Give some friend who's seen the show half a minute to explain it to you. Your friend may say, "They have this idea that the museum has an unconscious, which they psychoanalyze." You may think that sounds clever. You will not know that in hearing it you have skimmed the cream of the show's entertainment value: a dollop of the arch braininess that is today's up-and-coming art-institutional style.

Actually, do go see "The Desire of the Museum." (I was just kidding, making you think you needn't feel guilty about missing something. Life is not that easy.) It will help you understand and, if like me you are so inclined, to resist the acute theory-itis that's been inflaming a large part of the art world and intimidating much of the rest of it.

Visually, the show is dull. It favors conceptual work that either incorporates or seems to require lots of baleful text — the scrupulously impersonal kind, clad in an aura of disembodied authority. Wraparound aluminum strips on the wall, denoting "eye level," enforce self-consciousness. The installation calls insistent attention to mechanisms of museum display, in case you never noticed them before. In every possible way, the show detracts attention from art, the better to glamorize "critique."

Some strong old work by Marcel Duchamp and Ad Reinhardt feels outrageously dragooned. You would never guess that Duchamp's portable miniaturization of his oeuvre in *The Box in a Valise* — reduced by the curators to demonstrating "that the meaning of art is established by its institutional context" — is poignant with the artist's wartime exile. And the bristling specificity of Reinhardt's cartoon broadsides against the early-1950s New York art world mocks this show's gassy generalizations.

Alas, most of the newer stuff — such as Allan McCollum's tediously one-note *Plaster Surrogates* for painting, Julia Scher's closed-circuit "surveillance" video setup, and Aimee Rankin's precious "voyeuristic" peep-boxes (despite the diverting presence of rotating dildos in one) — only too eagerly does mascot duty for the curatorial team.

Artists should never, ever fall in line with reigning critical ideas. It's a fool's bargain, swapping truth to self and to the world for critical approbation that is bound to prove fickle. (How do I know? I'm a critic.)

As perfected by Foster (editor of influential critical anthologies) and other essentially art-hating intellectuals of a fuzzy leftist stripe, the new theorism relies on a rhetorical invention that I think of as the Incredibly Stupid Viewer. Tacit in all the catalog essays by the Whitney's tyros (Timothy Landers, Jackie McAllister, Catsou Roberts, Benjamin Weil, and Marek Wieczorek), the Incredibly Stupid Viewer is never ceasing to learn for the first time that, for instance, museums reflect the interests of the people who fund them. That hot tip pretty much exhausts this show's sociological vision.

Psychologically, meanwhile, the museum is exposed as a seamy bed in which the Incredibly Stupid Viewer, naively presuming to have aesthetic experiences, actually engages in scrimmages of "exhibitionism, voyeurism, and fetishism," ("what Freud called 'perversions,'" the catalog helpfully notes.) This vulgar-Freudian ploy — relabeling common pleasures with shaming jargon — is standard weaponry of the new authoritarians, a cheap but effective trick to humiliate any sense of individual mind, heart, and soul. The aim is to manipulate a cowed consensus, building an institutional power-zone crisscrossed with career tracks for the manipulators.

Today's "critique" Zeitgeist isn't only a hypocritical mandarinate, though the likes of Foster can make it seem that way. The fashion for menacing analyses of culture rides a genuine wave of wised-upness, among the young, about the means and ends of media, and it draws on feminist, minority-group, and other authentic rebelliousness. The dearth of democracy in American high culture — documented in the show by Guerrilla Girls posters detailing museum neglect of women and minorities — amply justifies a radical mood.

The Zeitgeist even shades into live creativity, making for the gray area of Barbara Kruger's oracular pasteup mixtures of coyness and rage (one is in the show) and a work by a promising young sculptor, Liz Larner: a little machine whose entire function is to scratch a hole in the museum wall, ambiguously either to illustrate the show's thesis or to bust out of it. And two quite watchable videotapes — by Mark Dion and Jason Simon on secret sins of art restorers and by Andrea Fraser and Louise Lawler lampooning a museum docent tour — point up recent art's frequent kinship to good old American social satire.

Also on the show's marginal plus side is Hans Haacke's multipaneled 1975 *Les Poseuses*, a gritty revelation of the intertwinings of art and money in the 86-year provenance of a small painting by Seurat. Haacke's 14-year-old investigative reporting stands out as prophetic, though not of current trends in "critique," whose main concern is to dissemble their own power-seeking agendas. Rather, it anticipates a present healthy frankness in art journalism.

Taken strictly on its own terms, finally, "The Desire of the Museum" is redeemed by none of its honorable associations. It is an exercise in flat-out hypocrisy: the alleged subversion of museums by museum trainees. Proof of its falseness is the complacence of the Whitney in this use of the museum's corporate-hosted, Wall Street-area branch. At real issue, politically, is nothing but the rise of a new institutional conceit that departs from former ones mainly in being so overbearing.

There is thus no cause for feeling threatened (as opposed to irked) by the show's ideological thrust, unless you are a bona fide Incredibly Stupid Viewer full of dewy innocence about the self-servingness of all institutions. Minimally canny art lovers will readily see in this new face of the museum a simple palace coup of minor consequence for a life of aesthetic cultivation.

As for the "perversions" that the Whitney's thought police will brightly read into the "unconscious" of such a life, we should just make the best of them, okay? Hard on the heels of any pleasure in this unkillably puritanical culture always comes somebody trying to make us feel bad about it. How else would an American know that he or she has been having fun?

September 6, 1989

PORTRAIT OF JOSEPH ROULIN *by Vincent van Gogh*
The Museum of Modern Art

FROM A DISTANCE, THE FACE IS CLOSED, hieratic, and perhaps
intimidating. Up close, the eyes seem frightened — they stare without
focusing — and the features spread, threatening to lose track of each
other. It is a deracinated face in a conflicted picture that is unified
by genius, or something. Maybe just by the craft of painting. Decide
for yourself when you make your welcoming visit to *Portrait of Joseph
Roulin* by Vincent van Gogh, a new acquisition of the Museum of
Modern Art.

It's wonderful, the effect of that small work, not yet encrusted with
familiarity, as it hangs in MoMA's masterpiece-intensive but pedantic
permanent collection. Other paintings in the vicinity, including van
Gogh's own old standby *Starry Night*, feel jarred awake momentarily,
made alert and voluble by the presence of the newcomer. So it seemed
to me the other day.

(It's a big relief, by the way, to see that this painting joins MoMa's
few exceptions to the terrible house rule of standard-issue strip frames
imposed by martinet ex-director of painting and sculpture William
Rubin. *Roulin* is in a beat-up old brown frame, with chipped gilt,
that is perfectly lovely and just right for it.)

Van Gogh is the proverbial exhibit A in any case for "genius" as
a near kin of "madness" — a nicely democratic formulation, balancing
pious envy and condescending pity, that has come to seem awfully
old-fashioned. You don't have to be a deconstruction theorist to feel
that ideas of "genius," "madness," and the like betoken a sentimental
conception of life that is practically defunct — but nothing is arising
to replace it, and how do we now describe someone like van Gogh,
whom the ideas fit like a glove? (I mean it. I'm curious.) Are we pleased
or displeased, now, by the obvious fact that van Gogh invested more
of himself in painting than is healthy for anybody to invest him- or
herself in anything? That fact is the joy and the anxiety of him, and
occasionally the exasperation.

"Oh, lighten up, Vincent," I've felt at times in front of a van Gogh.
"It's only art." There's a taxing relentlessness to his intensity, like that
of a friend, with a personality stuck in high gear, who sometimes
delights you and whom sometimes you will cross the street to avoid

145

meeting. But we will always come back to van Gogh if we love painting and want to know the extreme form and consequence of this love, which is not apt to become old-fashioned as long as human eyes are wired to human feelings.

Joseph Roulin was a postman who befriended van Gogh in Arles. The artist painted several portraits of him and his family, fascinated by the lower-class civil servant who wore his uniform proudly and was vociferously revolutionary in his politics. Van Gogh's fascination is the real subject of the painting. It's the same with most of his portraits. Ardent and shy, he tends to split the difference between his sitters and himself, producing masks of charged Otherness.

Painted in van Gogh's Japanese-inspired mode, the postman is boldly contoured against a floral-patterned background. The composition is rife with spiral motifs (rousing the sympathy of the nearby spiral-happy *Starry Night*) and is keyed to a clash of fresh blue (Roulin's uniform) and moody green (the background). Variously spiced browns in Roulin's beard, the forthright yellow-gold of his buttons, and the rust reds and pinks in the flower shapes keep your eye jumping. The overall design is about as hyperactive as relative symmetry can get. Roulin's flesh is rendered with medievalish green and red hatchings.

Maybe from simple suggestibility, triggered by his style of *japonaiserie*, van Gogh presents Roulin as almost a caricature of an Oriental personage, when viewed from a distance. Ten feet away, you may see a cruel mandarin. Approach, and the face seems very young, European, and vulnerable. Something uncanny about the eyes is explained when you realize their "whites" are the very green of the background. The eyes are thus windows not of a soul but of the painting itself (which for van Gogh may amount to the same thing).

The painting's near-far contradiction, like its blue-green clash, is only one of the discrepancies whose friction generates aesthetic and psychological heat, as you keep looking. Formally, there's a mighty "push-pull" in the way the modeling of the face seems to carve back into shallow space while the background presses forward. (If you try, you can see the blue uniform as a pool or cavern of endless depth.) But you would have to be pretty phlegmatic to read the *Portrait of Joseph Roulin* as a formal demonstration.

When van Gogh looks at Roulin, what does he see? Pride. He endorses this pride (Roulin is his friend) with his brush, celebrating the dignity of the slightly rumpled uniform ("POSTES" lettered on the cap with the severe pomp of a Roman insignia) and the preening

146

masculinity of the well-tended, fluffed and curled double cascade of the forked beard. But, as usual with van Gogh, the intensity of the celebration gets a little out of hand, revealing ambivalent edges.

With the painting's floral symbolism and its light —a sharp illumination coming from both left and right, and redolent of summer heat— van Gogh associates Roulin with nature, making him a Pan-like apparition of rampant virility. The postman is a baby-maker. The sexual hint lends aching tenderness to the close-up, boyish aspect of Roulin's face and an aspect of something like terror to his distant, imperious mien. At one point in studying the face, I had a sudden recognition: "It's the Devil." Then, looking again, I couldn't see that, as if the picture were a kaleidoscope that had gotten jostled.

Van Gogh will give you exactly as much of such subjective adventure as you can take. His paintings are inexhaustible, at least in museums. (Dear MoMA: Please lend me a van Gogh painting for a year or two, so I can test this hypothesis at home. Thanks in advance. Love, Peter.) They are especially communicative when new to you, free of that treacly picture-postcard aura to which van Goghs, perhaps on account of their design-y qualities, are peculiarly susceptible.

So make your first visit to *Roulin* count. Then observe the work's action on its peers. The pictures in the same room by Gauguin, Seurat, Munch, Redon, and Rousseau may seem as elated as the teammates of a slugger who, having hit a home run, returns to their midst, with high fives all around.

MUGHAL PAINTINGS
ANDREW WYETH: THE HELGA PICTURES
Brooklyn Museum

A SHOW OF MUGHAL MINIATURE PAINTINGS STRUCK ME as the archetypal topic for a late-summer art column, but when I found it (no cinch in the magically rambling pile of the Brooklyn Museum), my heart sank. That show is *tiny*. Its 30 items aren't even all Mughal — or Mogul, as the regime of Mongol emperors of India from 1526 until the 19th century used to be spelled. A few echt pictures are eked out with tangential things, forestalling a proper ravishment by the most exotic of fabulous court styles.

But then I had another sinking feeling that combined with the first to give me an idea. It was triggered by Andrew Wyeth's "Helga" pictures, which I had forgotten were there. Those grim images of a catatonic-looking country woman have been trucking around the nation ever since their pseudo-"discovery" three years ago (engineered by Wyeth's wife, Betsy, with a collector and a magazine editor) made for the damnedest fireball of art-related hype since King Tut. They are exotic to me in their own way — because they are so beloved by so many of my fellow Americans, with whom I empathize in many things but not this.

My idea was to bracket these two exoticisms: one (Mughal) straining the focus of my art-love because so remote and the other (Wyeth) blurry because so near. I will limit the comparison to two pictures: a delicate little c. 1775 opaque-watercolor of a nude woman with two female attendants on a terrace, probably by a team of late-Mughal artists in an imperial atelier, and a coarse, largish 1978 dry-brush on paper of Helga nude in bed, by Wyeth.

Poor Andrew Wyeth? I think so, and I sure hope *you* think so, though upon first glances the needle of anybody's interest may veer toward Helga. Wyeth's strenuous "realism" (an *effect* of show-off technique, as opposed to any true grapple with the visible world) and frankly lascivious signals — the arm-up pose, the peekaboo sheet — advertise satisfactions that the Indians' archaic mannerisms and motifs do not. Only with sustained attentiveness will the needle swing the other way, but once that happens there is apt to be no further contest.

The Indian work lacks earlier Mughal art's strongest characteristic, which was an unparalleled use of color: an eye-widening clangor of hyperintense secondaries (green, orange, purple) that awaken in each other the action of complementary primaries (red, blue, yellow), which are thus experienced without being seen. (Critic Rob Storr pointed out the dynamic to me.) Exemplifying this, a 17th-century portrait of Shah Jahan in the show is like an earthquake in the optic nerve. The Mughal taste for such sensations had declined by 1775, surviving in our picture as a subtle jangle where the deep purple and green of a cushion say "red?!" to the enveloping dusky pink that renders both flesh and fabric.

Enchanting in this work is a ritualized story that I, for one, don't get but that has no trouble getting *me*. Two clothed women attend a nude woman on an ornate terrace that is tipped up and miniaturized (tricks that monumentalize the figures), while in three trees and the sky behind them three pairs of white birds, three pairs of black birds, and a lone white bird perch or fly. Dainty containers of, apparently, flowers, drink, and food rest in the foreground.

The bejeweled (mostly in pearls) nude woman is ideally beautiful, with long, pale limbs and jet black hair. Her exaggerated eye regards something offered by one attendant, and she meshes fingers with the other woman — an intimate, confiding gesture, at once formal and sensual. An etiquette — a virtual metaphysic — of sensuality starts to breathe from the picture as you look, fulminating an atmosphere of perfume, music, and heat. The little scene that your first look contained looms and opens out. You could tumble into it and be gone.

Okay. Hold that thought and hurry downstairs to Helga, who is as threatening to your sense of self as a quilted pot holder. Even in this, probably his single raciest image, Wyeth is immune to fevers of imagination apart from the most idly literal-minded kind. (Helga-hype hysterically wondered aloud whether Wyeth slept with Helga Testorf, a paid model and his sister's housekeeper. If you care, change your medication.) His fans must be reassured, somehow, by a "sensual" nude, limned with finicky technique (count the pubic hairs), that generates approximately no sensual charge except maybe of a repressed, sex-in-the-head, Republican variety that I'd rather not think about.

Wyeth isn't exactly a painter. He is a gifted illustrator for reproduction, which improves his dull originals with sumptuous inked surfaces and kicked-up color. (He is quite as contemporary in this way as Andy Warhol, though tons less fun.) This picture's dominant visual impression is of moisture-starved pigment clogging rough watercolor paper. Moving your eye across it is like sledding on dirt. Such effects puritanize Wyeth's art, guaranteeing that the artist's hand can't have done anything nasty because it plainly makes contact with nothing living.

Sensuality is human energy ruled by what the senses like. No energy equals no sensuality, no matter what's dished up. So voluptuous Helga, pepless, is death on a shelf. This should not be held against the model.

Unpossessed of any noticeable vitality even when not (as is usual) asleep, Helga as a person may seem extraordinarily boring even by rural American standards. But might not her stupefaction be an appropriate response to the person painting her? I like to think she sparkled like Dom Perignon whenever she escaped Wyeth's studio.

In any case, isn't the violently impoverished libido of Wyeth as outlandish in its way as the violently quickened appetites of the Mughal cosmos? They are irreconcilable opposites, certainly. What would a Mughal mogul make of a Wyeth Helga? I fancy that he — Akbar (1542-1605), say, the all-time most enlightened despot east of the Medicis — would tremble, terrified by evidence of a sullen power somewhere in the world that, by dint of being so little delighted by life, would prove an invincible Nemesis to beauty everywhere.

EDWARD HOPPER: SELECTIONS FROM
THE PERMANENT COLLECTION *Whitney Museum*

EDWARD HOPPER SHOULD HAVE BURNED most of the work in this show, nearly all of which is selected from among the 2,500-some items bequeathed to the Whitney by his wife, Jo, in 1968. (Hopper died in 1967 at the age of 84.) Lots of artists unburden posterity by winnowing their stocks of early, mediocre stuff, stocks that in Hopper's case were immense. He was a late bloomer whose hard-won maturity — one of the all-time great self-inventions — might very aptly have been celebrated with a nice bonfire of what went before.

But he and Jo were frugal Yankees, who saved everything. He was also the single best American artist after Eakins and Homer and before the abstract expressionists, a towering original who outlasted the modernists who scorned him and the antimodernists who mistook him for a traditionalist. His stature just keeps growing, pressuring the Whitney, which owns only two or three first-rate paintings by him, to make good its threat (in this show's catalog) to exhibit things from the bequest "as often as we are able."

The Whitney's huge Hopper retrospective in 1980 was grotesquely glutted with such things, making for a sense that Hopper's reputation had fallen hostage to the indiscriminate zeal of archivists. Exacting critics and connoisseuring curators have rarely had cracks at him, even in this decade when his influence is vast. We can yearn for a lean and mean, definitive Hopper show, but we probably won't live to see one.

It doesn't matter. No one needs guidance to dig Hopper, a majestic poet in the painterly equivalent of plain prose. Alert visitors to the present show will plod through acres of mildly interesting, merely talented work to glimpse the Hopper who made masterpieces. Nothing else matters if the Whitney simply keeps hanging *Early Sunday Morning*, one of the indispensable paintings of the century.

Done in 1930, *Early Sunday Morning* was originally titled *Seventh Avenue Shops*. Hopper said, "It wasn't necessarily Sunday. That word was tacked on later by someone else." The tack-on was germane, gesturing toward the practically religious intensity with which the scene is beheld. This is a picture to look at until you are exhausted, your attention burned to a fine ash. Then look some more.

It is a dead-on view of cheap two-story buildings, with storefronts, raked by the light of sunrise. The colors bring it off: reds, greens, and yellows laid light-over-dark to yield a glowering brightness (punctuated with black rectangles), a buttery effulgence good enough to eat. The tacky shops, for which *humble* would be too fulsome a compliment, are transfigured by the colors and by a play of highlights and shadows as clever as the fingering of a virtuoso guitarist. A barber pole, leaning as if the sunlight were a gale trying to flatten it, concentrates in its incongruous gaudiness — so it seemed to me the other day, looking at it — the whole doomed human will to beauty.

Early Sunday Morning is about a way of looking that deserves an entry in every American dictionary: *Hopperesque*. That way is voyeuristic and awed. It pertains to human facts (buildings being no less human than people) that 1) are unself-consciously naked to our regard, and 2) do not care about us. It pertains to an absolute heat of vision combined with an absolute chill in the heart.

This sensational indifference — which has no tincture of the sentimental "loneliness" that some viewers insist on projecting into Hopper's pictures, then either praising or condemning him for it — feels American for the same reason that the U. S., perhaps alone among nations, is almost never called anybody's "mother country" or "fatherland." It's a free country: that's the good news. The bad news is it doesn't give a damn. Hopper suggests that really to look at America is to have your soul vacuumed out through your eyes and to get back *nothing*. Except maybe art.

If you love art you love Hopper, and vice versa. I suspect that Hopper has given more American kids their first conscious aesthetic thrill than any other artist. In his case, it's a thrill of feeling everything sucked out of you except your capacity sheerly to perceive, condensing your being in that capacity. The feeling is sub- and super-human: you are an animal and a god.

It is a feeling we get often, though fleetingly, at the movies, and it's significant that Hopper, a lifelong gourmand of movies, emerged from his excruciatingly prolonged art-studentship in the epoch when film aesthetics grew up. At the Whitney, we see the cinematic Hopperesque kicking in with etchings around 1920 (e.g., *American Landscape*), watercolors c. 1923 *(Gloucester Houses)*, and oils later. *Railroad Sunset*, 1929, is the first painted zinger here, though Hopper's breakthrough at the easel came about four years earlier.

Preparatory drawings for paintings comprise the most instructive portion of the Whitney's Hoppers. These aren't "studies," in the usual sense, so much as conceptualizations that recall the sketches with which certain great directors — Eisenstein, Hitchcock, Sirk — planned their shots. They show the elements of a painting like MoMA's *New York Movie* (my own favorite Hopper) being worked out in advance with a fierce eye for exactly the right effect. Every detail in a good Hopper is specific, none is extraneous, and everything sings.

His paintings are *built* like nobody else's, with lots of strange angles, slants of light, and gripping colors rigged into unities so tough you could break your toe on them. They hammer at you with a sense of crisis in time, the breathless mid-point of an unknown story, and simultaneously defeat any attempt to "read" them. What you read in front of a resounding Hopper is only the answering vibration of yourself.

He was a peculiar guy. The sometimes embarrassing awkwardness in his rendering of nudes (going over the top apropos breasts) is often noted, but the eruption of a panting avidity is no less imminent (just less laughable) in Hopper's treatments of gas pumps or bay windows. Astonishingly, he both repressed his polymorphous passions and didn't bother to hide them, and he rarely let a painting alone until it had been packed to creaking with bleak, explosive libido.

I'm talking about the mature Hopper, who is a bit player in this Whitney show. After *Early Sunday Morning*, only *Second Story Sunlight* and *A Woman in the Sun* (silly breasts and all) approach his top level. Among the watercolors, spare a minute for *High Road*, 1931, the most perfect American picture I know of the comfortless beauty of a summer noon. Aside from such scattered satisfactions, my main pleasure at this show was in contemplating how the early work of a *modern* artist — who needs, beyond talent, an idea — can so thoroughly veil the grandeur that is to come.

SHERRIE LEVINE *Mary Boone*

A COUPLE OF PEOPLE HAVE TOLD ME they find Sherrie Levine's new show "dull," and I think they are on to something but have it backward. "Too interesting" feels more like it. Just a glance at the room of elegantly glass-encased small glass sculptures, derived from forms in Marcel Duchamp's 1915-23 brain-busting masterpiece, *The Large Glass*, tells you this stuff is loaded with heady meanings eager to be teased out. It's enough to make you tired in advance, like anything that all too confidently expects your participation. Many will give this show a dispassionate once-over, then head for fresh air.

But you don't escape Levine that easily. She has been in the very air of the serious contemporary-art world—precinct of life stood on its head, with the luxury of aesthetics providing the foundation for everything else—throughout the 1980s. The most successful art-student-as-artist in an epoch crazed with art-studentship, she is the key figure linking this decade's melting nostalgias for bygone modernism and its heavy-metal strain of virtually anti-art critical theory. Half-tropical and half-icy—yearning, pissed off—her sensibility seems so riven that perhaps only the art world's sheer barometric pressure can have held it together.

Is it contradictory that this artist whose work has been synonymous with appropriation, deconstruction, and anti-originality critiques—an artist at times the heroine of the poststructuralist, sort-of-Marxist, para-Freudian cadre of *October* magazine (Rosalind Krauss, Douglas Crimp, Craig Owens, Benjamin H. D. Buchloh)—is being shown, for the second time, at the Mary Boone Gallery with spot-lighted preciousness worthy of Tiffany's?

There might be anguish for anybody else, but Levine is so sincerely romantic about both art and ideas, and so attentive to the secret life of both in our time, that I quite believe she has located a subterranean corridor between the gluttonous market and the anorexic intelligentsia.

Eight years ago Levine was photographing reproductions of classic photographs by Edward Weston. She had to stop because Weston's estate missed the theoretical point and threatened legal inconvenience: she thus switched to the copyright-proof legacy of WPA photographers such as Walker Evans and Russian avant-gardists such as Aleksandr Rodchenko. The theoretical point was, roughly, that "originals" are unavowed appropriations of old models and lurking structures, which avowed appropriations can expose. Other artists then, such as David Salle, *used* this chilly wisdom expressively, but Levine advanced it with menacing purity.

The critics who were delighted understood her too quickly, however. She has since made clear that she *loved* Weston, et al., and wanted into the structures that define a "real artist"—though on terms pitted against the oppressive, godlike myths of the modern masters. Her ambivalence became plain in painstaking, oddly tender watercolors she made from color reproductions of Schiele, Miro, Malevich, and other canonical masters. She also made abstractions that reeked of poignance: lovely and forlorn stripe compositions that mingled late-modernist high-mindedness and, as journalist Gerald Marzorati wrote, the "pathos of Seventh-Avenue knockoffs."

Her best works followed: paintings on lead in casein (a hypersensitive, milk-derived medium) of game boards (checkers, backgammon). (Four new ones in the present show are based on an elongated early-American checkerboard design.) Those pictures speak for the melancholy of all artists in love with moribund traditions, symbolizing a yen to make Art when Art may be impossible. They are about what Art would be *like*, were it possible. The motifs say, "It would be playful." The lead says, "It would be heavy." The candied colors say, "It would be sweet."

Levine's new, Duchampian objects —rather nastily pretty, pestle-like things that look fallen to the floors of their high cases—depart both forward and backward from the soulful ache of the game-board paintings. Backwardly, they return to school, rejoining critical theory in its present phase of excitement about issues of body pathology: fetishes and the like. For being correct, Levine earns a catalog introduction by Prof. Rosalind Krauss that raffishly exemplifies the new academic do-wop. Hence, "the desiring-machines produce by intercepting the continuous flows of milk, urine, semen, shit; they interrupt one flow in order to produce another, which the next machine will interpret to produce a flow for the next, and so on." (Get down!)

Krauss' essay is keyed to *The Large Glass*, also titled *The Bride Stripped Bare by Her Bachelors, Even*—history's most elaborate and sublime dirty joke. The eponymous "bachelors" are the quirky exterior forms, drawn on lead by Duchamp, of eight molds for making chocolate male figures (a policeman, a bellboy, etc.). (With reference to the invisibly encoffined figures, he dubbed their ensemble *Cemetery of Uniforms and Liveries.*) Levine modeled the forms in clay and had them cast in clear glass, which was then sandblasted to a translucent, sugary patina.

It would be interesting to compare the utilitarian molds that were Duchamp's models (do they exist?) with Levine's twice-removed versions, which have taken on a distinctly cartoony sexiness. Or is scholarly research not your idea of fun? I confess it isn't mine, as a rule. This work's delirious suggestiveness and its dusty erudition fight each other to a stalemate that can, indeed, feel "dull."

But Levine also inches forward with this show into aesthetic territory lately occupied by Jeff Koons, whose kitsch statuary last year gave the art world a shock it is still fibrillating from. This is a zone of supercharged presence that marshals every sort of prestige and glamor associated with art (erotic, religious, financial, whatever) and sends it shrieking over the top. What's the compromise between gluttony and anorexia? Bulimia, of course: getting so much of what you want that you end up with none. That's Koonsism, more or less, and Levine's edible-looking and palpably exquisite glass fetishes deploy something like it in exquisitely graded doses.

Maybe too exquisitely graded. A sense of reticence that works beautifully for the game-board paintings, which pointedly do not declare the emotion that haunts them, feels crabbed in work that alludes openly to patterns of obsession and compulsion. Why not go for broke and, by the way, get out of the library? Note, however, that I am quibbling at a fairly high level with art that, if it isn't what we're all waiting for, is right in the neighborhood of what that will be.

"PICASSO AND BRAQUE: PIONEERING CUBISM"
The Museum of Modern Art

THIS SHOW OF ABOUT 400 WORKS BY Picasso and Braque from the wonder years 1907-14 is so infernally hard to take in that you may be casting about for a reason to just skip it, perhaps thinking, "I do not at this point in my life actually need to feel stupid, okay?" Not okay. Get to MoMA now. There are ways to enjoy the show without being tested in the artistic equivalent of quantum mechanics, and what's the big deal about feeling stupid? Everybody's stupid today, or anyway ignorant, outside the narrow channels of their specialties.

Cubism prophesied this. Picasso and Braque took art out of the common world of stories about life, as life was lived or dreamed, and thrust it into a laboratory that presently became an academy called modernism. Cubism was a specific disaster, in terms of ordinary human confidence and comfort, within the general disaster of modernity, which chopped civilization up into a pile of job descriptions. With cubism, painting won the right to which all modern disciplines aspire, which is the right to make lay people feel like morons.

To recover the revolutionary, sick excitement of that moment that helped unclench the mental illness termed "progress" is one way to love cubism. Seen this way, the exhibition might consist of a single colossal explosion — Picasso's 1907 *Demoiselles d'Avignon* — followed by spreading rings of shrapnel. Or you can see the whole show as the explosion, with *Demoiselles* as a split-second image of its onset: a former world of stories — life lived, life dreamed — still barely displaying its old shape while commencing to go kerblooey. Relive the fiesta of destruction, frame by frame. Be Nero and whip out your fiddle as the flames of Rome lick the sky.

(The Italian futurists saw cubism that way and haplessly tried to make a method of it, not getting that the detonation, once registered, was all over in both senses: finished, splattered. The Russian constructivists understood that the next step was to become engineers of the wreckage, reaching for the social status of technicians. It's tempting to have such sweeping thoughts at this show, because you know you're standing at ground zero of the modern.)

Really looking at the pictures is something you should get around to, though you could do it every day for a month and not puzzle out most of them. The cubist trick is to make everything you see "read" at least two ways. Every line makes one kind of space on one side and another kind on the other: "bumps and hollows" is the usual phrase for it. Each little shape reads as a piece of depiction that is abruptly contradicted by its neighbors — saying "yes" to itself and "no" to those neighbors, contributing to a cumulative, resounding "MAYBE." As you look, your describing intelligence is forever rushing to the aid of your bewildered eye, like a boxing manager yelling instructions at his punchy fighter. One truly complicated cubist painting can be like 15 rounds with an octopus trained by Angelo Dundee.

The experience is highly eye-educating, meaning it's not much fun but leaves you feeling virtuously de-stupid-ified. For a while, your eye will be able to consume less demanding, non-Cubist paintings like popcorn. (Check it out in MoMA's permanent collection.) You may find yourself thinking contemptuous thoughts about the relatively slovenly pictorial dynamics of, say, the expressionists. This will be because the iciness of cubism has numbed your heart. You'll get over it. Or you won't, thereby becoming an academic snob.

The academicized aura of cubism — on full display in the catalog introduction by grand old blowhard William Rubin, last of the modernist Mohicans — is the main barrier to my own enjoyment of it. (Give this to Rubin: he's a connoisseur. The show's hanging sparkles with discriminations.) I must keep reminding myself not to blame Picasso and Braque, who had a swell time playing their eye-brain connections like banjos. Or at least Picasso had a swell time. Braque more or less confessed that he liked cubism because it helped him finesse his weakness as a draftsman.

Why do people like Braque? I don't get it. Sure, he has lots of frenchy virtues, such as suavely tasty color, nape-of-the-neck-sensitive texture, and Cartesian lucidity (often wrong, never in doubt). But I find him wimpish even when not trapped in an arena with Picasso, who kicks him from one end of MoMA to the other — except during their Doppelganger act of 1910-12, when their works really are tough to distinguish. Guessing each of those pictures' authorship before consulting the label, I didn't beat coin-toss odds by a whole lot my first time through. But the parity seems an effect as much of Picasso bending over backwards as of Braque soaring, though he did soar. I mistook a few Braques for Picassos merely because they looked so good.

(To minimize your error rate, I've since patched together the following less-than-infallible rules of thumb: closed forms, surprising colors, and linear pizzazz equal Picasso; open forms, harmonized colors, and painterly "cuisine" equal Braque. Picasso's liveliness is quick and sharp, snakelike. Braque's liveliness is ruddy and all over you, like a friendly pooch. Finally: genteel references to Bach and Mozart? Braque.)

Easily the most amazing thing to me about the invention of cubism as the spectacle of Picasso — whose name should be rendered ¡Picasso! — plowing against the grain of his own genius for drawing in order to noodle with perceptual space in ways that almost anyone handy could learn. He thus submitted himself to Braque's superiority as both an idea man (Braque was lost without ideas) and a dogged executor of formal permutations — until, that is, Braque made the competitive mistake of inventing pasted-paper composition, whose allusive poetics and potential as a ground for drawing instantly let Picasso be Picasso again.

John Berger, in his book *The Success and Failure of Picasso*, found a fleeting ethical heroism in Picasso's cubist self-abnegation, but I don't see how it is all that much less tedious, in its way, than his later egocentric smarm. Like you, me, and John Berger, Picasso was at his best when giving *and* taking, in a proper dance between world and self.

The best works of the show, as art, are the Picassos before mid-1909 and after mid-1912. The work in between by both artists is good or less good *as cubism:* art translated into an alien language, as I think one may say after 77 years without fear of not being up to speed yet. Hard-core cubism shows us . . . cubism. It isn't a style, a way of showing something particular, like Picasso's many styles or the style of Mondrian or Pollock or Johns (or Braque in his post-1914, weary attractiveness). It's a made-up system that laid down the surefire principles of modern revolution: 1) consider whatever you're doing a game, and 2) change the rules so you win.

VELAZQUEZ *Metropolitan Museum*

DIEGO VELAZQUEZ (1599-1660) WAS AS GOOD AT OIL painting as any-one has been at anything. When Edouard Manet, seeing Velazquez's paintings at the Prado in Madrid in 1865, said he wondered why others including himself bothered trying to paint, he expressed an enduring thought: painting has been done, and Velazquez did it.

The feeling of Velazquez is light, sparkling, swift, and easy. He is never "intense." Unprolific, he worked and reworked his pictures at length, as is attested by many pentimenti; but you rarely catch him sweating. He is profound, but in ways that seem to say, "Isn't every-body?" His truth has a self-evidence, as if you always knew it. It isn't a matter of "knowing about" something — the kingliness of Philip IV, say. You just know. Or, because this is painting, you just *see*.

Velazquez is Mr. Cool. If he were a rock singer, he would be Roy Orbison. He respects all possible sentiments but is never sentimental, and is alert to every manner of charm without being charmed himself. He is somehow detached in the very act of being engaged, staying out of the way of what he avidly fixes on. Compared with him, all other painters "seem completely like fakers," as Manet said, too.

The toughest thing about getting Velazquez is believing your eyes, accepting that such lucidity is really happening. That's why it's neces-sary to see many Velazquez paintings, so the easy, gliding truth of him can break down your suspicion that, when you look at art, you're bound to miss something. The only way to miss Velazquez is to be blind.

Those of us who know the Prado have an unfair edge at the Met's Velazquez show, because we can view it in light of what's lacking: *Las Meninas*, of course, but also a long list of the artist's greatest works (including London's *Rokeby Venus* and Rome's portrait of Pope In-nocent X). Maybe a dozen of the 38 pictures in this startlingly brief compendium ("When did they start putting the gift shop in the middle of a show?" an unprepared friend said as she reached the end) are top drawer. The rest are early and/or odd and/or in bad shape and/or quite grand but gloomed by the constricting nature of their commis-sions (not that Velazquez couldn't handle it, but you sense his oppres-sion). I'm ready to believe Met director Philippe de Montebello when he crows in the catalog that this show realizes what seemed "an unrealizable dream"—but when I have unrealizable dreams they tend to be, you know, fabulous.

The idea of "reviewing" Velazquez is silly. What follows are notes toward an opinionated user's manual for this show.

Remember in the first room that you are seeing a very young, provincial show-off from Seville out to make it at court in Madrid (where painters had roughly the social standing of carpenters). The coups of verisimilitude in *Old Woman Cooking Eggs* and *The Water Seller* are staggering, but space in the pictures is hopelessly tortured. Already there is philosophical and poetic, self-delighting brilliance. If you want to tell yourself intricate stories about the meaning of the old-woman picture, do. Velazquez approves.

There is something painful, in the second room, about the big Philip IV portraits and even the terrific *Forge of Vulcan*, because Velazquez was laboring to prove himself as a reliable propagandist, in the first case, and as an artist up to speed with Italian academic fashion, in the second. High status seems to have been his main goal, leading him to all but quit painting in his later, best years for the more prestigious jobs of court decorator, art adviser, and household manager.

The show's first clean hit is *Prince Baltasar Carlos With a Dwarf*: the 16-month-old prince posed regally in military garb (poor kid) while a little person shuffles past with a rattle and an apple (parody of scepter and orb). Taking sides in an art historian's argument, I believe (with Julian Gallego in the catalog) that this is a "picture-within-a-picture": the dwarf is painted in front of a painting of the royal tot. The textures are an express elevator to heaven.

Moving along, zero in on the snapshot-modern *Riding School* picture, which narrates the dynastic hopes, power relations (centering on unsavory Count-Duke Olivares), moral values, and lifestyle of Philip IV's reign as they pertained one crisp, cool morning. This isn't an artwork, it's a world. Note also the easily missed small, unfinished *Needlewoman*, a great poem about work: she is caught in skilled action and a concentration so transfiguring it's scary.

I think the show's two perfect works are the Met's own *Juan de Pareja* and the portrait of the dwarf Francisco Lezcano. The slackly arrogant Lezcano is often described as "witless," but ask yourself this: what if he's intelligent? The answer is that he is then the most dangerous little creep you ever saw—Velazquez gazing calmly into the attitude of a killer.

In the last room, with things from the period of *Las Meninas*, there is supreme artistry (brushwork in dizzying interplay with color) but no supreme art. The Met's poster child *Infanta Margarita* is gorgeous (salmon pink dress, blue-green drapes) but feels like a rushed job. (In *Las Meninas*, the same *infanta* tosses out a frank little-girl gaze that knocks two eye-shaped holes in your heart.)

Overall, in the mature work, register the theatricality that includes you in its dynamic. The baroque space is basically cylindrical, swooping around behind figures and out into your space. Time lives in the cylinder, as everything *turns*. When the eyes of a subject meet yours, they will just have done so: turning toward you, *click*. (A half-dozen sets of eyes do it in *Las Meninas*, and, jet-lagged my first time in Madrid, I became obsessed with catching the figures turning — looking at them faster than they looked at me. I hallucinated, *hearing* the rustle of a *menina's* crinolines. I suppose I should be glad I didn't see her move.)

As with hallucinations, you know that what you see in a great Velazquez isn't real because it is *too* real — in terms not only of optical illusion but of virtual feel and smell, and the tingle when someone you can imagine being in love with looks at you. He knew how to keep his distance, did the courtly Velazquez, and the keeping of distance is excruciatingly palpable in his official portraits, but when it was okay to home in, the doors of any soul were going to spring open, no problem.

Almost nothing is known of his personal life. He did well in court for his family, nepotistically. He fathered an illegitimate child in Rome (living there in middle age for nearly three years on an art-collecting mission, fending off the king's demands that he come home). He performed in women's clothes in a court burlesque. Aside from the knee-bucklingly sensual *Rokeby Venus*, done for a patron who was a notorious libertine, he painted at least three other female nudes, now lost. I figure that his talent for decorum was an expedient check on a major wild streak.

He got away with the feat, rare in Spain, of painting very little religious art — unlike his exact contemporary, Zurbaran. (Imagine being as great as Zurbaran and knowing you'll always be the second-best painter in town.) Why do the many masteries in the huge *Saint Anthony Abbot and Saint Paul the Hermit* add up to less than the sum of their parts? I think Velazquez did the picture sullenly, not necessarily because he was unreligious but because he was bound to nurse a grudge against any reality that insisted on being invisible.

My favorite explanation of nearly naked, crestfallen *Mars* (proposed in Jonathan Brown's 1986 book on Velazquez) is that it pictures the god as an adulterer, having been caught with Venus by Vulcan. Be alert in all his art for a strain of down and dirty, slightly cruel, also strangely redemptive comedy that he projects forward from Cervantes to Goya. Velazquez as archetypal Spaniard: you can count on his humanity, but if you take his sympathy for granted you're in trouble.

We can use Velazquez for remembering how to love life: directly, with an attentiveness and a responsiveness that drive thoughts of "love" and "life" out of our heads and consume us like a clear flame. How to make inanimate matter, such as paint, dance attendance — as if the flame painted the pictures — is a secret probably lost forever, but we won't be wrong in taking it as a compliment. One of our kind did that. He had a feeling we would like it, and we do.

"TO PROBE AND TO PUSH: ARTISTS OF PROVOCATION"
Wessel O'Connor

ON SECOND THOUGHT, I LIKE THE TITLE. The pure unpleasantness of "To Probe and to Push," which sounds like a manifesto of bad dentists, is perfect for the growingly ugly situation in American art brought about by recent censorship battles. Labeling a show of abrasive work by ten mostly serious artists—including Robert Mapplethorpe, Andres Serrano, Cindy Sherman, and Dread Scott—the title also occasions the unremarkable thought that, of course, truly new art does probe and does push, always intent on questions of limits.

But the concerns of art, as art, may not be exactly paramount in a coming national Kulturkampf made further inevitable last week by an appalling new law forbidding federal funds for art deemed "obscene"—a *compromise*, no less, tinkered by supposed congressional friends of the arts to forestall a hair-raising alternative urged by Jesse Helms. Helms and the anticosmopolitan, populist right have established liberals reeling on the issue of rude art. That's ominous, and so is a possibility, here in Cosmopolis, that reactive hatred of the right will bury the defense of artistic liberty in a polarizing offensive of rudeness, per se.

Thus it is with mixed feelings that I consider Dread Scott, the young black artist-activist whose *What Is the Proper Way to Display the U. S. Flag?* was a censored *cause célèbre* in Chicago last year and makes its East Coast debut at Wessel O'Connor. The piece invites viewers to stand on the stars-and-stripes while recording their flag-related sentiments in the latest of several books already containing hundreds of scribbled entries. Smart and affable, with a challenging insouciance that reminds me of knight-errant agitators in the '60s, Scott told me at the opening, "I hope I make work in the future that is more controversial."

As art—or para-art, perhaps—*What Is the Proper Way* recalls "behavioral" conceptual installations of the early '70s, such as a 1972 piece by one Mike Malloy that gave the viewer, in a booth, the option of pushing a button to kill an ant. (Many ants died.) The principle is an aesthetic framing of presumably authentic behavior with a moment of licensed exhibitionism as the lure for participants. My brief inspection of Scott's opinion ledgers found a heady harvest of foul-mouth vituperation, both pro and con, interspersed with much bland earnestness in adolescent script.

I dislike the manipulativeness of *What Is the Proper Way*, which theatricalizes political emotion in a manner not so different from the modus operandi of a Morton Downey Jr. But it's clever. And there is no use pretending that Scott isn't onto the raw nerve of a society that, lately deprived of the safety-valve specter of external communism, is spoiling for a domestic brawl, for which no incitement seems too silly. With right-wing demagogues using images of heterodox art as tinder for burning down liberal insitutions like the National Endowment for the Arts, the stage is set for libertarian radicals to up the ante of shock.

Bound to get lost in any such fight is the most valuable aesthetic use of the transgressive and the grotesque, art's delicate power to reconcile imagination with its own most disturbing contents. That power is evident at Wessel O'Connor in a telling, very early assemblage by Robert Mapplethorpe, the cancellation of whose show by Washington's Corcoran Gallery in June was the sneak-attack Pearl Harbor of present hostilities. A ritually compulsive altar of junk furniture and draped fabric, with a blindfolded plaster Jesus and a hammer wrapped with bits of purple velvet, this circa-1970 work prefigures an amazing sensibility that would test the innocence of beauty by beaming it into twilit regions of the soul.

Like Mapplethorpe a lapsed but deeply conditioned Catholic, Andres Serrano made the rather pretty photograph called *Piss Christ* that Helms has found a most expedient foil. Serrano's image in this show, called *Red River*, suggests a picturesque mountain from some Chinese scroll painting. It is a photo of menstrual blood. As a work about beauty and fear, vibrating between desire and disgust, it is elegant and plenty visceral, though its one-liner punch feels a bit lightweight. In any case, Serrano is a serious artist whose art deserves better than to be a polemical football.

Cindy Sherman is a great artist. Her photographed tableau, in which a living man goes down on an inflated plastic sex doll, epitomizes the profound use of shock in art. Intensely considered artifice operates at every formal and poetic level of the picture, lodging a nightmare image in the mind at the depth of personal memory. Any defense of artistic freedom must stick up even, or especially, for the rights of bad art. But Sherman's prerogative is, for me, a particularly morale-building idea of something to fight for.

I just realized — as I break off, rather than end, a discussion that is only beginning — that in Scott, Mapplethorpe, Serrano, and Sherman we have a black, a gay, a Hispanic, and a woman: an accidental rainbow coalition highlighting the fact, commonsensical when you think about it, that energy in new art almost always entails some element of social otherness. At any rate, coming confrontations over censorship in the arts will involve a lot more than questions of legality and taste. All the fears, hopes, and furies of society in its present drift will be variables. It will be hard to stay sane, but it might be a good idea to try.

October 25, 1989

JULES OLITSKI: PAINTINGS OF THE '60s *Andre Emmerich*

YUM YUM. THIS STARTLINGLY FRESH, deliriously tasty show reminds me that color-field painting, long a polite cult for aesthetic snobs and twits, had a real, risky edge for a while in the '60s, when Olitski said he wished he could spray paint into the air and have it just stay there. Swooning effulgences of grape-ade purple, lemon-spiked chartreuse, and other hard-to-believe colors in this show demonstrate how close Olitski came, in an elegant, nasty-sweet art slightly suggestive of hallucinogenic boudoir decor and, with minutely mottled surfaces, fabulous skin diseases. These paintings run a fever of hedonism reinforced by naughty-baby-talk titles, such as *Green Scrozzle* and *Judith Juice*. Give them a chance to work on you. They are high-caloric eye-candy and, as we used to say, *far out*.

CHRIS BURDEN *Kent Fine Art*

ONE DAY IN THE LATE '70s at an alternative arts space in Los Angeles, I chanced to see Chris Burden chatting with a German "body artist."

"I see you're hard at work," I heard Burden say jauntily.

"Yes," said the smiling young woman, gesturing at the blood that was streaming from her face. "It's all over the place."

I think it was the chirpiness that shocked me most — or, rather, that abruptly deepened the shocky condition I shared with many people who followed the avant-garde not wisely but too well in the '70s. An insane logic of aesthetic progress, a game of dare-and-double-dare feeding on itself since the late '60s, reigned then in tiny, often institutionally cocooned scenes. In some sectors of that archipelago, it was patent for a while that Chris Burden was the next great modern artist, heir to Duchamp and Pollock — the honcho, L. A. critic Peter Plagens called him.

By the time of the incident recounted above, Burden's moment of notoriety — a wildfire of hearsay in the art world, appalled coverage in the national press — was over. Not since 1975 had he literally suffered for his art, as by being shut up in a small locker for five days, squirming along a street across broken glass, getting crucified on a Volkswagen, and having himself shot. A new, market-driven art game, centered on painting, was eclipsing such work. Burden was entering a decade of relative oblivion for him that is ending now.

Burden's three installational pieces at Kent, all from 1983, are about a sense of disciplined adventure vested in, and pitted against, technology. Their time has come.

The show's masterpiece (just bought by the MoMA for $75,000, incidentally) is *The Flying Kayak*, an elegant, full-size kayak of creamy white canvas and nautical-looking varnished wood suspended about five feet from the floor. Four industrial-strength electric fans roar behind it, and a film-loop of a hovering helicopter is projected onto the wall ahead. Control levers would enable someone in the kayak to vary its pitch and roll with airplanelike tail-section elevators and a rudder. The experience of piloting it is fantastic, one imagines (which is all one is permitted to do at Kent).

The three works communicate an ecstatic reveling in technical know-how, never mind that the technologies involved are antiquated. The feeling is not so different from the brainy bliss of a computer hacker, except that it insists on self-evidence in the nuts and bolts and on engaging the body as well as the mind. Is it all a bit adolescent? Sure, and so is technology's revamping of the world continually on terms that only youthful minds are flexible enough to grasp at once.

Gazing at *The Flying Kayak*, I reflected that I lead a sheltered life. Out there somewhere, people are paddling—yahoo!—down white-water rapids. Other people are making incredible things in Silicon Valleys and in workshops of the world, to change everybody's life for the better and for the worse. What's the point of trotting around galleries to look at art that is not cognizant of such daring and such industry? Oh, there's a point, I suppose, but Burden makes me impatient with its distance from basic sensation, emotion, and action. I want to climb into his kayak and fly to where deeds occur.

But I just look, and as I do I seem to remember a basic, unjaundiced, adolescent capacity of my own to find even, or especially, in an art gallery a feeling of absolute possibility hardly inferior to running the rapids or inventing a machine. Suddenly the whole equation of art and life simplifies down to a moment like the one in 1912 when Picasso painted an aviation headline: *"Notre Avenir est dans l'air"* (our future is in the air). At such moments the notions of all human enterprises melt into one crazy happiness.

Followed by fear. I recall, for cautionary balance, my eavesdropped vision of Burden bantering with the woman who was bleeding for art's sake because art then seemed to demand the aestheticizing of everything, including pain and self-destruction. When you send your soul for a ride on an amoral dialectic, you can end up somewhere grotesque in a jiffy. But the alternative, in periods of droning moralism and stifling caution, is spiritual hardening of the arteries. I sense an appetite for risk, widespread and intensifying. I think that art of the near future is going to make the resurgent Burden look, first, prophetic and, second, tame.

ASHLEY BICKERTON *Sonnabend*

ASHLEY BICKERTON'S NEW SHOW OF ELEGANT and lively philosophical constructions disappoints me in ways that may be the fault
of my own exaggerated expectations. But I'm inclined to spread the
blame around a bit, because Bickerton's letdown confirms a current
general tendency of formerly adventurous artists to opt for cozy en-
trenchments of one kind or another. I had thought this was the season when the blunted cutting edge of recent years was due for a sharp-
ening, and now I wonder.

Bickerton, still as always an artist of amazing sensibility, came to
the fore about three years ago as one of the neo-geo smarties, with
Jeff Koons (the only one still truly edgy), Peter Halley, Meyer Vais-
man, and Haim Steinbach. Neo-geo skewered the then regnant fashion of neo-expressionism with frigid, untouched-by-human-hands-
looking pictures and objects that at once excited and mocked an enfevered art market. Bickerton contributed a line of elaborate wall
pieces he called "Susies," which deployed seductive materials and
ready-made components, redolent of high-tech or otherwise irresistible commodities, to poetic and satirical ends.

Most Susies made a big deal of their portability with handles, brackets, rolled-up wrappings (quilted leather with grommet clasps a spe-
cialty), and other practical appurtenances, including printed instructions for transportation and maintenance. Lest we mistake what all
this was about, some incorporated electronic displays of their current
market value —as they still do at this moment in some collections—
with sums that tick up penny by penny at a pace comfortably ahead
of the inflation rate.

Though too smart by half, now and then, the Susies seemed to fid-
get with a mysterious, smoldering anger that warned viewers not to
take them complacently. For a while, printed passages of erotica appeared, hinting at a buried content of instinctual magma struggling
up against the dominant tone of consumer greed. A sort of explosion
seemed in the offing, which might reveal a messier and perhaps crazi-
er but less divided Bickerton.

Well, the pressure's off. What we've got now is a wholehearted
Bickerton whose formerly polarized charm and menace have met in
a middleness of unexceptionable citizenship. Color him Green. The

message is ecological in constructions that contain plant matter, earth samples, and waste products (toxic or only cruddy) to illustrate such environmental depredations as the global spread of fertilizer- and pesticide-intensive monocultural (one-crop) farming, with attendant threats, it says here, to the survival of diverse seed strains.

Bickerton may be entirely right about the incorrigible evil of agribusiness (which nonetheless does efficiently produce food for people, I think), but in the absence of reasoned argument the point is just generic on-the-side-of-the-angels-ism. Not that I want reasoned argument about agriculture from an artist.

It's impressive, in a dismal way, to see how an abstract and righteous content undermines Bickerton's ravishing form. He is as virtuosic as ever in orchestrating such assorted materials as, in *Stratified Landscape #1*, wood, fiberglass, corroded steel, corroded copper, leather, rope, anodized aluminum, canvas, netting, beans, resin, decomposed seaweed, and coral. He can still make any fabricated stuff sing the erotic song of its functional uses and glamorous associations. Mountain-climbing gear in some pieces practically reeks of long-weekend sexiness.

But gut-clutching qualities that once were central to Bickerton's art, as they remain to the metaphysical vertigo of get-and-spend society, are now weightlessly incidental to a smarmy didacticism that lets everybody off the hook. Which brings me to the subject of epidemic coziness in the art world, where it suddenly seems more important to close ranks around fuzzy shibboleths than to brave the internal contradictions that define the one zone in the culture where art can make an actual difference.

There may be strong topical reasons for communal affirmation in the age of AIDS and Jesse Helms, but the thing has gone awfully far when the artist of discomfiting Susies starts selling collectors three-dimensional certificates of political virtue (as presumably they up their contributions to ecological causes). This Bickerton show omens a situation in which one no longer attends art events, but joins them.

THE ARTISTS SPACE CONTROVERSY

On NOVEMBER 9, EAST GERMANY OPENED its borders and the *Times* front-paged the National Endowment for the Arts' abrogation of a grant for a show at Artists Space, a Tribeca gallery. The grounds, set forth by the endowment's soon-to-be-a-household-name new director, John E. Frohnmayer, are that the show's catalog contains political opinions. The synchronicity of events suggests a heretofore unremarked Law of the Conservation of Totalitarian Energy: as the Berlin Wall is pulled down at one point on the globe, a Bush Wall is hydraulically pushed up at another. In each case, the action represents a lurch forward in an existing process no one thought would go so far so fast.

Like the breaching of the Berlin Wall, Frohnmayer's power play is just one step, albeit a spectacular one, in an ongoing revolution. In his case, that means overthrowing a two-decade era of good feelings — rooted in the vast influence of a benevolently nonjudgmental NEA — in the relations of American government and high culture. The NEA began as a Camelot vision of JFK's, but, lest we forget, it really kicked in only under Nixon, who correctly figured it would help buy off the pesky '60s counterculture. Ever riven in its values between elitism and pluralism, quality and energy, the NEA fudged all differences by relying on the changing idiosyncrasy of peer panels and made almost everybody happy some of the time.

A consequent fuzzy glow of appreciation for art in general, contingent on not looking too hard at any art in particular, radiated outward through private institutions, academe, and corporate philanthropy. It made *official culture* a phrase unused on American tongues, because among us nothing remotely dignifiable as culture could be deemed intrinsically *un*official. Whatever their feistiness in theory and symbol, artists accordingly became in practice the most tractable of citizens.

Well, good-bye to all that.

Having finally overcome a rosy inertia that survived even eight years of Reagan, the Right now plainly intends to sculpt a truly official culture by censorial subtraction. The rightists will be hard to dislodge before they have wrecked the NEA and roiled the cultural world's civil peace. In public dread of anarchism and depravity, they possess sharp demagogic hooks, baited with plausible arguments about proper use of "taxpayers' money." Eventually they may be checked by an organized appeal to American libertarian instincts along lines lately demonstrated by the pro-choice movement: shift the debate from the object under attack to the issue of politicians and bureaucrats forcing their own values on anybody. In the short run, however, the Right will retain political momentum as well as bureaucratic clout — and that means fighting back.

Was it really only five months ago that Washington's Corcoran Gallery canceled a Robert Mapplethorpe show, the Fort Sumter incident that started all this? Since then, an impressive contingent of outrage in the arts community against Corcoranism (defined by me in August as the "doctrine that preserving the means of cultural support justifies suppressing the ends of culture") has tarred and feathered that hapless institution, most effectively through artists withdrawing from shows there.

What if, universalizing the tactic of a boycott, all art people and institutions stopped accepting NEA money and raised private funds for those hardest hit by the shortfall? (The temptation to scuttle the NEA altogether should be resisted; that would be playing into the Right's hands. Insist instead that the rightists have ample funds to create an official culture, and a sorry-looking mutt it will be, too.) What if artists and intellectuals withheld participation of any kind in programs now to be governed by ideological exclusion? No more Kennedy Center galas, USIA lecture tours, White House concerts (if the president wants music, let him turn on the radio), no more public radio or television, Smithsonian symposia, NEA peer panels, or NEA-sponsored anything. No more goodies from it and no more goodies for it, unless the Bush Wall comes down.

Then if present trends continue, with worst coming to worst here and best to best over there, everybody can apply for asylum in East Germany.

"IMAGE WORLD: ART AND MEDIA CULTURE" *Whitney*

THE SOPHISTICATED GROAN, A VERNACULAR LOCUTION that most Americans pick up around the age of 8, is a defense against the mental and spiritual depredations of media that I, for one, am not about to suspend just because somebody decides to get earnest on the subject. The groan salutes the unction of anything that presumes to understand and, on that basis, to manipulate us. It is a shallow sound, indicating that we opt to repel threats to our autonomy, including those of the media, at a line far forward from our deep selves.

Such seems to me the properly jaded response to an exhibition that starts with a couple of hundred blitzing, rock-music-synchronized video monitors by Nam June Paik and proceeds to a sort of disorientation room, wallpapered with a time line merging art and media histories and equipped with three monitors emitting fragments of familiar TV shows. The effort to reproduce the media's supposedly soul-shattering glut is almost touching, it's so resistible.

Let's pause for a moment before the work of techno-orchestrator Paik, whom many people admire, maybe for his determination to entertain them, but who I think is among the world's most boring artists. He represents the dimmest option of art confronted with the media's spectacular claims on our attention, which is to cross over and become, in effect, part of the problem. He used to be distinguishable from run-of-the-mill professional producer-technicians, gussying up cliches at the control board, mainly by being limited to low-budget hardware. Now, with market success, he has no distinction.

The mismatch of scale between the structures of even ambitious art and those of even minor media assures art's humiliation when the game is joined on the media's turf.

Art used to have a home-court advantage: painting. That seems the message of the show's finest room, whose sheer quality unbalances the whole. I refer to magnificent pop-era canvases by Rauschenberg, Warhol, Rosenquist, Lichtenstein, and Ruscha — with the special revelation, for me, of a huge 1969 black-and-white face by Chuck Close. Close's compulsive photo-realism is aging splendidly, shedding its formerly mechanical aura to appear as a species of landscape wild beyond the dreams of surrealism: the human countenance as wilderness.

In the room of paintings, what gets celebrated is not the colonization of art by comic strips, Elvises, and *Playboy* bunnies but the capacity of abstract pictorial conventions, in the late heyday of the New York School, to gobble and transcend no matter what visual material. Except for an elegiac 1986 reprise by David Salle, that's about that for painting in the show — in fact, subsequent rooms radiate a feeling of historic loss as the works they contain struggle to make do with compromised tools in traumatized circumstances.

"Image World" will be remembered for its total inability to gain general traction in the mud of media, even with the grit of half-truths quoted in the catalog from Jean Baudrillard and other happy sages. "Why are media images so powerful and persuasive?" demands a wall label. It's funny. I had just been wondering why media images (including verbal ones on wall labels) are so weak and unpersuasive. Maybe it's because, like most people, I've spent my life in intimate, daily, love-hate combat with such images, acquiring a certain immunity in the process.

When my daughter was little, we had a family joke (which I meant) about the two rules of life: 1) always love your mother, and 2) never believe *anything* in a TV commercial. (The self-evident weight of rule one, provided by an extravagantly lovable mother, drove the nail of rule two, see.) The task of growing up in image-riddled culture is to preserve, via primary emotion armored with skepticism, a resilient core that will later make possible the unmediated recognition, in art as in everything, of earthly joy.

ERIK BULATOV *Phyllis Kind*

I WAS LOOKING FORWARD TO SEEING NEW paintings by Erik Bulatov, the 56-year-old leading light of Russian art, and the event turns out to be so relatively meager — just four somewhat undernourished canvases — that logically I ought to be let down. But I'm not. My enthusiastic conviction, formed eight years ago on the basis of mere photos of his work, that Bulatov is a great, indispensable, maybe history-altering artist proves irrationally hardy, somewhat like everybody's old, wan, childish wishes for an end of the Cold War that have lately come true like a miracle.

Art and geopolitics are related here. Bulatov is a symbolizing figure as well as a signifying painter, and I see no point in trying to untangle the matter just now. I must keep wondering for a while how much of what captivates me about Bulatov is his work and how much is what might be called his job description: philosopher, poet, and political satirist all at once in pictures alive with lost or debased Russian tradition (both revolutionary-era avant-garde and Stalinist socialist-realist) and acute about contemporary Western aesthetics. Never mind that his art is ironic, thorny, and often arcane. Like the also ambiguous German visionary Anselm Kiefer, he induces a sort of global intoxication you'd have to be soul-dead to resist entirely.

In Western stylistic parlance, Bulatov would have to be termed a conceptualist-formalist-photorealist, improbably combining three mutually antagonistic tendencies of art in the early 1970s — when, informed of Western work only by way of reproductions, he hit his mature stride as an artist. To convey the nature of Bulatov's inspired synthesis, nothing will do but to describe a couple of earlier pictures by the artist not in this show:

Welcome (1973-74) is a vast, sumptuous, postcard-derived view of an ornate fountain in Moscow with the Cyrillic phrase for "You are welcome" block-lettered across it in red. The barrierlike lettering regiments the seductive scene, flipping a promise of pleasure into a stentorian alarm.

Krassikov Street, 1976, is a lovely photorealist view down a shabby Moscow boulevard on which people in summer clothes walk away from us. A distant billboard of Lenin jauntily striding is rendered on a flat white ground that slams forward visually, seizing the picture plane and canceling the scene's illusion of depth.

Every explicit message in both paintings is innocent and upbeat. A subliminal, Kafkaesque sensation of vulnerability malignantly targeted arises by way of painting's formal dynamics alone: the recessive and the frontal qualities of pictorial space set in ferocious tension. The effect is like being knocked sprawling with a feather.

I have never been to the Soviet Union, missing out thus far on the various trans-Iron Curtain junkets that are shuttling American art people there and back, so I can't tell whether Bulatov's subtly anguished vision is (or was, as the case may be) true to the tenor of Soviet life. As a social-metaphysical fiction, however, the vision convinces me utterly, meanwhile moving me by the power it claims for Russian pictorial imagination. Bulatov's conundrums serve me as semaphores of everything I don't know but can begin to grasp *as a mystery,* out beyond the looking glass between Them and Us.

This brings me to Bulatov's four new paintings, all painted in New York since last year. He is a globe-trotting star now after decades of absolutely underground status during which he supported himself as a children's-book illustrator. So we here confront Bulatov in his own plunge through the looking glass, the rigors of which may explain a relative loss of intensity (though not integrity and intelligence) from the masterpiece level of *Welcome* and *Krassikov Street.*

Just one of the pictures is realist, with a Bulatovian twist: *Winter,* depicting a stand of distant trees and some buildings mostly hidden by a snowy hill beneath a fuming sky at sunrise or sunset (or, possibly, mid-winter noonday, if the site is northern enough). The buildings include a barrackslike structure, and there are poles suggestive of a fence. A Siberian gulag? That's my guess, but we can't see enough to be sure, what with the crepuscular atmosphere and the hill — or make that the "hill," since its maternally swelling form is painted as flat as a wall. As I stand there, contemplating that blankness, it starts to smolder with symbolic charges: ignorance, forgetfulness, denial, death. As often with Bulatov, what at first seemed a mild tour de force develops toward something like panic.

Perestroika renders the eponymous word in reverse perspective. Two of its block letters — *T* and Cyrillic *R* — loom in the foreground, where manly hands hoist them, interlocked hammer-and-sickle fashion, against a sunburst skyscape. The picture avoids being just a graphic image by its painterly qualities of rugged brushwork, radiant light, and sheer size (9 feet high). Bulatov's command of the poetics of large scale, impressive in someone who has worked most of his life in cramped quarters for an audience of practically nobody, makes him a painter readily congenial to New York taste.

The same can't quite be said of two paintings titled *New York*: the words NEW YORK in soaring perspective, converging at top and bottom, respectively, of compositions with complementary planes of ray shapes and a skyscraper-like grid. Maybe because I'm a citizen of the city in question, I find these the most puzzling of Bulatov's works and, in a revealing way, the most *Russian*. Suddenly the vaguely deco-moderne design motifs he often favors feel specific, evoking the sort of '30s newsreel-logo style that survives locally in Radio City, say, but that in the Soviet Union got frozen by Stalin into a monotonous, intimidating, bastard classicism.

Coming to New York to paint a New York he smuggled with him in his head, Bulatov thus recalls the last moment when Soviet and American modernisms were in sync. Depending on the degree of irony entailed, the upshot is either largely antic or mainly weird. Somehow I don't expect that Bulatov, an angel of ambivalence, is going to step forward and explain this, a very image of the East-West looking glass.

Bulatov isn't the first creative Russian to Westernize Russian culture while, by the backwash of his influence, perhaps somewhat Russifying the West. But he is the first in a long time. No more than Fyodor Dostoyevski or Kasimir Malevich or Sergei Eisenstein is he an artist to make up one's mind about. Rather, his use may be to help give us new minds, with which to think things unthinkable before.

A VISIT TO BERLIN

A SMALL HAMMER I ACQUIRED DURING THREE DAYS in Berlin at the beginning of this month dislodged only sparks and dust from the Wall—that baby is *hard*—so I had to glean bits and pieces from tailings left by better armed and more tenacious others. *Had* to? It did occur to me as I grubbed in dirt that such keenness for crumbs of concrete, with or without the authenticating traces of spray enamel that gladdened my heart when found, might be largely idiotic. But yeah, *had* to.

That's the way with symbols. (It's also the way with collecting, which no sooner focuses on something inherently worthless than it makes a hierarchy of qualities—size, presence of spray paint—for greed and envy to batten on.) Once you let something symbolize—let a wall be the Wall for just one second—you have lost yourself to it and must *have* it, somehow, to be whole again. Not that filling a Baggie with souvenir rubble—of a symbol of world-menacing, practically cosmic, bewildering malice, gloriously broken—is a panacea, especially in Berlin.

I ♥ Berlin, smoky and haunted, gap-toothed city (our old, truly superb job of bombing it still shows widely), city teeming with symbols, and pretty soon, now, the first city of the world. Rabbits still inhabit the weedy acres of Potsdamer Platz, bomb-obliterated and Wall-riven former center of Europe that is going to be the most expensive real estate in the universe, minus Tokyo, when the Germanys reunify, which they will. In Berlin you can feel the national magnetism, not always in what people say to you—which is generally some twisty, cagey, befuddling German bullshit—but in the air. Yearning is there, as impetuous as the hero and heroine running to embrace each other on the train platform so that the movie can be over.

The serious hammerers of Berlin were at it behind the Reichstag north of Potsdamer Platz and southeast in the gritty, Bohemian-nation neighborhood of Kreuzberg. (A friend who went with me to explore the latter place after midnight later discovered dog poop on his shoe with a guitar pick embedded in the poop: a Kreuzberg haiku.) Though maybe mauling for money now (with prices neatly listed for different grades of fragment) rather than with unpent rage and joy, the hammerers raised a vast, lovely clatter in the winter city.

Through holes here and there one could confront strangely smirking East German border guards and confused police dogs, patrolling the once terrifying no-man's-land of formerly electrified fence, floodlights, and guard towers. I saw a West Berlin girl and a guard intensively flirting through one gap, a sight so confirming of love's eternal and all-conquering power they should have been embarrassed.

I fell for Berlin on another visit seven years ago, when the city's profligate production of symbols was beyond grim, as if at the bottom of a cold ocean, and a fever burned in the night-life that made the shrieking local variant of neo-expressionist painting seem like simple realism. Few people except tourists so much as glanced at the Wall then, as if it were an evil eye whose gaze could shrivel, and all those walking, intent tunnel visions were like a crosshatch of laser beams. It was ground zero of the world, attended by absurdity and ever-impending catastrophe. I was aware of my heart beating, as of a clock ticking, and felt almost unbearably alive.

Now it's as if that Saturnian site had blown sky-high, with people looking around them as if to say, "I'm flying? I'm flying." That's in the West, where the window-shoppers from over yonder have the unmistakable look of backwater folk thrust into Times Square. On my first visit to East Berlin (last chance to observe communism in place, unless Albania consents to become a theme park), I saw some people smiling, which someone knowledgeable told me is unprecedented. But the ambient desertedness, squalor, decrepitude, grossness, rudeness, and all-around violent irrationality were as advertised. What a dump!

Art? What happens next in the sphere of German creativity, already at least as energetic and consequential as ours, is a prospect so tantalizing that one's curiosity about current things dims, not that I had time or opportunity to see much. You can turn the world upside down in a matter of days — everybody knows *that* — but artistic expression is relatively slow to register, digest, and further the will of history. Give it a few months. Do bet that the major new German talent will come through the Wall, if it hasn't arrived already with the hosts of emigrés and the adorable rubes reeling along glittery Kurfurstendamm. Most of the best contemporary German artists of the past 30 years emerged from the East, which is also the land of millions of hungry Prussian workers whose future economic effect, when geared into the West German megalith, maybe you would rather not think about.

Is this really the rush to the clinch that ends the thousand-reel movie

Cold War Blues and sets up a sequel in which Berlin marries itself and settles down as the most powerful city on Earth—with New York cast as Cincinnati and France as Portugal, with Britain as the loony old invalid in the tower? Yes, I'm giddy, and there is scary stuff to consider. But being thoughtful may accomplish nothing except to wear you out when reality changes this fast. ("Fast" doesn't quite do it here. We need a new word for this.)

My wife and I are setting out our pieces of the Wall in a candy dish for holiday visitors.

JENNY HOLZER *Guggenheim*

JENNY HOLZER'S LED WORD-CRAWL up the Guggenheim's atrium corkscrew is an amazing sight that makes for an amazing scene. Though it opened December 12, I didn't visit it until Christmas week, when New York museums are mobbed with college kids and tourists, and I'm glad. This is one show you want to see in a crowd — the more the better — because the flashing tapeworm's behavioral effect on people is so delicious: hundreds of citizens standing around in stopped-in-their-tracks attitudes — inwardly focused, slack-jawed, vulnerable-looking, adorable — as they perform the unnatural act of reading in public.

They read in the snaking display some punk-poetical greatest hits of Holzer, litanies of artfully formed verbal sludge: phrases like "SAVOR KINDNESS BECAUSE CRUELTY IS ALWAYS POSSIBLE LATER," that are frontloaded with spondaic stresses, hence effortful to read, and obscurely freighted with menace. Standing and reading these blazing, lugubrious urgencies in Frank Lloyd Wright's bobbin is like becoming a minuscule fantastic voyager inside the head of somebody probably insane.

This is one of the best public art pieces I've ever witnessed, because the public is at least half the show in an environment — the practically art-proof Guggenheim, no less — that is efficiently and drastically transformed. Young museum-goers sprawl in the ramp's empty, darkened bays, and people who aren't reading look at those who are or at one another, as dazed and weirdly exhilarated as folks during a minor natural disaster. There is a mildly anarchic, aimless air, a kind of exciting staleness like the last day of the closeout sale in a store that is going to be torn down. It somewhat reminded me of the 1960s, when Western Civilization felt that way.

All the while, the words glide by — in various fonts of the LED's red and green lightbeads, which can combine to make a sickish yellow — with spookily silent celerity, changing course at angles of the balustrade's convex bulges like river-rapids water spraying off rocks. At a brisk trot (not advised), you might physically keep pace with the upward scoot of, say, "PROTECT ME FROM WHAT I WANT." Walking downramp and looking across, you may briefly fancy that you are, in fact, tracking the word-crawl and even, in some manner, causing it to move — an illusion of being locked into the twinkling display that made my brain hurt.

Holzer is of the generation of artists who in the late '70s produced work defiantly heralded as "Bad Painting" (later subsumed to neo-expressionism), and I think of her stuff as Bad Writing: a use of language aggressively ugly, expressionistically distorted, and in your face. The word choice is often so "off" as to approach gibberish, but the syntax is so threatening that you automatically read very carefully, seeking cues for fight or flight. Such is especially the case of her things from the early '80s, of which her masterpiece is the monologue of pure malice that ends, "DO YOU WANT TO FALL NOT EVER KNOWING WHO TOOK YOU?" To be in a public place drenched in such guttural palaver is to feel normal social facades crack, with a paradoxical effect of calm stillness (because everybody's reading).

"THE MOUTH IS INTERESTING BECAUSE IT'S ONE OF THOSE PLACES WHERE THE DRY OUTSIDE MOVES TOWARD THE SLIPPERY INSIDE." Why would anyone want to say something like that? Anyone wouldn't, I think, and that may be the essence of Holzer's harsh, toneless, true (but somehow pointlessly true) statements, which seem to issue, with jarring emotional punch, from a disembodied consciousness belonging to everyone and no one. Isn't the sense of such a consciousness, at once insinuating and alienating, the definitive effect of public spaces in our time, of plazas, malls, airports, and lobbies (and museums, which may be defined as buildings that are all lobby)? Holzer is onto the nerve of our world — with sandpaper and a hammer.

The psychopathology of everyday life that Holzer explores is a trackless, amorphous realm, in which she fairly often gets lost. Her attempts to be sculptural with aphorism-engraved marble benches and pseudo-sepulchers — which I can't help thinking of as chatty garden furniture for rich collectors — are inauspicious. And much of her LED work has been overdependent on the tricky appeal of that medium, provoking negative comparisons to the laconic control that Bruce Nauman, for instance, brings to his uses of neon. Worse yet, Holzer's present installation at Dia hints at a loss of edge in her writing.

The Dia piece is stirringly theatrical, with vertical LEDs seeming to fire words up through the floor and down through the ceiling, but the messages thus displayed (and repeated on marble in an adjoining chamber) tend to be laboriously self-conscious. "WHEN MY MIND IS RIGHT I CAN SAY WHAT NO ONE WANTS TO HEAR" is like the nervous brag of an author on the talk-show circuit, and "A

CLEAR THOUGHT MUST COME TO STOP THE MEN AND MAKE THE AUDIENCE LAUGH UNTIL THEIR INSIDES BUBBLE" invites the rejoinder. "No it mustn't." Lots of Holzer's new hortatory nuggets are likewise arguable and even a mite pleading, lacking her old savagery. Does becoming an art star make it hard to stay pissed off?

But, oh boy, is she ever a showperson! The brilliantly simple Guggenheim installation, besides being my own favorite thing by her since her posters of nearly a decade ago (all those visceral one-liners plastered around the city), is the perfect realization of a very significant ambition. By trial and error, Holzer has fashioned an extraordinary cultural role for herself—some combination of dirty-talking stand-up comic and Wizard of Oz—and she plainly grasps the demands of the job, at which she is literally incomparable. As good as she gets, with disappointments allowed for, is as good as contemporary public art gets.

THE WHITNEY CONTROVERSY

A COUPLE OF DECADES AGO, WHEN IT WAS NORMAL to assume that downtown art people had no money, invitations to openings at the Whitney Museum would come with two or more free-drink tickets. The tickets' design never changed, so you could save up the ones from openings you skipped for an eventual toot, and they made nice gifts. Understand, one was indeed fearfully broke, intoxication was socially viewed as okay or better, and a Whitney opening was an art-communal rite, combining serious cool with uptown swank, where the beat met the elite. If you happened besides to love art, it was urban Heaven.

I'm remembering those tickets amid the obscure current flap, marked by snarky unattributed quotes in the press, over the leadership of the Whitney, because they symbolize for me a practically familial connection to the New York life of art that may go back to the museum's bohemian-genteel early days on West 8th Street in the '30s. The connection has thinned over the years but something of it — some tincture of Eros — persists amid artworld depredations of commercial Mammon, corporate Midas, and bureaucratic Saturn. Will we soon be obliged to kiss it good-bye forever?

Even if Tom Armstrong survives attempts by Whitney board members to oust him as director and to change his allegedly frivolous exhibition policies, probably. An ongoing spread of faceless managerial control in cultural institutions seems inexorable, and a national mood of conservative entrenchment, of which last year's censorship wars were just a sample, looms apace. Both factors appear congenial to at least some of the corporate-enriched new patricians lately rising to institutional power.

Sometimes I hate this town. Our often enough gritty and bracing instinct to disparage institutions can be so destructively mindless. That's the case now in conversations about the Whitney ruckus that assume, as common knowledge, that the museum's record is somehow deplorable: *trendy* is a frequent epithet, but even unexamined cliches represent too onerous an effort of thought for many disapprovers. New Yorkish swing-barreled resentment is abetting a repressive evolution within the establishment, immediately threatening the only uptown institution that with regularity has observed the fact and spirit of new art in our city and our time.

Does it bother anybody that the main public cheerleader for present assaults on the Whitney is Hilton Kramer, fresh from his chilling pro-censorship manifesto in the Sunday *Times* last summer? Calling Armstrong's regime "a bazaar specializing in fads, fashions and art-market promotions"—a fair summary of how Western civilization of the past half-century looks to the antediluvian art critic of *The New York Observer*—Kramer presumes that "euphoria" will be unbounded among right-thinking folks if the "unmitigated disaster" of the Armstrong era ends. Though he has no credibility in any sophisticated art milieu, Kramer's constant evocation of a conservative silent majority seems to be exerting hypnotic influence in circles of power—circles, I can only imagine, of people with oak-paneled brains dreaming inchoate dreams of privilege immune to untidy edges of creativity and thought. (An ascendancy of such people at the Metropolitan may explain why that place's modern and contemporary programs are so spectacularly lame.)

Not that all the anti-Whitney sentiment is Kramerite. When you hear the museum's exhibition style called "shallow" or "insubstantial," you are listening to the constituency of art historians and other departmental professionals obviously crucial to any serious museum but, if put in full charge, a deadly force for pedantic insularity. (Hence MoMA's occasional reminiscence of a pre-1989 Eastern European country, with shows like orchestrated rallies where worn-out doctrines are droned by rote.) What offends this constituency is the tendency of Whitney curators to know art-worldlings by their first names, to be informed by artists, and to mount an occasional show of what art fans actually want to see, months rather than years after we most want to see it.

As for the supposed "commercial" bias that seems to mobilize everybody against the Whitney, I would like to know exactly how a museum responsive to contemporary art goes about ignoring the all-affecting frontline judgments of major dealers and collectors, whose authority must be admitted even to be opposed. In fact, Whitney curators often favor work that is critical of market-mindedness. Last year's Biennial, sharply oriented to such work, is a good example — and the chorus of oblivious disparise that greeted it is a perfect example of a herd-spirited, blind malice that has gotten way too respectable around here.

Just for kicks, let's rewind the '80s and imagine them passing anew, minus the Whitney's purported atrocities. We will see a museum record unmarred by any such trace of a living phenomenon as the 1985 Biennial's vivid tribute and, as it soon turned out, valedictory to the East Village scene (in both ways, an unforgettable milestone). Kramers and scholars prefer that such things not be seen to exist, at least while anyone involved with them is still breathing. A Kramer epigone, Jed Perl, came right out with it recently, opining that no museum should show any art until 10 or 20 years after its creation.

In our re-edited '80s, we are not distracted from grooving on 20-year-old goodies by midcareer surveys of Eric Fischl, Cindy Sherman, David Salle, Jonathan Borofsky, Julian Schnabel, Elizabeth Murray, Robert Mapplethorpe, or other of the period's most interesting artists, whatever you think of them (which will be nothing intelligent without the test of overviews). Nor are our snoozes ruffled by ambitious theme shows, from the neo-expressionism-situating "Focus on the Figure" of 1982 to the current "Image World"—which I suspect will be better remembered than it has been received but which, even as a failure, is game, instructive, and full of pleasures.

In sum, we will just now have reached the end of a sanitized decade to which the Whitney's imperishable contributions—apart from the routine solid fare of Marsden Hartley, Edward Hopper, Willem de Kooning, et al.—were Grant Wood, "Flowers in American Art," and Ralston Crawford. (I kind of appreciated those shows, as it happens, but I promise not to hate you if you didn't.) We would have in our memory of the era a moribund Whitney to set beside a silly Metropolitan, a majestic but constipated Modern, and a floundering Guggenheim. Would we be euphoric yet?

Defending an art-world institution is not glad work for me (I'm a New Yorker, for chrissake), but the thought of not having a vital Whitney to kick around anymore recommends a departure from form. Never mind reinstituting free drinks (which you used to be able to consume in the same room with the art, sometimes plus a person you considered falling in love with, and when later you went out into the night on Madison Avenue your feet perhaps didn't touch the ground much). Who needs fun? Just remind us now and then that caring ardently about art in the present isn't some kind of felony.

BOB THOMPSON *Vanderwoude Tananbaum*

Bob THOMPSON AGAIN. HE'S BACK, like an unpropitiated spirit. As has happened periodically in the nearly 23 years since his death from a drug overdose in Rome at the age of 28, work by this African-American painter's painter — one of the best-kept secrets in American art, with a following too mild-tempered to be called a cult and too small to be called much else — is on display. It's high time for those of us who have long loved Thompson's art to start sharing it with others.

Something besides pleasure might be gained from discovering Thompson now, when dismay at the chronically low level of nonwhite participation in the art culture is intense. Here was a black artist who *participated,* though in ways occluded both by orthodox (pop and minimal) taste of the time and by the political shattering, in the middle '60s, of a downtown hipster consensus that had made interracial hanging-out a value of sweet rebellion for whites and a horizon of sorts for blacks, Thompson had a white wife and mostly white friends among artists, and that was a shaky position in the incipient sea changes of Black Power.

A middle-class kid from Kentucky, Thompson was already an extremely well-educated painter when in 1958 he found his way to the artists' colony of Provincetown, Mass. (then still a lively outpost of the clubby downtown scene), and fell in with an informal movement of Arcadian, art-history-intoxicated expressionism whose doyen was Jan Muller. Lovely Ensor-esque fantasias by Muller, who died at the age of 36 soon after Thompson met him, are sometimes on view at the top New York museums, as the most obviously accomplished work of this group (which included the young Red Grooms). Provincetown style was determinedly old-fashioned, with old-fashioned feverish bohemian mores to match, but it suited Thompson, whose talent didn't so much bloom as explode.

Thompson's paintings of nudes, birds, and fantastic creatures in bucolic landscapes and indeterminate night places feel spontaneous and emotional—otherwise they wouldn't be expressionist—but what carries them is erudite playfulness and uncanny virtuosity. Taking motifs and iconography from old masters including Piero della Francesca and, most of all, Goya, Thompson generated a heady tension of studentish homage and erotic fantasy that gets resolved where it can do the most good: in the paint.

A painter's painter is one whose special felicities have nothing to do with style and everything to do with what happens at the end of a brush. In *Family Portrait*, three or four weird female figures overlap a Batman-like bird silhouette (often a self-portraying device in Thompson's symbolic lingo) in a shallow space breathing intimacy and menace. Ask a painter how hard it is to make a convincing space of such ungainly shapes without visible fuss or sweat: like throwing a deck of cards in the air and having it come down as a card house.

Color is the engine of Thompson's art in a way that recalls, without straining the comparison, Matisse. There is the same irrational impression that some particular color or color combination has dictated every move in the picture with a ruthless aim to make itself comfortable. In *Family Portrait*, a range of red-orange, wine red, and purple, set off by tones of greenish-gray and black, throbs with a chromatic secret: blue, which is nowhere purely present but everywhere tacit. You feel the effect before you're aware of seeing it, as if it registered on another sense than sight. Probably sound. Thompson's bacchanals are like backdrops for an opera whose music they have somehow soaked up, holding it in buzzing suspension.

What does it matter that Thompson was black? Nothing much in terms of his art's quality. Something important in terms of his subject matter, full of dark male presences interacting with multicolored females in ways that bespeak interracial desires and fears. And a great deal in terms of his significance as a heroic figure in one of the most stubbornly white-dominated of the arts—a slightly equivocal hero, more Roman than the Romans, who incurred more than one kind of marginality by the ardor with which he embraced European traditions.

It seems appropriate that Thompson, making a virtue of his marginalities, was an expressionist. As a smoky, noisy elevator for all manner of repressed content, expressionism is often congenial to artists from excluded groups or backgrounds. Expressionism recurs in fresh variants periodically in modern times, most recently in the neo-expressionist early '80s, when it rode a rocket of fashion and incidently provided an opening for the extraordinary talent of Jean-Michel Basquiat. Basquiat, dead of an overdose at age 29 a year and a half ago, presents some practically doppelganger parallels with Thompson, largely in the vicinity of Charlie Parkerish myths of the meteoric and doomed young black genius but more lastingly, I hope, in an authenticity redeemed by—and redeeming for our democracy—the long history of painting.

February 21, 1990

ROBERT YARBER *Sonnabend*
"STORYLINE" *Edward Thorp*
GARY STEPHAN *Mary Boone*

Painting is dead," that dire old line is in the air again, this time
with a force it hasn't had since the early-'70s heyday of conceptual art,
and even a painting fan like me has to concede its half-truth. The
charisma of the handmade picture, which flared brightly in the early
'80s, is guttering like a candle in a high wind. Maybe it's an effect of
absurd success in a market that transmutes art values into money
values so fast that the former can no longer take hold. In any case, we
increasingly have a situation in which gaga expectations of painting
confront limping creativities.

For a taste of the situation at its worst, briefly visit the Robert Yarber show at Sonnabend. For a sense of how far we've fallen, linger
with the masterpieces by Philip Guston and Eric Fischl, and the near-
masterpiece by Jan Muller, in a theme show of narrative painting at
Thorp. And for a properly hedged hopefulness, check out the recent
efforts of old pro Gary Stephan at Mary Boone.

What is a happy hack like Yarber doing in a sophisticated gallery
like Sonnabend? Besides selling, I mean. His superficially varied but
essentially interchangeable views of chubby figures tumbling in the
air above nocturnal cityscapes are the platonic purchase for new collectors who, with still rudimentary taste but full-blown covetousness,
are looking to plunk for something fun that comes with a "serious"
imprimatur.

Upon first glimpsing Yarber's work, anyone might be tickled and
even awed. The illusion of a vertiginous void —call it the acrophobic
sublime — between levitating figure (sometimes cutely being harassed
by a helicopter) and lurid Rio-like metropolis is a lulu, clinched by
"backlit" contours that pop the figure out from the ground while keeping it in the jazzily brushstroked picture plane. Yarber is no mean
technician. What he also isn't is an interesting artist.

Yarber is an academic sort of entertainer, churning out a strenuous
shtick without the slightest savor of adventure in the process or inner
necessity in the vision. He trots through a repertoire of glib effects with
portentous overtones — "dreamlike" spatial zingers, "expressive" facile
brushwork, "beautiful" jukebox color (such as purple or deep blue
setting off livid green or yellow) —strictly to trigger the same shallow,

wowed response. A gallery handout wishfully calling the paintings "ambivalent meditations on glitz" (the only honest word there is "glitz") performs a similar operation on the intellectual plane.

If Yarber flogs painting as if it were going out of style, thereby indicating that it may be, Philip Guston's *Midnight Pass Road* (1975) shows how an eccentric style becomes a classic: by translating all its base content, which in Guston's case was an excited and appalled self-absorption, into poetry. The picture is a kind of studio seascape in which obsessively regarded domestic and personal objects —cup, watch, bananas, vase, books, shoes, lamp, brush, sandwich, etc. — drift, and staring heads slowly drown. It is lovely, with its harmony of pink and gray and sleekly caressed paint, and as monumental as a bass chord played on a cathedral organ. It has the ease and patience, the inevitably unfolding eloquence, that comes to a great painter on a good day (such as seems rarely to dawn for anybody now).

Eric Fischl's *The Funeral* (1980) was one of this extraordinary visual storyteller's first figurative paintings, a black-and-white panorama, done from an amalgam of snapshots, of a stricken family gathered to strew someone's ashes in a desert. (Surely the mother's, because no grown woman is visible.) The technique is raw, but the investment of imagination in every formal and iconographic decision is unrelenting, generating out of traumatized bleakness a cumulative charge of meaning that can stun. It edges over into the surreal at one point, when you note that the man dumping ashes has several arms and two heads, but nothing breaks the unity of a scarifying emotional nakedness. That was a magical time, 1980, when such prodigies of painterly maturation as Fischl's occurred.

The Search for the Unicorn (1957), by the German-American expressionist Jan Muller, is a somewhat winsome view of two schematic female nudes in a dark forest with two likewise puppetlike horsemen; but after observing it from a distance for a while, step close. When the figure-ground relations dissolve into a surface of brushstrokes, you'll know whether or not you love painting, because if you do you'll be thrilled. Muller puts strokes down with such individual character that each is like a picture in itself, producing —as in Cézanne —a field of delicate insistences nudging toward bliss. No one can paint like that anymore.

The Thorp show includes other beguiling things, including a politically timely Komar & Melamid, and some curiosities, such as a picture by the almost hypnotically tasteless Norwegian Odd (is right!) Nerdrum.

The show also occasioned, for me, one of those sudden thoughts that present themselves as settled conviction: *any* painting, to be strong, needs a "story line"—not necessarily an overt narrative but absolutely a narrative tendency, a velleity toward telling about something—that draws painter and viewer together. Monet tells about how a haystack is in a field so that the sun can shine on it. The abstractions of Malevich, Mondrian, and Pollock are cosmic parables.

The point is that when an urge to *tell* with paint is lacking, out of control, or, as in Yarber, unfelt, something extrinsic—a story of critical prescription or of sentimental cliche or of money—automatically takes over, and that's what a painting must then haplessly communicate, parrot-like.

Gary Stephan's show, which deserves more attention than the passing remark I can give it here, exemplifies the serious effort of a distinguished abstract painter to make his medium tell of something, if only an aura or aroma of something, beyond itself. Though not so rapturously as his gallery-mate Ross Bleckner—lately some people's nominee as the American most maintaining painting's shaky viability—Stephan here pushes his virtuosity with heraldic shapes and atmospheric tones to a level of mysterious incipience, as if the canvas were about to be delivered of a great secret. The conceit is brittle, but the ache that drives it feels real. Give these subtle works a modicum of time and empathy. They'll reward you, honoring their medium in a demoralized season.

"TERRITORY OF DESIRE" *Louver*
"ODALISQUE" *Jane H. Baum*

Dᴇsɪʀᴇ" ɪs ᴀɴ ᴜɴᴀᴍᴇʀɪᴄᴀɴ ᴡᴏʀᴅ, a swanky Latinism for sex in the brain. That's how it works in American art talk, such that when a show is called "Territory of Desire" you expect some ratio of pretension and horniness. Myself, I'm not sure I know what "to desire" feels like other than as a euphemism for the Anglo-Saxon "to want." "Desiring" has a fancy-dress connotation of "longing," a feeling so impressive it distracts me right out of feeling it. "Wanting" secretes down-to-earth "lacking," which any born and bred American consumer understands.

Compare "I desire you" and "I want you." The first phrase invites congratulations. The second declares an emergency. The first makes being in love seem an achievement. The second makes it seem humiliating, which from what I know of life is God's plan, at least for Americans.

The ritzy new Louver, Eastern outpost of a long-established Los Angeles gallery, is trying what many would-be with-it dealers feel they must try nowadays to stand out from the competition: the high-quality group show with loans and secondary-market goodies by non-gallery artists, building prestige and providing glamorous coattails for gallery artists to ride. "Territory of Desire" is interesting for a few excellent works, and of course for its exceptionally irritating theme.

The Louver press release terms Bruce Nauman's major neon piece "seminal," which is pretty funny unless the humor is intentional (in which case it's gross). The work is a programmed frieze of five life-size multicolored, neon-tube cartoons of naked men standing in profile. In flashing sequences, the guys goosestep and/or have their penises jump to attention. The effect is hypnotic, hilarious, and disquieting in about equal proportions. It provokes thoughts about the power of sex and the sexualization of power, while perhaps rendering you too numb to think them.

In the Nauman, I feel a fury against sex-in-the-brainness, an exasperated frankness. It's a fine antidote to recent American developments of neo-puritanical censorship and also of a sort of neo-smuttiness whose high, chic end is, for instance, the longueur of a title like "Territory of Desire": sex as a devil's plot versus sex as a mental diddle.

It's as if our turn toward sexual honesty in the 1960s never happened, and we're back in the old American swamp of militant shame and furtive kicks.

Such is the apparently unwitting import of the photographic group show at Jane H. Baum called "Odalisque," which gathers dozens of pictorial conceits involving the old-fashioned "exotic" nude. Now, your typical odalisque is a partly grotesque, partly poignant projection of male lust: the maximally inaccessible (because unreal, and haloed by its unreality) image of the maximally accessible female. As an "artistic" subterfuge of panting appetite, it is so inherently ridiculous that anyone really witty will likely disdain to joke with it. "Odalisque" unsurprisingly contains numerous witless jokes.

I might not mention the Baum show were it not for the instructive shock of a single little picture in it: a print from a ravaged plate made around 1912 by Bellocq, one of his photos of New Orleans prostitutes. In it, a voluptuous *naked* (not *nude)* young woman lies full-length on her side atop a chaise, looking not so much posed as plunked or parked there like an object between uses. Her face is expressionless, more unhappy than happy but not especially unhappy.

Bellocq's picture cracks the odalisque genre in two ways, even while parroting its tritest composition. This woman isn't in the least inaccessible-because-unreal, clothed in "nudity." She's as real as a side of bacon and there for the taking. That's one disruption. The other is that her attitude is beyond inaccessible: it's imperceptible. Undefended, she conveys no invitation, no complicity, no personal sexuality even. Entire responsibility devolves, along with entire power, onto the bemused beholder.

I'm struck by how rare such unguarded impassivity is in any photograph of anybody, let alone of someone posing naked. It bespeaks an extraordinary relationship between Bellocq and his model, a hardly comprehensible condition that could be an oblivion of trust or an oblivion of cruelty or just some quirky passing moment, maybe of mere exhaustion, in which the normal hold of personality let go.

That dim and shabby little picture is an artifact with moral force. Beyond shame and guilt, it sobers and disenthralls in calmly exposing an actuality of sex, a starkness as of all cards on the table: "wanting" in both senses of the all-American word—lacking, craving—connection, possession, knowledge. "Desire" does not apply.

"PHOTOGRAPHY UNTIL NOW" *Museum of Modern Art*
"MOVING PICTURES: FILMS BY PHOTOGRAPHERS"
Public Theater

IN *STILL MOVING,* A 1978 FILM BY ROBERT MAPPLETHORPE, then underground icon Patti Smith maunders gawkily in a muslin-draped studio corner, carrying on about God and evil and other obsessions of a lapsed-Catholic punk and restlessly prowling the set. Toward the end of the film, a few still images from what we've already seen (but without, we realize at once, really *seeing)* are flashed in sequence: Smith turning quickly with a haunted glance at the camera, Smith pressing her body into the corner as if to merge with it, and so on.

The stills are perfect, arresting, great photographs, precipitated essences of something important — a new ratio of life and art — that Patti Smith in 1978 was about: flat-out candor of being. In the film, the stills are like pearls in an oyster, vastly more precious than what contains them. Suddenly the film is a sort of allegory of the photographer's discovery, in unruly time, of absolute moments.

Mapplethorpe is not represented in *Photography Until Now,* John Szarkowski's majestic exhibition of work by over 200 photographers since 1839. The omission of our time's best studio photographer is vexing, especially during the present cultural crisis in which Mapplethorpe's work has been made a bullseye of threats to artistic freedom. It isn't exactly scandalous, given that the show signals in many ways — for instance, by the inclusion of pictures by 41 unknown photographers — that it is a history of a medium, not a roll-call of canonical masters with which to play the who's-in/who's-out game. Still, Mapplethorpe's absence is a clue to a certain insensibility — an evasion of the passions and urgencies of social, political, personal, actual life — that is the weakness of Szarkowski's strength, his lofty aesthetic detachment.

Szarkowski's historicist *Photography Until Now* registers photographic individuality only as it focuses or, in the greatest cases, deflects phases of the grand parade from earliest daguerreotype and calotype to the present. What you get mainly is Szarkowski's own impressive will to stake out and dominate his field.

It starts, in his superbly written catalog, with a twisty theory that views the invention of photography as one step in a linear evolution of Western arts and sciences of vision, an event brought about as much by Renaissance perspective drawing as by advances in optics and chemistry. The argument, which is essentially circular and self-proving, has a comfortably reasonable air. What's twisty is how it lifts photography onto a high conceptual plane from which the critic-curator can gaze omnisciently, with knowledge of first principles and historic inevitability, upon the blinkered striving of people who take pictures and people who make use of them.

Szarkowski is an old-fashioned modernist, in other words, for whom the medium is the message and the role of the artist is to be in sync with the medium's unfolding. It's interesting, when you look at pictures Szarkowski's way, to see what shines with the most concentrated greatness: notably Eugene Atget, August Sander, and, to the extent that this very great and contradictory artist was a formalist, Edward Weston. What is seen in a major Atget, Sander, or Weston is the sheer quality of *photographed-ness*, its exaltation usually underlined by humble subject matter regarded in some pointedly no-comment manner. The payoff is a rush of the radiant-brain bliss of art for art's sake.

If you'll play along with Szarkowski at the show — I hadn't meant to myself, but suddenly I was doing it and getting drugged with pleasure — you'll have bone-deep comprehensions of the varieties of photographed-ness, all in apple-pie order of historical appearance.

Then go to the movies. Or to the films. Go anywhere to remember some humanly understandable reason why someone would take a picture or look at one. I suggest looking at something by Mapplethorpe, whose insistence on violating photographed-ness with lapsed-Catholic-punk obsession — such that the height of the aesthetic becomes inseparable from the depth of the obsession — speaks of the impure, cross-wired way, the cussedness, with which real-life meaning happens to most of us, photographers included, and that we love art for teaching us how to suffer and enjoy.

KEITH HARING, 1958-1990

THE SWEET WORLD-ENHANCER IS GONE.

His last years — the last years of one who died at 31 — were variously dimmed. The creative ebullience of the New York night world of the early '80s, of which he was the artist prince, was history already. Partly, it succumbed to its own success at defining youthful authenticity in an age of youth marketing.

As an American artist, Haring briefly occupied a previously uninhabited (even by Andy Warhol) stratum between street-low and museum-high, impeccable in both places. Because civilization is orderly and pleasant complication, he was a tremendous civilizer. He delivered a vision of democratic, soulful liberation whose impression lingers on the soul's retina though it fades and though it will not be reinforced, as darkness increases.

His rock-&-roll-Dubuffet designs declared a trickle-up-down-and-sideways economy of hip generosity, a Walt Whitman Memorial punkdom. He meant it, as he proved by devoting himself and his art to endless community service in which there was no hint of condescension. His wonderful "Crack Is Wack" mural in Harlem, still unmarred by graffiti the last I saw, has a power of credibility not to be expected in any sort of culture hero, let alone a whiteboy artist from Pennsylvania. Still, it's hard not to feel that the duties imposed by social and medical emergencies, in his last years, rather sidetracked his proper talents.

His proper talents were for knowing and giving happiness. He beamed happiness from some common human source, to which he had miraculously unimpeded access, in a steady outward wave that irradiated everything. We will remember and reap advantage from Keith Haring's talents when the day comes, as it must, that we are disposed to be happy again.

BRUCE NAUMAN *Sperone; Castelli; 65 Thompson Street*

IF THERE IS A BEDROCK VERITY in our civilization, it's that sophistication begins with disdain for mimes. Mimes—people acting like cartoons of people—appeal cheaply to a capacity to be charmed that, as we acquire taste, we learn to sell dearly. The presumption of someone with a cute little suit and whiteface and winsome leaning-on-air stunts to make us go warm and chuckly inside is felt as an emotional attempted robbery for which we'd like to make a citizen's arrest or at least deliver a citizen's kick in the ankle.

Leave it to Bruce Nauman, who has an instinct for civilized bedrock and for opening cracks in it that reveal abysses, to produce an art work in which a mime suffers for the effrontery of her ilk and, as one result, stirs an appalled empathy in the viewer. The work is a four-monitor, four-projector video installation called *Shadow Puppets and Instructed Mime* at Sperone, part of an unsettling and magisterial current three-gallery show with which Nauman confirms for me that his is the most formidable creative intelligence now operating at top form in American art.

The intricately programmed video piece comprises, besides sequences involving the mime (a young woman, Julie Goelle, in New Mexico, where Nauman has a home), a montage of shadows cast on a scrim by backlit, pendulum-swinging sculpted heads. (Head games? On some level, all of Nauman's works are that: willful manipulations of states of mind.) Every so often, one head is violently bashed into by another, which never fails to startle the contemplating viewer. Images jump from screen to screen around the room at gradually quickening and then slowing tempos. A full cycle takes 20 minutes.

An off-screen male voice (not Nauman's) reads instructions to the mime that range from dog tricks ("lie down, roll over, play dead") through increasingly tortuous contortions with a table and chair ("foot on your hand on the chair, your hand in your mouth, your head on the table") to combinations that are either physically impossible or impossible in the time that the calmly hectoring voice allows. While concentrated on doing what is asked, with as much mime-y cuteness as she can muster, the woman thus must select from the torrent of commands, and she understandably shows frequent signs of stress.

Like almost everything Nauman makes—and in 25 years he has seemingly made more kinds of thing in more mediums than any dozen other artists — *Instructed Mime* has an element of cruelty. Its immediate predecessor is a suite of tapes, recently featured in the Whitney Museum's "Image World" show, that is unequivocally titled *Clown Torture*: clowns striving to be funny while trapped in infinite repetitions of single jokes. Both works project a fascination with the human will to perform, kept steadily in view (and futile) by rigidly imposed rules. They show how bizarre a phenomenon any sort of performing is, at root, and how powerful — clenched, primitive, practically reptilian — is the impulsion to do it.

The mime in the Sperone tapes sometimes seems about to be overwhelmed with frustration, but she does not succumb. She is very good at what she does, and when she gazes off-camera with a weary, half-despairing look that says "Okay, now what?" your heart may suddenly go out to her. Little by little, her perseverance becomes an amalgam of horrific and heroic, fusing a child's desperation to please, an athlete's gameness, and the self-abnegating commitment of a true artist. The nakedness of the situation might make you cringe, but stay with it. For me, the payoff is a feeling of lucid compassion and a surprising exaltation of art, as a zone where steady detachment can yield direct access to primordial stuff.

Fire-and-ice meshing of hot content and cold form is a definitive Nauman effect, which can seem to summarize in a flash a whole possible range of meanings available to any art. It requires of the viewer not so much suspension of disbelief as active trust. You must give yourself over to the laconic and comfortless premise of the work in order to test its truth, which is generally some fairly unsettling recognition. (Nauman once said he wanted to make art that is "like going up the stairs in the dark, when you think there is one more step, and there isn't.")

It helps that Nauman sculpts, draws, and designs like an angel. This has been apparent ever since a legendary debut at Castelli in 1968 that incidentally marked his first visit to New York (where he never resided until his marriage to the painter Susan Rothenberg a year ago). Now 48, a dominant figure in the generation of post-minimalism and vastly influential in Europe, he is a maverick who at one time or another has affected the course of just about every visual medium except painting, earning a prestige among serious younger artists like that of no one else since Jasper Johns.

Nauman weighs in at Castelli and 65 Thompson Street with some animal sculptures that have a savor of instant classics. They are made from taxidermist's forms, which are spookily nude-looking, generic casts in polyurethane foam of flayed critters —moose, deer, coyotes, bobcats, etc. —in "life-like" poses, for covering with actual animal skins. Nauman cast some in aluminum and assembled sawed-up pieces of others to make ceiling-hung configurations of from one to four beasts (at Castelli) and an awesome 12-foot pyramid of five caribou, eight deer, and four foxes (at 65 Thompson).

With his characteristic jury-rigging and efficiently messy workmanship (every move necessary, none wasted in fuss), Nauman's reassemblies invigorate the lifeless shapes with a vitality of hand and eye, an energy of *making*. The coherence of this secondary energy is intense and exciting in proportion to the weirdness of the reconfiguration: torso sections skewed, head on backwards, legs bristling from sides, and the like. The animals surge more to life, with a sort of antic agony, the more their bodies take forms that would spell death for anything living. The upshot is an all-out war between the aesthetic and the natural, which both win.

The animal pyramid at 65 Thompson is destined to be cast in bronze for permanent outdoor installation in Des Moines, Iowa, and plainly that's going to be wonderful. The triple-decked lumbering caribou, rearing deer, and flying foxes radiate primeval force, as of some tribal creation myth sprung to life, but with a lightness in their tone as artificial, made things that forbids sentimentality. As in all of Nauman's best works, a certain matter-of-fact abruptness —completely without "style"—gives rise to a foursquare dignity, a *thereness* that calmly anticipates viewers and, unlike a mime, observes the precaution of assuming that some viewers might have brains in their heads.

JOHN WESLEY *Fiction/Nonfiction*
STEVE GIANAKOS *Barbara Toll*

W HAT IS *CARTOON-EALITY,* BESIDES A WORD (spun off "reality") that I just made up? It's a lightbulb that appeared over my head as I was thinking about John Wesley and Steve Gianakos, eccentric visual poets of the contemporary penchant not only for cartoonish entertainment but for cartoon-likeness as the standard treatment, in every medium, of just about any public content even remotely emotional. At some point in recent decades, the cartoon became to modern feeling what abstraction is to modern thought, the preferred model of subjective reality, perhaps because it is the least threatening for people too numbed by modern life to cope with anything grittier. Cartoon-eality *is* contemporary culture, more or less.

At a time when few important contemporary artists are untouched by some aspect of cartoon consciousness, Wesley and Gianakos strike me as painters at the tiny, stony heart of the matter. Otherwise unrelated, they are a couple of American mavericks (Wesley is 62 and was mistaken for a pop artist in the early '60s, Gianakos is 52 and made his mark in the '70s) who have smallish but avid followings. Both use old, usually non-specific cartoon genres to project funny-strange, ineffably hostile visions with "minor" written all over them, but certain effects on their exact wavelengths are jolting enough to set me, at least, groping for a theory.

Wesley, represented by work from the '60s and '70s, is an aggressively bumptious artist particularly esteemed, it is fascinating to note, by first-generation minimalists. (In case you're out that way, he has a show this month at Donald Judd's personal museum complex in Marfa, Texas.) Wesley's dab-flat, banner-like acrylics in odd colors (notably on a blue-to-purple scale) are obstreperous somewhat in the way of minimal sculpture, confrontational with a bang. They have coldly hysterical subject matter to match—with tones that can feel misogynist, child-phobic, and animal-derisive, in about that order, though also with signs that the artist may feel worse about things than anybody.

My favorite Wesleys in this show are: *Olive Oyl,* in which four irate naked babies perch on the levitating, naked body of Popeye's girl-friend; *Daddy's Home,* in which five darling little girls reach out to the viewer with trustingness calculated to freeze the blood; and *Four Seasons of War and Laughter*, four near-identical small paintings of a moronic, laughing-and-crying male face whose title and date (1969) recall the relentless agony of Vietnam. Like nearly all Wesley's pictures, these crank up violent impactions of blatant form and enigmatic content, signaling the existence — somewhere, in somebody — of strong emotions that the art sits on like a lid.

A far smoother operator than Wesley, Gianakos has always veered inventively between sensitive abstract design and thuddingly dopey, often smutty cartoon humor, usually in forthright black and white. His new, small acrylics of female nudes — in eroticism-proof, mix-and-match styles variously redolent of Betty Boop, *Archie* comics, old cheap men's magazines, and "Draw Me" ads — are tough little presences, with an impassive intensity like that of predella panels in a medieval altarpiece. They aren't at all repulsive, though by rights they should be. Is it possible to be nastily nice?

Gianakos's high cunning in these pictures is to blitz our conscious attention with maximum crudeness of image while working on our unconscious sensibility with terrific refinements of design. I dismissed at first glance, as mere style-parodies, the inset rectangles and other abstract elements of the paintings, and it took me a while to recognize that they are as purely, plastically functional as anything in Mondrian. The resulting humor is a sort of anti-camp: a display of adolescent gutter-mindedness dissembling the idealism of a seeker after beauty. You want to know sophisticated? *That's* sophisticated.

A joke is the epitaph of a feeling, Freud said, laying down the main theoretical line of cartoon-ealism. In modern society, with its overwhelming demands and non-stop stimuli, feelings are nuisances that cause mosquito-bite-like itchy bumps on unprotected spiritual membranes. Culture rushes to the rescue with the insecticide of all-blanketing ironic attitudes that kill feelings on contact. Actual cartooning is just one form of cartoon-eality — and hardly the most effective when compared to, say, the exquisitely soul-annihilating verbal styles of some gossip-driven magazines — but the cartoon joke is an unbeatable symbol of this contemporary mindset, which explains why so many artists are attracted to it.

Wesley and Gianakos are at the same time minor and revealing figures, in this connection, because they operate too close to the lethal core of cartoon-eality not to be a bit deadened by it themselves. (Certain major works by, for instance, Sigmar Polke or David Salle show

how cartoons may be used to breed new feelings out of extinct ones, and Jeff Koons and Mike Kelley differently manage with cartoony kitsch to generate actual emotions, be they only disgust and despair.) Wesley seems driven to desolate anything heartfelt in his vicinity, giving a funereal pathos to his peppy images. Gianakos's virtually anti-sex nudes are similarly toxic, though with a surgical deftness that throttles eroticism while keeping its sublimation in painting on life-support. Both artists shed light. For heat, go elsewhere.

(unpublished)

"THE NEW SCULPTURE 1965-1975: BETWEEN GEOMETRY AND GESTURE" *Whitney*

LISTEN TO THIS: "I think art is a total thing. A total person giving a contribution." And this, a list of influences: "Marcel Duchamp, Yvonne Rainer, Jasper Johns, Carl Andre, Sartre, Samuel Beckett." And this: "All I wanted was to find my own scene — my own world — inner peace or inner turmoil, but I wanted it to be mine." And this, apropos of having a terminal illness: "Now art being the most important thing for me, other than existing and staying alive, became connected to this, now closer meshed than ever, and absurdity is the key word."

That's Eva Hesse in a 1970 interview (reprinted in the handsomely documented catalog of this show of the sculpture movement usually termed postminimalist) shortly before her death of cancer at the age of 34. If the Whitney's attempt to trace the development of postminimalism in the work of ten artists could have a verbal track, it should be Hesse's voice: quirky, categorical, glazed with anxiety, and brave. It might provide an element that I miss in the show, a spirit or attitude to animate works threatened with seeming mere relics of barely comprehensible activities.

Postminimalism was a radical movement in a radical era, and I wonder if anyone who didn't live through it can grasp the fierceness and rigor with which certain artists then (three or four of the Whitney's ten consistently, the others intermittently) assaulted conventions. Maybe you had to be there. Not that being there, as I was, made for clarity in a moment crazed with revolutionary fervor (and a society busily ripping itself apart). But when you first saw "sculpture" that was a pile of stuff in a corner, say, you could feel art making a violent but precisely considered lurch, changing everything including your life. Now, two decades later, it may mainly look odd and a bit sad.

At the Whitney, there are piles or masses of stuff in corners by several artists (Hesse, Bruce Nauman, Richard Serra, Alan Saret, Lynda Benglis). That was a favorite postminimalist motif, as was stuff hanging off a wall onto the floor (most of the above artists plus Keith Sonnier) and stuff lying around on the floor (most of the above plus Robert Smithson, Richard Tuttle, Barry Le Va, and Joel Shapiro). A typical postminimalist work is made of one or more soft or soft-looking materials—standbys included rubber, cloth, cord, wire, neon, lead, and fiberglass—formed and presented in self-explanatory ways (such as pouring or propping), usually with overt cooperation from gravity.

The idea was to make things that happen in the creation and experience of art fully apparent and self-conscious, phenomena in real space and time. It worked, too, to the extent of establishing a new artistic convention that still informs contemporary aesthetics: roughly, a notion of exhibition space as a performance zone in which people play at being viewers of things that play at being art. But this success of the postminimalist revolution was also a failure, because it smothered in an institutionalized embrace some sharply refractory drives.

Seething emotion distinguishes the best postminimalism from first-generation minimal sculpture by the likes of Donald Judd and Carl Andre, who helped invent but also coldly formalized the performance-zone situation. Hesse (visceral shapes in fiberglass), Nauman (multiform exercises in what might be called participatory narcissism), and Serra (menacing deployments of lead) disrupted the situation's common tone of depersonalized professionalism with hints of sensuality, anxiety, and rage. Their work was about the "total thing" of which Hesse spoke (to be "the most Eva can be as an artist and a person," she further explained), a frankly heroic and scarcely sustainable ideal.

Smithson, the master of earthworks, and Shapiro, the reviver of figurative sculpture, also challenged the institutional envelope, but in ways that differently seem extra to a strict sense of postminimalism. In general, curators Richard Armstrong and Richard Marshall are overly inclusive, as in giving lightweight work by Benglis and Sonnier, for instance, representation equal to that of the strongest artists. But it's not the curators' fault that so much postminimalism even by Hesse, Nauman, and Serra barely transcends the you-had-to-be-there effect.

When you visit the show, consider going through it in sequence (first the second floor, then the fourth) twice: once fast and once slowly. Beginning in a small room where some wobbly painted wood reliefs by Richard Tuttle insinuate a strange new fever into geometric abstraction and ending in a big room where an intimidating double-cage structure by Nauman signals a frigid denouement, your quick circuit will yield an instructive sense of the frazzling speed of artistic mutation in the decade 1965-75. You may then better understand, while perusing the show carefully, the tendency of individual works to feel scrappy and tossed-off.

Such an impression is practically the content of flimsy wire constructions by Saret and floor-scatter pieces by Le Va, as if producing anything at all to look at had been a hardly tolerable demand on the artists' time. In the cases of Hesse and Nauman, you may feel an idea being realized in haste to get on with the next idea, and the next. (In this context of flickering attention spans, the relatively methodical Serra seems downright mulish.) What was the rush?

On one level, postminimalism (along with closely related conceptualism) was the last, meteoric flare of the old modern idea of progress in art, with innovations succeeding one another ever faster as they became ever thinner and more hybrid. (Benglis pours latex on the floor. Bam. Got it. Next.) On a deeper level, postminimalism expressed a period that had lost all faith in a predictable future. Any notion of continuity in civilized forms was rendered unbelievable alike by hope for revolutionary change and by dread of nuclear obliteration. The passing moment was everything, in which any gesture might be one's last.

So I think of Hesse in 1970 racing with her own certain death to extrude her sense of being and becoming — self-consistency, self-invention — in transmogrifying fiberglass geometries. By normal standards, her sculptural achievement is incomplete and cruelly truncated — "experimental" in both the good and the limiting senses — but the pressure and velocity of it, at any given point, are anything but normal. Never mind timeless art objects. No more than life itself was postminimalism about treasures in a museum. In Hesse I glimpse what it *was* about, which today's treasures-obsessed art culture has lost utterly: the conviction that being an artist may be the most desperately important thing in somebody's universe.

Peter Schjeldahl was born in North Dakota in 1942 and has lived in New York since 1964. He has worked as a regular art critic for *The New York Sunday Times*, *The Village Voice*, and *Vanity Fair*, as well as for *7 Days*. At present he is contributing editor of *Art in America*, a consulting editor of *Mirabella*, and a frequent columnist for *The Village Voice*. His *The Hydrogen Jukebox: Selected Writings 1978-1990* will appear in 1991 from the University of California Press.

THE FIGURES

Rae Armantrout *Extremities* $4.00
Paul Auster *Wall Writing* $5.00
David Benedetti *Nictitating Membrane* $3.00
Steve Benson *As Is* $5.00
Steve Benson *Blue Book* $12.50
Alan Bernheimer *Cafe Isotope* $5.00
John Brandi *Diary from a Journey to the Middle of the World* $6.00
Summer Brenner *From the Heart to the Center* $5.00
Summer Brenner *The Soft Room* $4.00
David Bromige *My Poetry* $6.00
Laura Chester *My Pleasure* $5.00
Laura Chester *Watermark* $6.00
Tom Clark *Baseball* $6.50
Clark Coolidge *At Egypt* $7.50
Clark Coolidge *The Crystal Text* $10.00
Clark Coolidge *Melencolia* $3.50
Clark Coolidge *Mine: The One That Enters the Stories* $7.50
William Corbett *Remembrances* $4.00
Michael Davidson *Analogy of the Ion* $4.00
Michael Davidson *The Prose of Fact* $5.00
Lydia Davis *Story and Other Stories* $5.00
Christopher Dewdney *Spring Trances in the Control Emerald Night
    & The Cenozoic Asylum* $5.00
Johanna Drucker *Italy* $3.50
Barbara Einzig *Disappearing Work* $4.00
Elaine Equi *Accessories* $4.00
Norman Fischer *On Whether or Not to Believe In Your Mind* $7.50
Kathleen Fraser *Each Next* $5.00
Gloria Frym *Back to Forth* $5.00
Merrill Gilfillan *River Through Rivertown* $4.00
Michael Gizzi *Just Like A Real Italian Kid* $4.00
John Godfrey *Midnight on Your Left* $6.00
Lyn Hejinian *Writing is an Aid to Memory* $5.00
Paul Hoover *Idea* $7.50
Fanny Howe *Introduction to the World* $5.00
Ron Padgett *The Big Something* $7.50
Ron Padgett & Clark Coolidge *Supernatural Overtones* $7.50
Bob Perelman *a.k.a.* $5.00
Bob Perelman *Captive Audience* $6.00
Bob Perelman *The First World* $5.00
Bob Perelman *7 Works* $5.00
Tom Raworth *Tottering State* $11.50
Tom Raworth *Writing* $10.00
Stan Rice *Some Lamb* $6.00
Kit Robinson *Down and Back* $5.00
Kit Robinson *Covers* $4.00
Stephen Rodefer *The Bell Clerk's Tears Keep Flowing* $12.00 (Cloth)
Stephen Rodefer *Emergency Measures* $7.50
Stephen Rodefer *Four Lectures* $7.50
Peter Schjeldahl *The 7 DAYS Art Columns* $12.50
James Schuyler *Early in '71* $2.00
Ron Silliman *Tjanting* $10.00
Ron Silliman *What* $10.00
Julia Vose *Moved Out on the Inside* $6.00
Guy Williams *Selected Works 1876-1982* With an Essay
    by Gus Blaisdell $10.00
Geoffrey Young *Rocks and Deals* $4.00
Geoffrey Young *Subject to Fits* $5.00